The
Special
Educator's
Toolkit

The Special Educator's Toolkit

Everything You Need to Organize, Manage, & Monitor Your Classroom

by

Cindy Golden, Ed.D.

PAUL·H· BROOKES PUBLISHING Co.®

Baltimore • London • Sydney

Paul H. Brookes Publishing Co.
Post Office Box 10624
Baltimore, Maryland 21285-0624
USA

www.brookespublishing.com

Typeset by Spearhead Global, Inc., Bear, Delaware.
Manufactured in the United States of America by
Sheridan Books, Chelsea, Michigan.

The individuals described in this book are composites or real people whose situations are masked and are based on the authors' experiences. In all instances, names and identifying details have been changed to protect confidentiality.

Selected clip art used in some figures is © 2011 Jupiterimages Corporation.

Library of Congress Cataloging-in-Publication Data

Golden, Cindy.
   The special educator's toolkit : everything you need to organize, manage, and monitor your classroom / by Cindy Golden; foreword by Juane Heflin.
      p.   cm.
   Includes bibliographical references and index.
   ISBN-13: 978-1-59857-097-7
   ISBN-10: 1-59857-097-8
   1. Children with disabilities—Education—Handbooks, manuals, etc.   2. Special education—Handbooks, manuals, etc.   I. Title.

LC4015.G65 2012
371.9′04—dc23   2011037674

British Library Cataloging in Publication data are available from the British Library.

2024   2023   2022   2021   2020

10   9   8   7   6   5   4

Contents

About the Author

Cindy Golden, Ed.D., is currently serving as the principal/psychologist of an educational and therapeutic program serving students with severe emotional and behavioral needs and autism. Cindy most recently held the position of Special Education Supervisor in a public school system, supervising the county's autism and emotional/behavioral disorders programs. She has also held other positions during her 28 years in special education. She spent 13 years serving in a classroom setting, where she was twice elected Teacher of the Year. She has also been a psychologist in a large metropolitan Atlanta school system and provided psychological service to a variety of K–12 schools. In addition, she has served several years as the psychologist in a special center that served students with severe emotional and behavioral disabilities in addition to intellectual disabilities and autism spectrum disorders.

Cindy graduated from Georgia State University with master's and educational specialist degrees in school psychology. Her undergraduate degree is in special education. Cindy received her doctorate in 2011 and was chosen as Doctoral Student of the Year. She was the author of a popular blog: http://www.omacconsulting.blogspot.com, which focused on the education and parenting of students with autism, and now serves as the editor for Special Needs Resource Magazine (http://www.snrmag.com). Cindy is a frequent speaker at state and international education conferences and has published articles with online educational magazines.

Foreword

There is a phenomenon described in the fields of psychology and neurology known as *episodic memory*. Episodic memories are those visual memories of a moment in time that are seared into the brain because of the high degree of emotion affiliated with them. Societies can share episodic memories, usually based on chronological age. For my parents' generation, a socially shared episodic memory occurred when President John F. Kennedy was assassinated while being driven through downtown Dallas. My parents can remember where they were when they heard the news and who told them; my mother can even remember what she was wearing when her sobbing teacher made the announcement to her class. Anyone old enough to read this book shares an episodic memory of the September 11, 2001, terrorist attacks on the twin towers of the World Trade Center on Manhattan Island in New York. I was at home, hoping to finish grading papers before meeting with an afternoon class of graduate students. I called the department secretary at Georgia State University to verify something, and can still see every detail of standing in my kitchen, still in my pajamas, looking at the microwave, holding the phone in my right hand. I have vivid memories of the horrible sense of disbelief and feeling dazed as I walked over to turn on the television in time to see the images of the second plane crashing into the buildings.

A significantly less catastrophic event, but nonetheless poignant for me, was walking into my first classroom as a teacher. As is suggested in this book, I went a few days early, by myself, to see the room that would house me, two paraprofessionals, and nine students with autism. In my early 20s, and having graduated a few months before, I can still see my hand putting a key into the lock on the room door, turning the round handle, and pulling the door toward me to step into the room. Almost 30 years later, I keenly remember the feeling of panic that swept over me as I stood rooted to the spot looking around the room. Most of the furniture had been pushed against the walls of the room. Two trapezoid tables were directly in front of me, one upended on top of the other. Ten rectangular student desks were likewise paired, one with legs on the floor and one with legs in the air, against the back wall, which had windows along the entire expanse. An indeterminate number of carrels had been pushed together and were guarded by a stack of chairs that was almost as tall as I. In fight-or-flight mode (with flight about to win), I remember thinking, *Where do I start?*

If I had the book you now hold in your hands, I could have walked confidently into that classroom, knowing that I had a resource that would guide me step by step as I created an educational context that would facilitate effective learning for the attainment of critical knowledge and skills. Dr. Golden integrates existing evidence of best and promising practices in the field of education to inform decisions related to organizing environments, instruction, and collaboration. Fortunately, with her copious classroom experience as a teacher, psychologist, and administrator, Dr. Golden translates the evidence base into meaningful implications for application in real-life settings by practitioners who find themselves juggling multiple demands. In this comprehensive book, Dr. Golden takes readers by the hand and guides them through prioritized activities that build on each other, with checks along the way for analyzing and celebrating what is happening in actual classrooms.

Dr. Golden tackles the expected components of establishing the physical environment and developing a workable behavior management system, while also covering the critical but rarely addressed elements of organizing classroom staff and home support. Because technology is central to the world in which we live, Dr. Golden expands beyond tried-and-true low-tech solutions using items such as electrical tape and Velcro, to provide suggestions for harnessing technology to enhance organization. Dr. Golden discusses the basics of monitoring personal behavior (e.g., the ratio of positive statements to reprimands when one is communicating with students, staff, and parents), identifying behavioral function to develop appropriate support plans, and communicating by using data. Equipped with this book, practitioners will not only survive, but also will thrive.

In this single book, Dr. Golden answers the question "Where do I start?" and systematically guides you through the subsequent steps as you prepare to spend approximately 1,440 hours over the next school year ensuring that all, staff and students alike, will benefit from the opportunities to acquire skills. Whether you are a brand-new teacher, or a veteran teacher retooling for the demands of changing student populations, I hope that your episodic memories of a new school year are seared into your brain fueled by feelings of hope and confidence, rather than panic and doubt. Gather a few three-ring binders and get ready to make a difference in the lives of the students entrusted to you.

L. Juane Heflin, Ph.D.
Georgia State University

*Dr. Josette Bailey—you gave me the opportunity to make
my dream of a model classroom a reality.
Thank you.*

About the Online Materials

The Special Educator's Toolkit offers online materials to supplement and expand the knowledge and strategies provided in this text. All purchasers of the book may access, download, and print these materials.

To access the materials that come with this book,

1. Go to the Brookes Publishing Download Hub:
   http://downloads.brookespublishing.com

2. Register to create an account or log in with an existing account.

3. Filter or search for the book title *The Special Educator's Toolkit.*

Introduction and Overview

Successful classrooms need organization. Just as this is true for regular education classrooms, it is also true for special education classrooms. The organization and successful management of a classroom, regardless of the type, will go a long way in helping to provide educators a less stressful environment while they are using best practices in the field to help educate students with special needs.

Higher education and preparation are both important to the field of teaching special education. In today's college programs, students in the education arena will study educational theory, developmental theory, behavioral theory, cognitive theory, and learning theory. Future special education teachers will exit college programs having strong theoretical foundations in teaching and learning, but sometimes upon entry into their first teaching assignment, they will feel overwhelmed and at a loss for where to begin. With so much knowledge in the methods of teaching, young teachers are simply overwhelmed at how to begin putting this practice into play. They are at a loss at how to begin organizing and managing their first classroom setting.

Veteran teachers are the backbone of the school campus and the go-to mentors for young staff members. Rich with experience and knowledge of how teaching practices have evolved over time, veteran teachers are a wealth of information. But, like the rookies, these same teachers can also become overwhelmed at the expectations of today's classroom. As the newest educational theories from research are expected to be put into practice in the classroom, veteran teachers sometimes find it difficult to create new, manageable ways of organizing their environment to include these new requirements.

The Organization and Management of a Classroom (OMAC) system is an organized approach to the management of a teaching environment for students with all types of special needs. This system groups the theoretically based best practices in the field of special education into several foundational components. The OMAC system creates a layered approach to the implementation of these practices. After working through each of the layers of ideas and organizational techniques, the teacher walks away with a manageable setting that employs the full breadth of best practice.

To get an idea of how this approach works, let us take a look at how a professional decorator designs and decorates a new home. The decorator

1. Examines and takes inventory of the space
2. Determines the functions for the space
3. Develops a theme for the space
4. Decides on the color scheme
5. Considers the traffic flow

6. Determines the furniture placement
7. Paints the room
8. Lays the floor
9. Places the furniture
10. Adds lighting
11. Adds textiles such as drapes, pillows, and rugs
12. Adds accessories: hangs pictures and places knickknacks and plants

The decorator then steps back to evaluate the now manageable, organized, up to date, and functional space.

To organize and manage a classroom environment for students with special needs, teachers can adopt the decorator's layered approach. As each layer is put into place and built upon by the subsequent foundational components of the OMAC system, the classroom becomes not only manageable, but also organized, up to date, and true to the function for which it was created. The function is to become an optimal environment designed to enhance learning potential, encourage independence, and meet the unique learning requirements of students with special needs.

Organization increases the ease of managing a classroom and, therefore, decreases the stress level of the teaching staff. Aside from the positive outcomes for the staff, an organized, well-managed classroom becomes an environment that will increase the chance that students with special needs can predict what is required of them in the classroom. Predicting expectations will enhance the student's ability to become independent in completing everyday tasks. With each of the OMAC-inspired foundational layers in place, you may begin to have the following outcomes:

✦ The classroom routine becomes more predictable to both staff and students, enhancing student independence and decreasing stress level of the staff.

✦ All aspects of the students' day will appear more structured, which minimizes perceived chaos in the students' mind, helping to decrease inappropriate behavior.

✦ The time and talents of the classroom staff are more efficiently utilized, relieving stress of the staff members.

✦ The students' communication needs are met via ample visual supports, thereby enhancing independence.

✦ The students' day includes scheduled times of teaching social skills, "cool-down" techniques, and leisure skills, enhancing appropriate behavior and level of independence.

✦ Sensory needs are met with intermittent sensory activities, therefore enhancing positive classroom behavior and time on task.

✦ The organized, less visually cluttered space produces fewer visual distractions, thus alleviating the students' need for order and enhancing positive behaviors.

✦ Academic frustration is minimized with the use of a variety of teaching methods.

✦ Learning weaknesses of the students, such as the ability to be independent, are strengthened through a predictable, organized, well-managed environment.

✦ An overall reduction in the frequency and intensity of behavioral outbursts in the classroom may decrease not only student stress but also staff stress levels.

✦ A reduction in the stress level of classroom staff members can be achieved by creating a pleasant space with organized materials.

The creation of an environment that is manageable and organized may not only enhance a student's ability to be independent in the school setting, but it may also help to decrease inappropriate student behaviors. These two global outcomes can be instrumental in helping students achieve success into adulthood. The third global term, recurrent in the outcomes of an organized classroom, is the potential for a decreased level of stress in the classroom staff. This has the potential for creating an environment that may prevent early burnout of teachers and one that may enhance the potential for overall success for both staff and students.

So, what are the components of the OMAC system? There are six organizational foundation layers (see Figure 1.1):

1. *Environmental organization* (Chapter 4) pertains to the basic physical setup of your classroom. Furniture placement, traffic flow, visual clutter management, the use of *purposeful spaces,* and *teaching boards* are just a few of the environmental organization ideas that will be discussed.

2. *Communication and visual support organization* (Chapter 5) utilizes visual supports designed to enhance the students' communication needs within the classroom. This chapter will discuss, in detail, a variety of ways to use and organize visual supports in the classroom.

3. *Teaching methods and materials organization* is addressed in Chapter 6. This chapter gives great ideas on how to organize teaching materials, simplify the organization of lesson plans, and use a center-based approach within a classroom.

4. *Behavior organization* (Chapter 7) is the structured management of various token economies and reinforcement techniques used in the classroom. This chapter

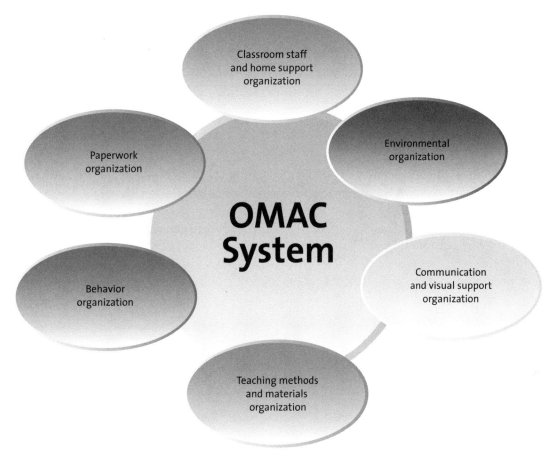

Figure 1.1. OMAC Support. (*Key:* OMAC, organization and management of a classroom.)

examines ways to organize and manage several different behavioral systems for your students.

5. *Paperwork organization* (Chapter 8) gives several practical techniques that will help you to efficiently manage the paperwork required in classroom for students with special needs.

6. *Classroom staff and home support organization* (Chapter 9) gives practical solutions for managing a classroom environment that employs several support staff. It also contains information and management tools that will help you provide support and build relationships with the parents of your students.

The OMAC system's six components cover every aspect of setting up and efficiently managing a classroom. As you read through this book, you will begin taking inventory of how you manage and organize your own classroom. Take an objective view of your setting. Use the preassessment tool that is available in Chapter 3 and ask yourself, *What is working well and what needs to be updated, changed, or just thrown out?* Ask for input from other members of the classroom staff or from other teachers. Go through each chapter and complete the classroom rubrics that are available. Read through each of the layered components and glean from each chapter the ideas that will work in your setting and for your students. Let the information be the springboard for your own creative ingenuity. The goal is to use the information in a methodical manner, each approach building on the next, so that in the end you will also have created an environment that enhances your students' ability to progress both academically and behaviorally while they are becoming more independent and lessening your stress in the classroom.

Research Basis for the OMAC System

The toughest part of determining whether or not to implement an intervention or management system in the classroom is to identify the research upon which it is based. Without a foundation based on empirical research, newly developed educational strategies are just good ideas. Good ideas are important but are not something on which to build the organization of a classroom. Chapter 2 synthesizes current research and practices that comprise the Organization and Management of a Classroom (OMAC) system.

The OMAC system is not a method unto itself. It is not a new idea of how to manage a classroom of students with autism spectrum disorders (ASDs) and those with other special needs, including developmental delays, sensory needs, and behavioral issues. It is a simple, organized method of implementing research-based best practices, many of which may already be used in the classroom. Regardless of the students' age or ability and regardless of the setting, this organizational system will benefit both staff and student alike.

In education we use the term *best practice* a great deal, but what does it mean? My simplified definition is that best practice is *a group of evidence-based teaching methods, techniques, or interventions, grounded in research, found to be effective, and used to enhance a student's ability to progress and achieve his or her potential* (Horner, Carr, Halle, McGee, Odom, & Wolery, 2005). This is what OMAC is based on. It simplifies and organizes a predetermined group of research-based best practices so that educators can easily implement them in the classroom. You do not have to go searching for what is included in best practice or wonder if you are covering all of the bases; OMAC organizes the research and makes it easy to implement.

To set the stage, let us first discuss the characteristics specific to students with ASDs.

CHARACTERISTICS OF STUDENTS WITH AUTISM SPECTRUM DISORDERS

Autism is a complex spectrum disorder that is becoming more prevalent among today's children. The National Institute of Child Health and Human Development (2011) defines autism as a "complex developmental disability that causes problems with social interaction and communication. Symptoms usually start before age three and can cause delays or problems in many different skills that develop from infancy to adulthood." Autism spectrum disorders affect the normal functioning of the brain, thus impacting the development of areas of social interaction and communication skills. The impact autism has on a child's communication and social interaction dramatically affects his or her ability to adequately function, to progress, and to become an independent member of society. In addition, the child's ability to function and make progress may be compounded by behavioral and sensory issues.

Take notice of the primary areas included in the definition. These are social interaction, communication, independence, behavior, and sensory issues. As you work through the organization of your classroom, all of these areas should be included in some way, and the OMAC system simplifies that process.

The Centers for Disease Control and Prevention (CDC) released new data in 2009 that showed that approximately 1 in 110 children, with an estimated prevalence of about 1%, have an ASD (Centers for Disease Control and Prevention, 2009). In May of 2011, the *American Journal of Psychiatry* published a study (Kim et al., 2011) from South Korea. This study focused on the prevalence of autism in the Ilsan district of Goyang City. The researchers found that the autism rate among 7- to 12-year-olds (2.64%) was more than two and a half times the prevalence rate in the United States. One of the differences between the research of the CDC and the study completed in South Korea is that the South Korean study screened every child in the Ilsan district, unlike the research data from the CDC, which counted children diagnosed with autism who were receiving health and education services.

The *Diagnostic and Statistical Manual of Mental Disorders, Fourth Edition, Text Revision* (*DSM-IV-TR*; American Psychiatric Association, 2000) outlines specific criteria needed to make a diagnosis of autism. The *DSM-IV-TR* states that the criteria for autistic disorder include qualitative impairments in both social interaction and communication along with restricted repetitive and stereotyped patterns of behavior, interests, and activities. The *DSM-IV-TR* criteria also include delays or abnormal functioning in at least one of the following areas, with onset before age 3 years:

1. Social interaction
2. Language as used in social communication
3. Symbolic or imaginative play

In addition, there are specific criteria outlined in the *DSM-IV-TR* for Asperger's Disorder (2000). These diagnostic guidelines differ from those for autistic disorder in that they include qualitative impairments in only social interaction and restricted repetitive and stereotyped patterns of behavior, interests, and activities. Unlike autistic disorder, the *DSM-IV-TR* criteria for Asperger's Disorder require no clinically significant delay in language. There are also no delays in areas of cognitive development, self-help skills, and adaptive behavior.

Further investigation of the *DSM-IV-TR* (2000) criteria reveals details about the more specific characteristics students with ASDs, including both autism and Asperger's Disorder, may exhibit:

✦ Inflexible adherence to specific nonfunctional routines

✦ Marked impairment in the use of nonverbal behaviors

✦ Failure to develop age-appropriate peer relations

✦ Lack of spontaneous seeking of enjoyment with others

✦ Preoccupation with interests or objects or parts of an object

✦ Lack of social and emotional reciprocity

✦ Delay or lack of ability to use spoken language (autistic disorder)

✦ Repetitive motor mannerisms

✦ Impairment in ability to imitate or use make-believe play (autistic disorder)

✦ Impairment in ability to initiate or sustain a conversation

✦ Repetitive use of idiosyncratic language (autistic disorder)

Using these criteria for diagnosis helps to frame the guidelines for best practice in the field. The OMAC system then organizes all of the best practice areas into a practical step-by-step six-level system that can be easily implemented in the classroom (see Figure 2.1)

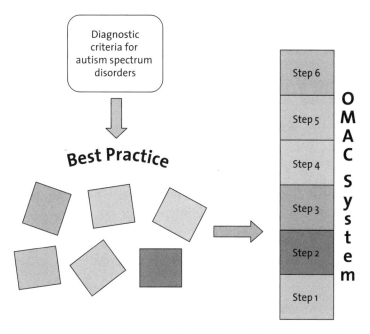

Figure 2.1. Research basis for components of OMAC system. (*Key:* OMAC, Organization and Management of A Classroom.)

The organization of the OMAC system was discussed in Chapter 1 so it is now important to have a basic knowledge of the research foundation on which the system is based. Before we delve into the research specific to the best practice in the area of ASDs let us explore the literature to determine the reasons why all educators should create well-organized and well-managed classroom environments.

CLASSROOM ORGANIZATION AND MANAGEMENT

The environment or ecology of a classroom, regardless of the setting, has a dramatic effect on students and their ability to learn. The American psychologist and educational reformer, John Dewey, said, "We never educate directly, but indirectly by means of the environment" (1944, p. 18). Every classroom has a life and culture of its own, and teachers have the power to determine the nature of the ecology and climate of their setting.

Research on classroom ecology suggests that the physical setup of a classroom be organized and structured so that maximum learning can occur and the class can be adequately managed (Savage, 1999). Research from Wang, Haertel, and Walberg (1994) indicated that, above all other variables, classroom management has the greatest effect on student achievement. This research suggests that a teacher's ability to develop a set of classroom management skills is an important factor on which progress of students in the classroom is based. The most important activity for a teacher in a classroom environment is the creation of an organized classroom climate. Marzano (2003) stated that teaching and learning cannot take place in a mismanaged classroom. Mitchell (2008) stated that the environment of a classroom is vitally important in facilitating an atmosphere that is conducive to student achievement. Kayikci (2009) also stated that a well-prepared physical environment complete with order and organization seems to create an easier atmosphere for teaching and learning. Kayikci (2009) indicated that an ill-prepared, poorly organized, and poorly managed classroom setting can negatively affect student participation and learning.

So we know that an organized, well-managed environment promotes student achievement, but there are also reasons critical to your personal success for employing a good system of organization, management, and the promotion of positive classroom ecology. Teaching has been described as one of the most stressful jobs in the world of work (Yang, Ge, Hu, Chi, & Wang, 2009). Yang et al. (2009) described several of the issues that increase teacher stress and among these are an increase in administrative duties, preparation of lesson plans, keeping up with grading papers, communicating with parents, and interpersonal staff issues such as lack of teamwork in the classroom and insufficient communication.

In addition to the day-to-day rigors of the classroom, our 21st century teachers have the added pressure of meeting benchmark assessments. The No Child Left Behind Act of 2001 (NCLB; 2002; PL 107-110) was written to create a standards-based educational reform complete with high expectations to achieve specific measurable goals. This would require formal assessment of student progress and these assessment data would be used to drive decision-making processes in order to improve educational outcomes. This added stress to the classroom teacher's workload.

Because of the stress of these basic management issues, teacher retention has become a concern. In a longitudinal study by Browers and Tomic (2000), teacher burnout was described as a critical issue in education. These researchers stressed the importance of self-efficacy or the belief in one's ability to manage a classroom, when creating interventions to deal with teacher burnout. In terms of burnout, Smith and Ingersoll (2004) found that special education teachers were at a higher risk and two and one half times more likely to leave their teaching positions than were general education teachers.

The challenge of special educators to meet the diverse issues of students with special needs is a constant dilemma. In addition to the challenges and stressors of being a teacher, special educators have unique issues they are required to manage. Special education teachers must not only manage the day-to-day requirements of the school environment, as in the management of paperwork, lesson plans, parent communication, and staff relations, they are also required to keep abreast of and implement research-based best practice in the field. Knowledge about the particular characteristic issues of children with special needs, specifically students with ASDs, is vitally important as the prevalence of the disability increases.

Specific to the field of special education, Holdheide and Reschly stated that "teacher preparation in the use of evidence-based instructional strategies—including learning strategies, classroom organization and behavior management, and scientifically based reading instruction— are integral to the success of students with disabilities in the general education classroom" (2008, p. 10). Research continues to show not only the importance of creating a positive classroom climate and ecology, but also the need for the addition of evidence-based best practice to the success of students. That makes it even more difficult to keep up with the demanding requirements of the position. Probst and Leppert (2008) reiterated the need to more strongly integrate into the curricula of higher education teacher programs coursework about scientifically validated intervention methods or best practice techniques and tools in the area of special education, specifically the area of ASDs.

EVIDENCE FOR BEST
PRACTICE IN THE AREA OF AUTISM

As the requirement for additional skills and duties increases, it is crucially important that special educators implement a system of classroom organization and management techniques that will help ease the day-to-day stress of creating a positive classroom environment. Thus is the research foundation indicating the need for organized classrooms. The goals for an organized, well-managed setting are to decrease the level of stress in teachers and staff members, increase teacher retention, and increase student performance. This need to help teachers create organized, well-managed settings is what has prompted the development of the OMAC system.

SAMPLES OF BEST PRACTICES

Let's first look at a couple of examples of comprehensive resources you can further explore to increase your knowledge base about specific interventions and teaching methods along with treatment options currently used for students with ASDs.

National Perspective

In 2009, the National Autism Center (http://www.nationalautismcenter.org) produced the National Standards Report that serves as a guide that provides the most current research-based evidence for the effectiveness of interventions used for students with ASDs. This project began in 2005 with a group of experts in the field of autism coming together with the goal of creating a document that would provide guidance to educators, parents, and professionals. This information is helpful for those needing to make informed decisions about current intervention and treatment options. This document is the first of its kind to be produced on a national basis.

The National Standards Report (National Autism Center, 2009) states that there are 11 *established* best-practice treatment methods for use with students on the autism spectrum. These are:

1. Antecedent Package: These interventions involve the modification of situational events that typically precede the occurrence of a target behavior.
2. Behavioral Package: These methods are designed to reduce problem behavior and teach functional alternative behaviors or skills through the application of basic principles of behavior change. Treatments falling into this category reflect research representing the fields of applied behavior analysis, behavioral psychology, and positive behavior supports.
3. Early Intensive Behavioral Intervention: This treatment involves a combination of applied behavior analytic procedures (e.g., discrete trial, incidental teaching), which are delivered to young children (generally under the age of 8) and may be delivered in a variety of settings (e.g., home, self-contained classroom, inclusive classroom, community) involving a low student-to-teacher ratio (e.g., 1:1).
4. Joint Attention Intervention: These interventions involve teaching a child to respond to the nonverbal social behaviors of others or to initiate joint attention interactions.
5. Modeling: These methods are dependent upon adult or peer demonstration of a target behavior. This should result in an imitation of the target behavior by the student with an ASD.
6. Naturalistic Teaching Strategies: These strategies involve using primarily child-directed interactions to teach functional skills in the natural environment.
7. Peer Training Package: These interventions involve teaching children without disabilities strategies for facilitating play and social interactions with children on the autism spectrum.
8. Pivotal Response Treatment: This treatment focuses on targeting "pivotal" behavioral areas—such as motivation to engage in social communication, self-initiation, self-management, and responsiveness.
9. Schedules: These involve the presentation of a task list that communicates a series of activities or steps required to complete a specific activity. These schedules make use of pictures, words, photographs, and/or work stations.
10. Self-management: These strategies involve promoting independence by teaching individuals with ASDs to regulate their behavior by recording the occurrence or non-occurrence of the target behavior and securing reinforcement for doing so.

11. Story-based Intervention Package: These treatments involve a written description of the situations under which specific behaviors are expected to occur (e.g., Social Stories [Gray & Garand, 1993]).

There are also several treatment methods that are included as *emerging* treatments, as they may become established treatment options after additional research studies are completed. At the current time they do not have as much research evidence to substantiate their effectiveness. These include, but are not limited to, the following:

✦ Augmentative and alternative communication devices
✦ Developmental, Individual-Difference, Relationship-Based Model Treatment
✦ Exercise
✦ Massage/touch therapy
✦ Music therapy
✦ Picture Exchange Communication System
✦ Scripting
✦ Sign instruction
✦ Social skills package
✦ Structured teaching
✦ Theory of Mind Training

Example of a State Perspective

There are several states that have prepared guidelines for the structure of educational programs in the area of autism but none as comprehensively as the state of Washington has. In July of 2009, the Washington State Autism Task Force, with guidance from experts in the state of Ohio, produced the *Autism Guidebook for Washington State*. This guidebook is modeled after the Ohio State Department's *Service Guidelines for Individuals with Autism Spectrum Disorder/Pervasive Developmental Disorder* (2004). Members of Washington's Autism Task Force wrote the guidebook to provide comprehensive information about autism to educators, parents, and professionals. This guidebook contains information that outlines the essential components of instruction and instructional programs. Some of the educational components described as integral parts of a comprehensive educational program are predictability and structure, interventions for communication, interventions for social development, and the use of data for progress monitoring. This guidebook also places a great deal of importance on the generalization of skills for independent living across the life span (*Autism Guidebook for Washington State*, 2009).

Continuing its rich history as a leader in the development of educational service guidelines, Ohio's Department of Education (2007) wrote the *Ohio Parent's Guide to Autism*. Although this guide does not address specifics about the school setting, it does provide a comprehensive overview of information that is considered best practice and interventions that can be implemented in the home setting.

As you can see, there is much research available in the area of special education and the interventions used for students with ASDs. Current researchers in the field have "consistently underlined the importance of tailoring choice of treatment to individualized needs" (Seida, Ospina, Karkhaneh, Hartling, Smith, & Clark, 2009, p. 103), as the interventions are not *one-size-fits-all*. So, I will divide the research into three broad areas that are directly related to the primary areas outlined previously by the autism definition from the Autism Society of America (http://www.autism-society.org). This will give you a better understanding of research behind the techniques used for students with ASDs.

The behavior characteristics of an ASD include the need for

1. *Environmental* structure to promote independency
2. *Communication* accommodations and visual supports
3. Interventions to enhance and encourage *social interaction*

Within this literature review I have also included a section for some of the more widely used applied behavior analysis (ABA) approaches in the classroom.

ENVIRONMENTAL STRUCTURE TO PROMOTE INDEPENDENCY

> *The greatest sign of success for a teacher...is to be able to say, 'The children are now working as if I did not exist.'*
>
> Maria Montessori

Autism is a disorder that dramatically impacts a student's ability to function independently in society (The National Institute of Child Health and Human Development, 2011). Independent functioning can be defined as "on-task engagement in an activity in the absence of adult prompting" (Hume & Odom, 2007, p. 1166). Many researchers agree that promoting independent functioning and decreasing dependence upon adults is vitally important to the education of students with autism (Bryan & Gast, 2000). Difficulty with functioning independently can and will dramatically impact overall skill mastery for students with ASDs (Hume, Loftin, & Lantz, 2009).

We have established that the ability to function independently is important for students with ASDs, but what does the research say about the distinct characteristics of ASDs that make it more difficult for these students to exhibit an age-appropriate level of independence? And how can structuring the environment help to accommodate and remediate these areas?

Hume, Loftin, and Lantz (2009) stated that achieving an age-appropriate level of independent functioning may be difficult for students with ASDs because of the core deficits of the disability. These core deficits, such as the difference in using verbal and nonverbal communication along with differences in social interaction and social understanding, may impact the initiation and generalization of independent skills. Let us briefly explore the major characteristic areas that may have an effect on a student's ability to be independent and the reason why the structure of an environment is included in best practice, and is therefore included in the OMAC system of organization.

Let me introduce three concepts related to autism:

1. Theory of mind (Blacher, 2007)
2. Executive functioning (Ozonoff, Pennington, & Rogers, 1991)
3. Central coherence (Frith, 1989; Hill & Frith, 2003)

Understanding these theories may provide you with insight into how certain environmental accommodations, such as structure and organization, may increase a student's ability to independently function in society. We need to understand that other students may also exhibit deficits in these areas, not just students with ASDs, and may benefit from these best-practice strategies.

Theory of Mind

Theory of mind, or the ability to understand the thinking of others (Blacher, 2007), plays an important role in participating in and completing tasks in the classroom, regardless of the setting. This concept also plays a role in the participation in tasks and activities outside the school setting and across the life span of the student. If a student has a difficult time in understanding the thoughts, feelings, wishes, and desires of others and how those are different from his or her own, it will affect his or her ability to make inferences in a classroom (Ozonoff & Miller, 1995).

Delving deeper into the theory of mind involves a student's ability to understand and make inferences about the behavior of others or the ability to understand what is expected from him or her and the unwritten rules of the school environment. These unwritten rules of the school environment, also known as the *hidden curriculum*, can be defined as "the unstated rules or customs that make the world a confusing place" (Smith-Myles, Trautman, & Schelvan, 2004, p. 5). The hidden curriculum is a set of rules that we just assume students have indirectly learned through watching others in the environment. They are simple social tips and tricks for successfully managing the school setting. Examples of these unwritten rules are what type of clothing the students are now wearing to be "cool," what kind of behavior a certain teacher expects in the classroom, things you should and should not say to members of the opposite gender, and ways in which you should act in certain social settings.

In 2007, Blacher stated that throughout the day, a student's "theory of mind" is required in order to "navigate the social world" (p. 96). To navigate the social world, a student with autism must employ the use of certain organizational tips and tricks to make the environment more concrete and easier to understand.

CASE IN POINT A student with autism has both science and math in an inclusive general education setting. Both teachers have different styles of teaching—one being very strict about the way the classroom is managed and one a bit more lenient. One requires order and quiet while students are working and the other allows cooperative learning and discussion among peers. For the student with autism, just watching the behavior of others and the way they function in the classroom may not be enough to solidify the difference in expectation. The teacher may need to consider additional structure (e.g., visual supports, reminder cards, different seating arrangement) within those settings for the student to understand the rules. He or she may need a more explicitly organized environment to independently succeed.

Executive Functioning

Executive functioning is another of the theoretical concepts involved in the functioning of students with autism. "Executive functions comprise those abilities that enable individuals to maintain an appropriate problem-solving set for attaining future goals. These functions include strategic planning, impulse control, organized search, and flexibility of thought and action." (Weyandt & Willis, 1994, p. 1). Being able to organize your activities, having the ability to plan ahead, having the ability to be flexible and predict what is coming ahead, and having the ability to control your impulses are all part of executive functioning. Do you see how these concepts play into having the ability to be independent?

Hill and Frith (2003) even went as far as to say that perseveration is another aspect of executive functioning. This behavior constitutes getting "stuck" on something and not being able to move on. The student with perseverative behavior issues may insist on sameness and an inflexible routine so that he or she can make sense of the environment. The student with an ASD may be rigid in his or her thought patterns, which may manifest itself into a very literal interpretation of the world.

CASE IN POINT Leon, a student with autism, is enrolled in a 10th grade world history class. The teacher has been discussing a large project that is due tomorrow. This project was given out 2 months ago and the other students have been working throughout the past 8 weeks to get the project completed. Leon has barely begun the project, thinking that the due date had still not come. He has the ability to be successful on the project but needs an organizational plan to help him manage time. He needs this added environmental structure to build his independent skills.

By organizing Leon's environment in a way that his repertoire of planning and organization strategies increases, Leon can internalize ways of organizing his time. This allows him to begin to rely on his own abilities and less on the prompting from others (Ozonoff, Pennington, & Rogers, 1991), which is the definition of independence.

Central Coherence

You may have heard the saying "I can't see the forest for the trees" or "I can't see the wood for the trees." If you have, then you have an understanding of central coherence. Central coherence is the difficulty with taking parts of information, putting them together, and understanding the concept as a whole. Hill and Frith (2003) said that the attention of a student with an ASD is sometimes taken over by small details of the feature of an object—a detail or piece that may be unnoticeable or unimportant to others in the environment. Frith (1989) also described the concept of central coherence as one of the reasons students with ASDs have stronger abilities in linear areas such as math and engineering than in more global areas such as language arts.

In a classroom setting this concept may come into play when students are asked to focus their attention, organize materials, choose or prioritize, and generalize. They may pay more attention to the small details of their own interests, objects, and subject areas or work, and they may not be able to grasp how to generalize that focus into a more global, usable concept.

CASE IN POINT Monique is in a fifth grade science classroom. She is fascinated by the topic of frogs and is a voracious reader on the subject of African tree frogs. The class is studying the topic of animals and has a test on Chapter 5, which covers the topic in general. Monique takes the test and fails. She has become hyperfocused on one aspect of the subject area while dismissing the other parts as unimportant. Monique would benefit from structure in her environment, such as a timer to limit the time she reads and studies African tree frogs. For the student to function independently and successfully, regardless of the high cognitive level the student exhibits, the environment must be organized and structured to meet her needs.

In organizing the environment, Dalrymple's (1995) research indicated that students with autism require four types of supports in the classroom to be independent:

1. Sequencing supports for structuring time
2. Procedural supports for activities
3. Visual supports for environmental organization
4. Social supports to assist with interactions between peers and adults within the classroom setting

Research by Dawson and Osterling (1997) suggested that to enhance the independency level of students with ASDs, a structured teaching environment that relies heavily on the use of visual supports should be used. A few years later research continued to suggest the general need for visually supported tools for students with ASDs to enhance progress toward independence (Dettmer, Simpson, Myles, & Ganz, 2000). This will now lead us directly into the next area of best practice: communication/social interaction and visual supports.

Use of Visual Supports for Communication/Social Interaction

As was stated previously, the diagnostic criteria for an ASD include deficits in the areas of both communication and social interaction. These characteristic behaviors are exhibited by not only students with autism but also students with other types of special needs. Communication is also one of the first areas of difference noticed by parents and early intervention providers. A difference or a deficit in the ability to use expressive or receptive language will likely be one of the first warning signs to parents and early childhood educators that will have them questioning a child development expert or pediatrician.

The literature states that "language and communication are major areas of concern for children with autism" (Marckel, Neef, & Ferreri, 2006, p. 109). In 2000, Koegel stated that even though the practitioners at the time had made progress in helping to remediate the behavior characteristics of children with autism, there continued to be a great need to find interventions that were successful in helping children make progress in the area of communication. The National Research Council (2001) indicates an estimate of one third to one half of those with autism do not possess functional speech and language skills.

What is the goal of implementing communication interventions for students with ASDs in the classroom? The American Speech-Language-Hearing Association (ASHA) stated in its 2006 position statement that one of its goals for communication therapy with those who have ASDs is to "maximize opportunities for interaction in order to overcome barriers that would lead to ever-decreasing opportunities and social isolation if left unmitigated" (p. 1). ASHA continued by saying that the challenges that are created by the social communication deficits of ASDs lead to difficulty in the generalization of communication skills to all settings. This calls for the creation of settings that accommodate and help remediate communication deficits in order not only to increase a student's engagement in the classroom but also to increase his or her ability to independently function in natural learning environments (ASHA, 2006).

The reason for teaching communication to students, those with and without disabilities, is to give them the skills they need to reach their full potential and to become independent members of society. Implementing specific interventions for students with disabilities or communication differences is a way that educators can help level the playing field. If a student, such as one with an ASD, has a difficult time in the comprehension of oral verbal instruction in the classroom, the teacher will implement interventions that will modify the environmental structure or create accommodations so that the instruction is given in a way that plays to the strengths of the student. Bruner and Seung (2009) outlined an extensive review of the literature on the efficacy of current trends in communication interventions with students on the autism spectrum. This piece of literature is a wealth of information and goes into great detail about the various new trends in autism communication interventions.

So, what are the characteristic strengths that students with ASDs possess and how did those assist educators and researchers in creating best-practice interventions? Students with ASDs appear to have stronger abilities to process visual stimuli than auditory stimuli. In a seminal piece of literature by Kathleen Quill (1995), she cited evidence that supported the use of communicative visual stimuli, stating that this type of intervention appeared to create a way of enhancing the ability to process communication. Quill indicated that children with ASDs are more able to process a two- or three-dimensional visual stimulus than an auditory stimulus (Quill, 1995). Verbal communication is a transient, more fleeting type of stimulus that lacks the static concreteness of a visual picture. In 2002, Boswell and Nugent cited Quill's research (1995) stating that children with ASDs seem to perform best on tasks that involve visual elements that continually remain in view. Interestingly enough, Boswell and Nugent (2002) also reported that, because of the predictable order, these children have a particular interest in numbers and letters. Predictability and order, along with visual items, seem to be important aspects of the needs particular to students with ASDs. These strengths will support the use of visual schedules in work-related activities, which will enhance the student's ability to follow oral directives given by the teacher in academic settings. Quill suggested that students with ASDs are better able to "focus their attention on visual materials than to attend to the rapidly changing social and communicative events inherent to instruction" (1997, p. 707).

Overall, the most successful long-term results for transforming a student's behavior into something that is more independent and functional depends on self-management that uses a student's strengths. Quill emphasized the importance of visually cued instruction to "enhance the understanding of verbal and environmental cues by children with autism" (1995, p. 57). More specific information was emphasized by McClannahan and Krantz (1999) in highlighting the value in the use of visual schedules to assist children with ASDs to learn basic social routines and to help them become independent by using strength-based learning tools.

Let's now discuss some of the accepted research-based interventions and practices that are used in the classroom to accommodate the differences in communication and social interaction for students with ASDs. Ogletree, Oren, and Fischer (2007) described effective communication-related practices for individuals with ASDs as a group of discrete evidence-based intervention techniques such as prompting, modeling, and visual supports. According to research, the use of visual supports helps assist students with ASDs to make sense of their environments, predict scheduled events, comprehend expectations placed on them, and anticipate changes made throughout the day (Heflin & Simpson, 1998, as cited in Dettmer, Simpson, Myles, & Ganz, 2000).

One strategy suggested by researchers well-versed in working with students with ASDs is the use of activity schedules. McClannahan and Krantz defined an activity schedule as "a set of pictures or words that cues someone to engage in a sequence of activities" (1999, p. 3). The researchers continued by describing the ways that the activity schedules can be developed. The detail of the schedule would depend upon the ability of the child using it. It could be made from pictures placed into a three-ring notebook binder and may contain many different photographic representations of a detailed task analysis. The pictures may graphically represent a few of the steps involved in completing a task and they may be mounted on a student's desk with hook-and-loop tape. The visual schedule may be a step-by-step schedule of a work task that uses simple words as a visual prompt. Regardless how the schedules are completed, McClannhan and Krantz suggested that the goal of the schedule is to "enable children with autism to perform tasks and activities without direct prompting and guidance" (1999, p. 3).

There are several reasons for the use of visual schedules with one of those being to accommodate communication weaknesses. Aspen and Austin reported that the "addition of visuals to support language may promote growth in the area of both receptive and expressive language" (2003, p. 11). The authors also stated that pictures are but one type of visual support that will enhance a student's communication ability. The authors suggested the use of video, daily planners, visual schedules, and desk organizers. They stated that the organization of the general environment must be centered on using visual tools. McCloskey-Dale (2000) described how visual supports used in the classroom can help support the student's visual strength while minimizing the deficits of auditory processing skills. Using this type of environmental communication teaching (McCloskey-Dale, 2000) model, each task within a student's day is structured and represented visually with supports. The student uses these supports to discern what the task is, what it requires, and the sequence of steps necessary to accomplish it. This helps move the locus of control from a person in the environment to the student.

Research also suggests other reasons for using visual symbols and supports to enhance communication and socialization. Visual supports and visual schedules are described as being instrumental in helping to overcome difficulty with joint attention. Joint attention is described as the "sharing of attention with others through pointing, showing, and coordinating looks, between objects and people" (Kasari, 2004, p. 4). Joint attention to tasks is integral to the act of attending and learning from someone teaching a task in the classroom. A student with an ASD who may have difficulty interpreting social stimuli may also be failing in his or her ability to attend to other people compounded by the difficulty with communication. According to the research, this is a difficult issue to overcome because knowledge of the world often comes directly from other people (Dawson, Toth, Abbott, Osterling, Munson, Estes, & Liaw, 2004).

The joint attention aspect of teaching students with autism is important in determining the types of intervention techniques to use. "Initiating joint attention is a communicative behavior that is notoriously difficult to teach" (Yoder & Stone, 2006, p. 426). In Yoder and Stone's research, they state that for joint attention to occur with students who have ASDs, it is important that they are met with visual stimuli of interest, not with continuous verbal prompts, therefore supporting the use of visual supports.

Visuals or picture supports also appear to be helpful in accommodating the difficulty students with ASDs have in perspective taking or theory-of-mind skills. Blacher (2007) stated that using visuals such as conversation topics on index cards, conversation starters, or other key helps may assist students in their social interaction. Teaching skills for social interaction include teaching social conversation, emotional regulation in social settings, empathy or perspective taking, and problem solving, among other things. These include the nonverbal language aspect of communication differences, such as utilizing eye contact, personal space, and body language.

In using visual supports for both communication and social interaction, there is another intervention that is included in best practice. Carol Gray (1995) developed a visual technique for teaching children with ASDs how to read the intricacies of the social environment. This technique is called *Social Stories*. Social Stories are intended to visually demonstrate social situations and provide support to students who struggle to comprehend the quick exchange of information that occurs in a conversation. These techniques use a brief narrative that describes a situation, relevant social cues, and responses. Gray's (1993) social stories can be used as a visual representation of a social interaction, turning an abstract situation into a concrete representation that allows for reflection.

The use of visual cues was assessed and also found to be highly effective in prompting the decrease of certain behaviors that may occur in children with ASDs. In Ganz, Kaylor, Bourgeois, and Hadden's (2008) research, they noted the highly effective response in perseverative speech to showing a "quiet" picture. In 2006, Pries' research suggested that the use of visual supports in the form of picture symbols was effective for the generalization

Research Basis for the OMAC System ✦ 17

and maintenance of verbal commands. Pries' research indicated that visual supports served as a trigger to recall or maintain previously learned skills.

According to the literature, the use of visual supports may enhance the ability to comprehend verbal directives, understand the social environment, generalize, and maintain previously learned skills (Bryan & Gast, 2000; Ganz et al., 2008). Visual supports have been seen as effective interventions in helping students attend to relevant information in their environment, attain and maintain joint attention (Yoder & Stone, 2006), generalize and maintain learning skills (Pries, 2006), organize their work environment (Mesibov, Shea, & Schopler, 2005), and predict and make sense of their environment (Heflin & Simpson, 1998). Overall, the use of visual supports in the classroom is supported by research and is not only included in most classrooms as best practice but is also encouraged by the OMAC system of classroom management.

OVERVIEW OF APPLIED BEHAVIOR ANALYSIS AND ITS USE IN THE CLASSROOM

A literature review of best practice as related to the education of students on the autism spectrum would not be complete without discussing applied behavior analysis (ABA).

ABA could be considered the 21st century's new buzz word in the field of special education, but it is far from new. Sometimes the term "ABA" is used correctly, but more often it is not. To the layperson, ABA sounds like a complicated, labor-intensive, specialized teaching method that only very few people are trained to do, and if you do not use it in your classroom, you may not be running a model classroom. We need to review what the literature says about ABA and dispel the myths surrounding it. Does OMAC employ the use of ABA? Absolutely, because OMAC organizes best practice, and best practice is immersed in the science of ABA.

ABA is not one type of teaching method. You cannot set aside an hour of your schedule each day to "do" ABA. It just does not work that way. There are so many methods of teaching that can be considered as based in ABA. Many people use the term Discrete Trial Training (DTT) synonymously with ABA, but they are not one and the same. If you are confused, then let us back up a bit and define the terms through review of the literature.

ABA has a rich history in educational research and was developed by the forefathers of behavioral psychology: John Watson (1913), B.F. Skinner (1953), and Ivar Lovaas (1977). ABA can be defined as the large science of behavior from which teaching methods are derived (Cooper, Heward, & Heron, 2007). ABA is not a teaching method or a specific intervention. It is a science based on the principles of behavior outlined by B.F. Skinner (1953), and those principles are systematically applied to identify the variables responsible for the behavior. ABA treatments involve "the application of empirically-validated principles of learning to the solution of socially significant problems" (Fortunato, Sigafoos, & Morsillo-Searls, 2007, p. 92). In the 1970s, Ivar Lovaas (1977) developed his innovative teaching method using Skinner's principles of behavior. He coined the phrase *applied behavior analysis* and used this to describe the technique that is now known as DTT. Allow me to give my simplified version of the definition: ABA is the use of data gathered on a particular behavior and the application of the analysis of those data to determine what is responsible for that behavior and how the environment needs to be modified in order to make a change in behavior. You identify a behavior, take data on that behavior, analyze the data, and apply that analysis to a situation in order to make a change.

Teaching Methods Associated with ABA

There are myriad specific teaching methods with ABA as their foundation. These also fall in the *established* or *emerging* category of treatment methods as reported by the National Autism Center (2009). Among these are

- ✦ DTT (Lovaas, 1977)
- ✦ Incidental Teaching (McGee, Morrier, & Daly, 1999)
- ✦ Treatment and Education of Autistic and related Communication Handicapped Children (TEACCH; Mesibov, Shea, & Schopler, 2005)
- ✦ Picture Exchange Communication System (Bondy & Frost, 2001)
- ✦ Pivotal Response Training (Koegel, 2000)
- ✦ Naturalistic Teaching Strategies (Halle, 1982)

I will outline the research for these teaching methods used most often in today's classrooms in this chapter.

DTT, which is typically associated with Lovaas (1977), is but one specific teaching method used in today's classroom. It can be described as series of distinct trials or events that are presented to the child in a systematic progression that is enhanced by positive reinforcement. The discrete trial sessions are typically used with younger children with the use of a small teacher–child ratio and with the use of data to analyze progress in order to continue to the next step. As Siegel (2003) stated, DTT is not a set hierarchy or program of skills and it does not tell what to teach; it is a method to teach the skills you have predetermined are appropriate for the student using the science of behavioral principles and data as the foundation.

The TEACCH Program (Mesibov et al., 2005) stands for the Treatment and Education of Autistic and related Communication Handicapped Children. It hails from the University of North Carolina at Chapel Hill and was designed by Eric Schopler (Schopler, Mesibov, & Baker, 1982). It was designed to be used specifically for students with ASDs and takes into account their characteristic features. The structured method of teaching that makes use of workboxes and visual supports, structures work tasks to create structure and routine. A study by Hume and Odom (2007) demonstrated that the use of structured individual work systems with students on the autism spectrum resulted in stronger levels of independent behavior and completion of tasks.

Natural Environment Teaching (NET; Halle, 1982) can be simply defined as teaching in a natural setting, with true-to-life objects and activities. This was designed to promote functional communication and language skills for students with significant cognitive disabilities but is now used for students with ASDs. Not only can NET enhance communication skills, but NET can also be used to practice and strengthen social interaction and to facilitate the generalization of academic skills. Chiang and Carter's (2008) research suggests that sometimes a highly structured teaching environment can be too restrictive and stunt the promotion of generalizing skills to a more natural setting. Natural environment settings create less of an artificial setting and will help to create situations that encourage communicative spontaneity by providing appropriate opportunities to communicate in less controlled environments (Chiang & Carter, 2008).

Functional Behavior Assessments

The term functional behavioral assessment (FBA; Horner, 1994) is as common a term in today's special education classrooms as ABA. This term can be defined as a group of different observational and interactive strategies that can be used to identify the variables (both antecedents and consequences) that control a behavior (Horner, 1994). The purpose of an FBA is to use data in a way that helps educators improve the effectiveness of a behavioral intervention.

CONCLUSION

The OMAC system was not designed as a new method or classroom intervention but as a simple, organized way of implementing research-based best practices in the classroom. Educators have a difficult task managing the rigorous requirements of today's classroom. For those involved in the area of special education, these requirements are compounded by the need to become well-versed in and implement evidence-based best practice in several different areas of student exceptionality. One of the exceptionalities becoming more prevalent is the area of autism.

The OMAC system has pulled together a summation of the best practice in the field of special education and organized it in a way that is manageable for implementation by both experienced and inexperienced teachers in all types of settings. After putting each of the six layers of organization into practice, you can stand back and know that your classroom has been organized and structured in a way that is simple to manage, that promotes student achievement, and that is founded on research-based best practice.

Getting Started—The Who, What, Where, When, Why, and How

Here it is: the Organization and Management of a Classroom (OMAC) system. It's an easy-to-understand, easy-to-implement, and very effective system for organizing and managing all types of classrooms for students with special needs.

There are six basic questions that need to be addressed before we begin. They are:

1. **Who** should use this information?
2. **What** exactly is the OMAC system?
3. **Where** or in what type of setting should the system of organization be implemented?
4. **When** or at what developmental level classroom can it be used?
5. **Why** should I use this system of organization?
6. **How** do I implement this system?

Let me answer these questions, and then we will walk together step by step to quickly get you started.

WHO?

Who can implement this system? This is an important question, and the answer is: *anyone*. This is not only a book for first-year teachers; it is also a book for veteran teachers. It is not a *how to teach students with autism* book; it is a *how to organize your teaching environment so that you are implementing research-based best practices that are designed to meet all the needs of your students* book. That's a mouthful, but that is what this system is about. It can be used by anyone and for students with a variety of special needs.

This book is for the veteran teachers—the old-timers who have been around for 25+ years and can remember the beginning stage of education specific to students on the autism spectrum. I put myself in this category. I remember my first student with autism. Being that it was my first year, I didn't have a clue where to start or where to turn for help. In the past 27 years, the field of special education has changed, especially the field specific to autism. Veteran teachers have a great deal of knowledge, experience, and gut instinct under their belt when it comes to managing a classroom, but, speaking from experience, we can all benefit from fresh ideas.

This book is for that teacher in the middle of his or her career, standing on the brink of burnout, thinking that the stress of managing a classroom and meeting the needs of students is just too much. This may give those middle-of-the-roaders some fresh ideas and a gentle spark of creativity where none is left.

This book is also for the rookie, the green teacher fresh out of college, filled with both fear and excitement. It will add to the knowledge and expertise they have amassed through years of study and give an extra boost of confidence to help them successfully embark on their first classroom adventure.

WHAT?

What is the OMAC system? It is made up of six organizational layers, and this book devotes a chapter to each of these layers. You should think of it as a step-by-step process, similar to a recipe. It is a recipe in which the product or end result is to create a model program or classroom that is not only organized and simpler to manage but also is steeped in research-based best practice. Let me go over what you will encounter during each of the chapters.

1. *Organization of the Classroom Environment* (Chapter 4) pertains to the basic environmental setup of your classroom. This includes how to arrange the furniture, plan for traffic flow, and manage the visual clutter all while using best practice in the field of special education. I will also introduce the concept of purposeful spaces and teaching boards as a way to make the most of the classroom you have. The suggestions given in this chapter not only pertain to a large regular education classroom with 25 students, but it is also applicable to a smaller size special education classroom that has only five or six students.

2. *Organization of Communication and Visual Supports* utilizes best practice in the field to intervene in the area of communication. Best practice supports the use of visual aids that are designed to enhance the students' ability to use communication for both expression and understanding. The creation of an environment that will level the communication "playing field" for students with autism spectrum disorders is a time-consuming task but one that is vitally important in meeting the needs of each child within the classroom. Chapter 5 will discuss, in detail, a variety of visual supports that can be used in classrooms for not only students with autism but also for students with other types of special needs.

3. *Organization of Teaching Methods and Materials* (Chapter 6) addresses how to organize teaching materials and manage the different teaching methods that are used in special education. There is so much required of teachers in this area: the creation of lesson plans, learning centers, the organization of materials, and the management of a variety of best-practice teaching methods used in today's classroom.

4. *Organization of Behavioral Interventions* (Chapter 7) contains tips and hints on how to structure the many items that teachers use in their behavior programs. This chapter not only gives ideas on various token economies and reinforcement techniques used in the classroom, but it will also help by giving creative ways of managing the behavior programs and paperwork.

5. *Organization of Paperwork and Data* is sometimes the thorn in the side of special education teachers. This chapter will discuss several ways of managing the mountains of data and paperwork required in a special education classroom. Chapter 8 gives practical ways teachers can easily organize and store daily data, manage individualized education program (IEP) paperwork, organize student work samples, create emergency plans, and manage the stacks of other paperwork required of today's classroom teachers.

6. *Organization of Classroom Staff and Home Supports* (Chapter 9) refers to creative ways that the teacher can not only support the additional staff that serve the classroom, but also support and build communication between home and school. Included are several innovative ways to manage multiple staff members and ways to enhance the relationship between school and home.

7. *The appendix* contains several items such as printable forms and organizational templates. These may be helpful in continuing to organize the classroom environment. The appendix also includes a reference list that may be helpful in the further exploration of autism spectrum disorders and the best practices included in the OMAC system.

WHERE?

Where can this system of organization be implemented? The answer is easy: anywhere.

As discussed in Chapter 2, all teachers need a system of organization. Special education teachers, above all, have extraordinary amounts of paperwork they are required to manage, and some system of organization is mandatory for survival. The general educators who serve children with special needs in their inclusive classroom setting can also use some of the ideas contained in the chapters. The information will help them manage their setting while implementing several of the best practices in the field. The OMAC system is simple and can be implemented wherever you serve students with special needs, particularly if you serve students with autism spectrum disorders. As the prevalence of autism continues to rise, all teachers, regardless of the setting, will need to be well-versed in best-practice interventions and will need innovative ways to manage the ever increasing requirements of a 21st century classroom.

Remember that the OMAC system can be implemented in any setting because it is but a compilation of best practices. These best practices should be implemented in all types of classrooms: in inclusive regular education settings, in pull-out resource settings, in self-contained settings, and in home-school settings.

WHEN?

There are really two parts to this question: when, during the school year, is the best time to implement these steps, and when, during what developmental age or grade level, can this system be used?

Although you can begin to implement the system of organization anytime during the year, it may be best to implement it during the summer, before the school year starts. This way you can begin the year on an organized footing.

But, is this always possible? No. So, you can begin at anytime and it is never too late to start. Take it a step at a time, carefully implementing each of the organizational foundations to completion. To create an optimal setting for your students, it is recommended that you finish one step before moving on to the next. Remember that you will glean the things that work for your classroom from each chapter and you should implement those. The chapters are a way to get your creative juices flowing. Know always that your classroom is unique and all things do not work for all classrooms. The main thing is to just begin.

As to when in the student's developmental age or grade bracket the OMAC system should be implemented, the answer is: at any age and at any grade—preschool, elementary, middle, and even high school. Organization is needed at every age and in every setting. There is nothing worse than an unorganized, poorly managed kindergarten classroom except for an unorganized, poorly managed high school classroom. There is no one exempt from the need to implement best practice in an organized way.

Now, what you do within each of these areas and the interventions you will implement will certainly depend on the developmental level of your students. For example, teaching organization is going to encompass the steps involved in organizing your teaching environment, methods, and materials. The types of teaching methods you implement are up to you. If the students are special education preschoolers, you will implement different teaching methods than if they are included in a high school general education setting. Organization is universal with no age limit.

WHY?

In Chapter 2, I discussed the teacher stress and teacher burnout that are associated with the job and the fact that this burnout is more prevalent among those teaching special education. I also spoke of the part that organization and classroom management plays in student achievement. For all of these reasons, the adoption of some form of organized classroom management is important.

The OMAC system's six components cover every aspect of setting up and efficiently running a classroom. Each of the components includes research-based best practice. Another way to answer the "why" question is to give you the goals for the OMAC system. OMAC was developed with six specific goals in mind. The overall goal is to ***create an easy step-by-step method that will help teachers implement best practices in the field of special education, particularly in the area of autism, into any classroom environment.***

The system has five other goals. These goals aim at creating a classroom environment that will

1. Create classroom organization so that you feel less stressed at the end of the day
2. Enhance the camaraderie between you and your classroom staff and the parents of your students
3. Make use of all of the research-based best practices in the area of autism in order to meet the students' complex needs
4. Enhance the ability of your students to be independent
5. Decrease the frequency and severity of inappropriate student behaviors by meeting the students' specific needs using best practice techniques

HOW?

Getting Started: On Your Mark...

The first suggestion is to get a small three-ring binder and begin an *OMAC Classroom Organization Notebook*. This is certainly not a requirement to follow the organizational system of the following chapters, but if you are a novice teacher coming into the classroom for the first time or if you feel that you need a great deal of change to your environment, this may certainly come in handy. This will become your handbook to organizing your classroom, and as you are working through the system it will be a place to keep the information you have put together so far.

The layout of the OMAC book contains several different types of planning documents in each of the chapters. Some of the chapters will contain a *Classroom Rubric* that will be completed to help guide you through the organizational process. It will serve as sort of an outline for creating organization out of all of the information that you will gather for each of your students. You will find that some of your students may require an environment that is much more structured than other students. This will guide you in organizing the environment in a way that meets the needs of each and every one.

Some of the later chapters will contain other types of forms, such as the *Staff Duty Schedule* (see Figure 9.2) or the *Student Safety Information* form (see Figure 8.12). All of these will not be needed for every student but are included to help in the organization process.

A *Suggested Material List* will be included with each chapter. This will help you take inventory of the materials already in your classroom as well as highlight what you will need to obtain. Some of the items, such as a digital camera and laminator, you will only need to access as needed. The OMAC system is budget conscious and gives creative ways of using what you already have in the classroom. We have included in the accompanying online materials an OMAC Toolkit (see Appendix 3A). This is a compilation of most of the general materials that have been used to set up model programs and may help you become prepared before beginning each of the chapters.

Getting Started: Get Set...

Before proceeding, it would be helpful if you completed a few prerequisite tasks in order to fully plan the organization of your classroom. This should be specific to the needs of your students and your setting. Remember that the OMAC system can be used with students of all ages, in all settings, and by teachers of all experience levels. We will examine step-by-step tasks that will guide you as you work through the system.

The first is the *OMAC Personal Classroom Assessment* (see Figure 3.1). This is a way of helping you paint a true picture of how you feel about your current classroom organization. Be honest as you complete this form. It will help you identify where you should focus.

APPENDIX 3B

Let's take a Personal Assessment of your classroom. Read the following statements and be honest with yourself about where and how your classroom currently stands in each area. Place an X on the face that best describes your feelings.

OMAC Personal Classroom Assessment

ENVIRONMENT

When I stand at the door of my classroom, how organized does my classroom appear to be and is it clutter free?

How well do I use the available space that I have?

How easily can I find the materials that I need?

Do I have a posted schedule that organizes my day and the day for my students?

How independently can the students function in the classroom?

COMMUNICATION AND VISUAL SUPPORTS

Does the classroom have enough supports so that all students have some way of communicating their want and needs?

Have I provided enough visual supports to the students to enhance their ability to learn during teaching?

Is there enough visual support in the classroom to allow the students to follow the schedule?

Figure 3.1. OMAC Personal Classroom Assessment.

APPENDIX 3C

Getting Started Worksheet

INSTRUCTIONS

1. Use one sheet for each student.
2. Read through the student's individualized education program (IEP) and determine how each subject area is to be taught.
3. Complete each of the columns of information.
4. After completing these for each student in the classroom, you can use this information to determine the most effective way to arrange your class schedule.

WHO	WHAT	WHERE	WHEN	HOW
Ann Smith	Math	Resource room	8:00–8:30	Small group
	Writing	Regular classroom	9:00–9:45	Large group with paraprofessional support
	Reading	Resource room	2:00–2:45	One-to-one instruction

Figure 3.2. Completed Getting Started Worksheet.

There is also a *Getting Started Worksheet* (see Figure 3.2) included in this chapter's appendix.

The *Getting Started Worksheet* will help you organize the information that you have about each of your students in an easy way so that you can get started. It is a way of compiling all of the information you need into one complete format so that you do not forget or miss something in the planning stage.

Let's think a minute. There are all types of settings where this type of organizational system can be helpful. You may serve as an educator in a regular classroom where one or two students with special needs are included, a small pull-out type special education classroom with a small class of students with special needs, or maybe even an entire school or wing of a school that is solely dedicated to the education of students with special needs, much like a private school setting that focuses on the education of students with autism spectrum disorders. Regardless of the setting, you need to back up and plan in order to get set on a firm, organized foundation. This *Getting Started Worksheet* will ask you to gather the following information on each of your students:

✦ ***Who** you are going to teach?* For this section, you are to list your students with special needs, particularly those who are have an autism spectrum diagnosis. It is helpful to use one page per student.

✦ ***What** are you going to teach?* For each student you will determine the subject areas that you need to teach by reading through his or her IEP. It will help you determine the materials that you will need and the way the environment should be structured.

✦ *Where you are going to teach?* This is also a very important section to complete before moving on to the environmental component. Until you know where you will teach what subject, you cannot organize your space. For example, will you be teaching math in your classroom to a small group of students or will you serve as the inclusive education teacher in a regular education setting? Will you be teaching vocational skills to one student in your classroom or will you use a vocational lab? Will you need to have a section of the room for one-to-one instruction, using Discrete Trial Training (DTT), or will you teach all subjects as a group? This information will be key to determining the layout of your classroom.

✦ *When you are going to teach?* This is the overall schedule for your classroom. This is a vital step because you will build your entire environment around this schedule. Your schedule may be organized by a bell schedule and administratively set time periods, or you may have the flexibility to set your own schedule around the needs of your individual students. Whatever the case, you will need to refine this schedule so that you can build your environment around it.

✦ *How you are going to teach?* There are many methods and techniques that educators use to teach students with autism spectrum disorders. You may be in a preschool classroom and may use DTT in a one-to-one format. This precipitates the need for a DTT center within the room with a structure all its own. You may teach using Treatment and Education of Autistic and related Communication Handicapped Children (TEACCH) workboxes for academic readiness skills. If so, you will need an area of the classroom designed to organize and manage the myriad workboxes needed for this method of teaching. How you teach will determine what your classroom looks like. It is important information to have before you begin moving furniture as it drives the organization of the teaching environment.

Getting Started: Go!

Have you completed the following:

☑ Created the *OMAC Classroom Organization Notebook*… check!
☑ Completed the *OMAC Personal Classroom Assessment*… check!
☑ Completed the *Getting Started Worksheet*… check!

You are now ready to organize your environment.

Organization of the Classroom Environment

Whether you're a first-year teacher who is serious and passionate about getting off to a good start or whether you have been teaching for the past 30 years, if you are to update the way you organize and structure your teaching day, you need to begin with step one, which is to organize the classroom environment. I know you may be thinking, *Are you kidding? Have you seen my room? I don't know where to begin!* Just follow along with me step by step and at the end of this book you will look back and say, "I love it, and it was worth the work!"

This chapter is structured as if I were decorating a room. Even though this is not about decorating a classroom, the steps involved are surprisingly similar. I know that you already have your work clothes on, so let's have a little fun.

PLAN AND PREPARE

Stand at the front door of your classroom. Look around. Look up above cabinets and shelves, look at the walls and bulletin boards, and look at the floor. Look in the corners of the room and look under desks and tables. What do you see? This is what a designer would do if he or she were to come into your home for a consultation. They would also be very honest and blunt with you about your space—the good, the bad, and the ugly. You are going to do the same thing. If you think you need a peer to do this with you then bring him or her along for the ride. Sometimes if you have been in your classroom space for a long time, you may not be able to see things as others see them.

Now, while you are looking around, think about your students. You may have students with autism, you may have students with cognitive disabilities, or you may be a regular education teacher with only a few students with learning differences in your classroom. You may also be a regular education teacher with 25 student desks and they are packed into a small classroom like sardines; you may be a self-contained special education teacher who has a large double-wide mobile classroom, much like I did for a few years; you may be a special education teacher who teaches in a storage closet that you share with the science lab complete with frogs in jar, again much like I did for a year; or you may be a special education teacher with an odd-shaped classroom, but one that is large enough to accommodate lots of stuff. Regardless of what you have to work with you can make this work, but you have to have a plan, and the first item of business is to—with an honest eye—check out your current space.

Step One

Get a clipboard and make some notes about what is working and what is not working (see Figure 4.1). A blank copy of this form is available in the Appendix 4A. Go look around and make some notes.

In Figure 4.1, this teacher liked the way her files were organized and the traffic flow of the classroom, but she thought the room was messy and she had a hard time finding things that she needed. This was a great place for her to start.

Step Two

I call this step *Clutter Cleaning,* so get your gloves on.

The classroom is your and your students' home away from home, so it needs to be uncluttered and clean. When a designer comes into a new space, he or she usually gets everything out of the room. Have you watched those shows on television where the host goes into a home and the first thing he or she does is to get rid of the clutter so everything ends up on the front lawn? You may not need to go to that extreme but, again, during summer vacation, you may want to do just that.

Clutter is a visual distraction. This is especially true for students with disabilities and in particular those with sensory differences such as students with autism. When it comes to children with sensory differences *visual clutter is a big no-no!* Clutter cannot be visible upon a person entering the room. Think about how your students will view the space. What will they see? To help guide yourself in knowing where to begin, ask yourself the questions in the clutter cleaning checklist, Appendix 4B.

I know that cleaning is something you may not want or have the time to do, but you need to find the time. Can you spend a few afternoons after school or come in before school starts during the summer? If you don't do this step, you are just moving junk around and you won't really even know what you have. This takes time, but you will find that time invested up front will be well worth it. Think about what an impression this will make not only on the students, but also on the administration and on the parents at Open House.

When you begin clutter cleaning, make three piles: *Throw Away, Share with Others,* and *Definitely Keep.* Begin rummaging through desk drawers, bookcases, closets, file cabinets, storage cabinets, and your desk.

✦ Do you still have those old purple ditto masters that you used to use when making copies of worksheets? *Throw them out.*

✦ Do you have 25 packs of red construction paper that you don't even remember ordering? *Share these with others.*

✦ Do you have files and files of old worksheets? *Keep, recycle, and reuse* by cutting them into small message paper or provide them to the students as scrap paper.

✦ Do you have stacks of old bulletin board materials that you will not ever have the time to use? *Share* by putting them in a box and allowing teachers to come by and get what they want.

Next, take everything off the walls and bulletin boards. It is much easier to start from scratch than it is to redo what is there. If you begin with a clean slate, you will see things more clearly and be more open to change.

Step Three

Now that you can see what you have you can begin taking inventory.

At the beginning of the year, you may be one of the fortunate teachers who has lots of money to spend, and every teacher keeps a wish list. But, if you do not take inventory of

How's My Classroom?

What's working	What's not working
Book bag is in a great place	Room looks messy
File cabinets are organized	No place to store group materials
Traffic flow works	Too much junk on top of cabinets
I have plenty of supplies	I can't find things when I need them
	The students rely on us to find materials

Figure 4.1. Sample How's My Classroom?

what you have first, you will order 10 new packs of markers and then find 20 packs hidden beneath the junk in the corner of the room. Don't waste your money until you know what you need.

This is a suggested list of items that may be helpful in the organization of your environment. It is not all-inclusive but gives you a place to begin. Use what you have and use your imagination to find new uses for available objects.

Suggested materials list for environmental organization	
❑ Large and small visual timers	❑ Colored poster board
❑ Egg timers	❑ Round sticky dots (in colors)
❑ Clip-on timers	❑ Painter's tape
❑ Hanging plastic wall pockets	❑ Sticky-back hook and loop tape (e.g., Velcro)
❑ Colored file folders	❑ Spray glue
❑ Dry-erase markers	❑ Solid color fabric
❑ Three-ring binders with plastic pocket on the cover	❑ Mayer-Johnson's Boardmaker program
❑ Plastic file crates	❑ Small bookcases
❑ Access to digital camera	❑ Group table
❑ Sensory items	❑ Student desks
❑ Plastic shoe boxes	❑ Paint
❑ CD player	❑ Long table
❑ Access to a variety of music CDs	❑ Colored rugs or carpet squares
❑ Stiff felt	❑ Computer with a color printer
❑ Magnets	❑ Sentence strips
❑ Variety of colors of construction paper	❑ Clipboards
❑ Access to laminator	❑ Hanging folders
❑ Small white boards	❑ Carrels or dividers (wooden or PVC)

Suggested Materials List for Environmental Organization

Figure 4.2. Suggested materials list for environmental organization.

Before you order you need to have a list of basic supplies that you can use for anything.

CASE IN POINT Have you ever assisted someone who is a *Hostess Queen,* as I like to call
 him or her, decorate for an impromptu dinner party? This person typically has a
closet of basic items that he or she can put together to throw a party with any theme,
for any occasion, and on the spur of the moment. Candle sticks, white table cloths,
clear flower vases, and solid color dinnerware are all basic items that can be used
at the drop of a hat to create the perfect party. They are not clutter but good, basic,
useful items.

Look at Figure 4.2. Here is your list of basic materials that will be helpful as you are organizing your space. These are items that are staple goods and if you do not use them at the beginning of your reorganizing adventure you will definitely use them later. This document is available for you as Appendix 4C.

Step Four

Let me go back to our example of the steps an interior designer follows. At this point, a designer would not just jump in moving furniture around, correct? He or she would typically sit down with you and determine the needs of the space. What will you do with the space? What kinds of activities will be happening in the space? Are there specific limitations? Are there specific needs of people using the space? What is the overall goal?

First of all, if you are walking into the classroom as a new teacher, you need to read through the students' files or sit down with someone who knows your students to discuss each one's particular needs. If you have known the students for a few years it will be much easier, but do not allow that to give you permission for everything to remain the same.

As you develop a plan, *don't compare it to what you've done in the past—compare it to the perfect environmental setup for a classroom for students with special needs.* Before setting up a classroom for students with special needs, you have to consider their needs. All classrooms are not created equal, so be sure to consider your population when you are setting about to structure your new classroom as the needs of your students will affect how you arrange your space. Consider the example shown in Figure 4.3 (a blank version of this form can be found as Appendix 4D).

You will notice on Figure 4.3 that there are three areas that you need to investigate when you are determining the specific needs of your students: (1) physical needs, (2) behavioral needs, and (3) safety needs. Specific physical needs information would encompass whether the student uses a wheelchair, has other mobility issues, needs additional space to walk around, needs space for added organizational materials, or requires a bigger desk because of his or her size. There are so many different physical needs the students could have that will impact the physical layout of the classroom. See Figure 4.3: Not only did Joanne need space for her wheelchair and Johnny needed space to walk around, there was also a space need for the paraprofessional's desk and a spot the occupational therapist could use to do therapy in the classroom.

What about the behavioral needs of your students? When you looked through the student records, did you note any students with volatile behaviors? If so, the students may require a desk built with the writing surface and the seat as one piece so they cannot push the desk over. It may also require that you place objects that could be thrown around outside the proximity of the student. You may also find that some students do not work well together. I certainly found that out in my middle school classroom. I taught a self-contained classroom in a mobile unit and had a large group of all boys. Some did not work well together and, to promote a peaceful classroom environment, it was better to separate their work space and work on the *getting along* during our social skills lessons. Look at Figure 4.3: Sam and Ryan need to be separated, and Marvin is a runner and does not need to be close to the door of the classroom. Apparently Pete has some behavioral concerns because he needs to be in close proximity to the teacher.

This will be a good segue into the area of safety. In my career I have had a great deal of experience with students who have severe emotional and behavioral disabilities. These students exhibit behaviors that are volatile and aggressive, and they can be a danger to themselves and others. You may have students who have the same level of behavioral needs. The behavioral needs of these students have to be addressed and three things come to mind:

1. For the students who are runners or tend to elope from the area, it is helpful to create a more difficult way to exit the room. The student's desk area should not be near the door. I have been in several classrooms where this is an issue and one of the first

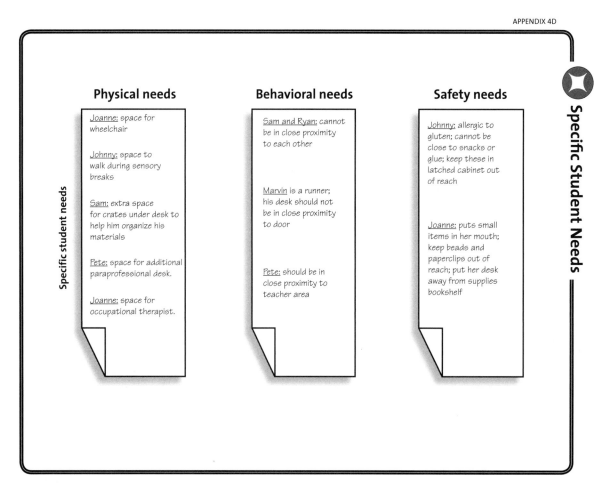

APPENDIX 4D

Physical needs

Joanne: space for wheelchair

Johnny: space to walk during sensory breaks

Sam: extra space for crates under desk to help him organize his materials

Pete: space for additional paraprofessional desk.

Joanne: space for occupational therapist.

Behavioral needs

Sam and Ryan: cannot be in close proximity to each other

Marvin is a runner; his desk should not be in close proximity to door

Pete: should be in close proximity to teacher area

Safety needs

Johnny: allergic to gluten; cannot be close to snacks or glue; keep these in latched cabinet out of reach

Joanne: puts small items in her mouth; keep beads and paperclips out of reach; put her desk away from supplies bookshelf

Specific student needs

Specific Student Needs

Figure 4.3. Filled-in example of Specific Student Needs.

things that I suggest to the teacher is that they position furniture to generate a traffic flow that does not create a straight path to the door.

2. Students who have the potential to use objects to harm themselves or others should not be allowed in the teacher/staff area. This area should be sectioned off and office supplies should be stored in this area. Storing staplers and scissors within easy reach of a student with this level of need is not acceptable.

3. Students who have the potential for harming themselves should not be isolated in the room. One of the scenarios that comes back to my mind is the student who was self-injurious and bit his hands and arms. The classroom was arranged in a way that the student had his own desk area away from the other students, behind a bookcase. This created the perfect environment for his continued self-injurious behaviors to occur outside the watchful eyes of the classroom staff.

Another issue in the area of safety is that there are so many students with autism on special diets. Some cannot touch items with gluten. Some students cannot be in close proximity to peanuts. And some students, as you can see from Figure 4.3, tend to mouth inedible objects. All of these need to be taken into account when you are designing a room.

Step Five

You have so much information already. Take a look back at what you have accomplished so far in this chapter! It is at this point that the designer would take all of the information that he or she has and create a plan. That's what you are going to do.

You will not be able to completely sketch out a layout for your classroom yet, but you can begin to make notes about the areas you need and want to see in your room. Figure 4.4 shows an example of a classroom for younger students. This classroom is more of a self-contained model with fewer students, but you should take the things that work from this layout and adapt them to fit your layout.

Now, look at Figure 4.5. It is for an older group.

Now, let me first point out some things that I want you take note of, then I will discuss each of the areas you may want to consider in the layout of your classroom.

Classroom Traffic Flow

Let's consider a grocery store.

The store has no arrows on the floor pointing you in the direction you should travel while shopping. There are no pedestrian traffic signs directing you where to start. But think about it for a moment. Don't you almost always enter the store and begin traveling to the right?

That is because a clever use of visuals and physical boundaries creates a traffic pattern, thus directing traffic flow.

Without clear visual boundaries, students with autism and other special needs have significant difficulty structuring themselves. Walking into a large open space with no clear boundaries, no visual structure, and no visual supports to define the space's function can cause the students much inner turmoil and unrest. It may frustrate some to the point of behaviorally acting out.

Classroom flow strengthens the structure of the room's environment. Think about walking into a party, a department store, or even a bank. Aren't you accustomed to finding a physical flow of the space that enhances to your ability to interpret the function? When you walk into a party at someone's home, there is often a place to hang jackets and store other items such as umbrellas. Someone normally greets you at the door and provides ver-

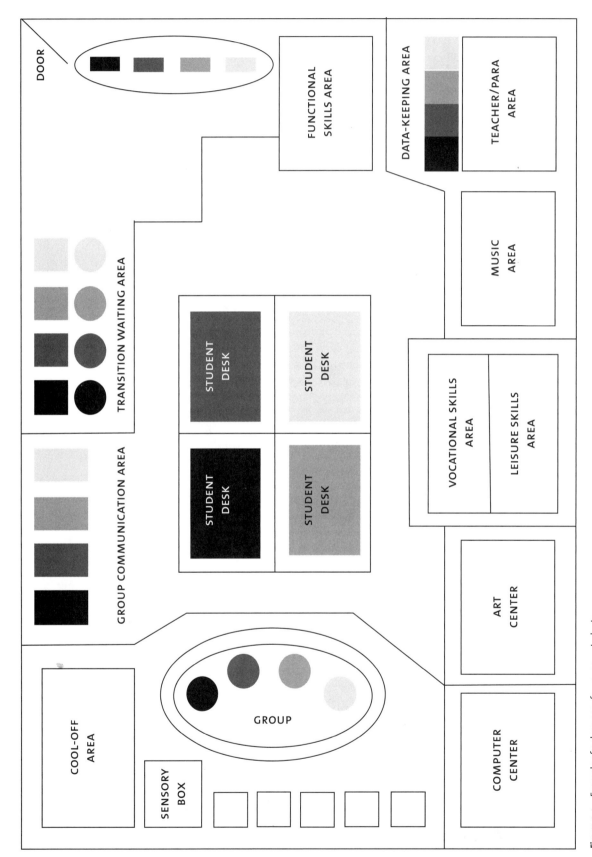

Figure 4.4. Example of a classroom for younger students.

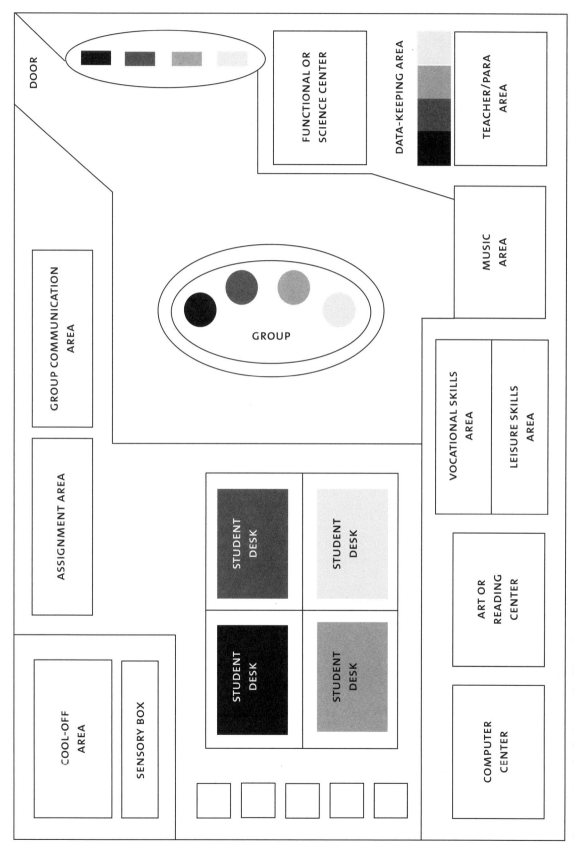

Figure 4.5. Example of a classroom for older students.

bal direction to your next task. You may be directed verbally or visually to the refreshment area. Each area is usually indicated by chairs or furniture arranged in such a way as to visually support its function, which may be social conversation and interaction.

Traffic flow in a classroom for students with autism or other types of developmental disabilities will operate in the same manner. It should be arranged in a way that makes sense to the students. Remember, the students have a difficult time reading nonverbal social cues. The students need visuals that help structure the unwritten rules of the environment in order for the student to know the expectations.

Visual Boundaries

Think about your local grocery store again. Imagine that large open store with nothing in it.

That's how you should now be viewing your classroom—empty, with all sorts of possibilities. Some classrooms are like that. In times past, many classrooms for students on the autism spectrum were sparse with large, empty spaces, no visual boundaries, and no visuals to indicate function. This seemed to create a perfect environment for the students to get lost in their own sensory world. It was difficult for the student to know what to do because the environment made no sense to them. Would it have made sense to you?

Like in a grocery store, the classroom staff will position counters, shelving, and various other physical boundaries in manners that direct students certain ways. In a grocery store, these aids section off the bakery, fresh produce department, and meat department as well as other departments. You recognize the function of each area and can determine the beginning and ending of the space by simply encountering visual boundaries.

The same concept should be used in the classroom. In a classroom of students with special needs, visual boundaries are an important part of the classroom setup. Visual boundaries give structure to the environment. These students benefit from external structure to their space. In each area of the room, they need to know

◆ The function of the space

◆ Where the space begins and ends

◆ Expectations within the space

There are many different ways to create visual boundaries in a classroom and you should always choose the ones that are applicable for the level of your students. I am going to give you just a few:

◆ Start at the front door. As soon as students walk in through the door of the classroom, there should be a traffic pattern for them to follow. Use low-tack painter's tape or hook-and-loop tape on the floor to create "aisles" to follow. If this is not allowed in your particular school, then purchase inexpensive carpet runners in several colors from a local discount store. Carpet runners work well for this purpose.

◆ In classrooms for very young students, you may want to tape footprints to the floor in the hallway so that the students learn to wait before entering. Visual instructions or reminders can be placed on the door so that the student is reminded how to walk into a classroom and what to do next. A small piece of plastic carpet protector can be placed over the footprints to protect them.

◆ Use low-tack tape to delineate different areas of the room. If this is not allowed in your school, then use different colored carpet squares or solid color rugs. These are usually available at a local discount store. This will help visually differentiate the areas.

◆ If a couple of students use one table but need their own space, place masking tape down the center of the table to delineate the student's space.

✦ Furniture placement is important in separating areas of the room. Like at home, class-room furniture is more interesting if it's not all placed against the wall. Try thinking outside the box, but remember that safety is paramount. If you have a student with the potential for being physically aggressive, make sure that all furniture is bolted to the floor or strapped to the wall.

✦ Try creating area dividers made of PVC pipe and fabric. Piece together the PVC to make a lightweight square frame with a T at the floor to stand it up. You can use a few yards of fabric and a simple seam at the top to make a curtain that will feed onto the top of the divider. Because the divider is lightweight, it is appropriate for classrooms with students who may become aggressive.

✦ If you are fortunate enough to have a handyman at your disposal, create dividers out of plywood and pieces of 2" by 4" wood. These dividers will be sturdy and can be painted, covered in felt to create a Velcro surface, painted with magnetic paint to create a magnetic surface, or covered with cork to create a bulletin board. This is a great place to hang visual schedules or teaching boards. An example is shown in Figure 4.6.

Classroom Zones

Notice the different areas or zones of the room. Each area has a purpose and will contain visuals to provide additional structure for the students. If the classroom is divided into different zones or areas of focus, then it will be easier to locate classroom materials and supplies because they will be kept in that particular spot! You can go even further and color code the different areas, and that will increase the structure. Color coding and information about the creation of areas or zones in the room will be discussed in more detail in this chapter, so just hold that thought.

Figure 4.6. A visual boundary created using plywood as dividers.

Let's get on to a little more detail about the areas in the classroom zones so that you can sketch out the layout of your room. The goal of step five is for you, as a designer would, to have a plan for your room and implement it.

First take a look at this classroom layout (see Figure 4.7).

Now look at the same room after a few modifications (see Figure 4.8).

Do you see how the areas are defined? Each student has his or her space, the areas are color-coded, and there are visual supports everywhere! It may seem like a lot of visuals. For this particular group of students this was necessary, but only use the ideas that are pertinent for the needs of your particular students.

I am going to get a little more detailed with the classroom zones and will describe several that may be useful to you and your students. After this section you can begin sketching out your classroom. Remember, implement only what works for you and leave the rest alone.

Look at Figure 4.9. This form is included as Appendix 4E and will help you organize yourself as you work through the next section.

Purposeful Spaces

Time to move furniture! Well, almost. You now have a clean room so you need to determine what to do with all of that space. The areas you put in the classroom need to have a purpose and that is why I call these *purposeful spaces*.

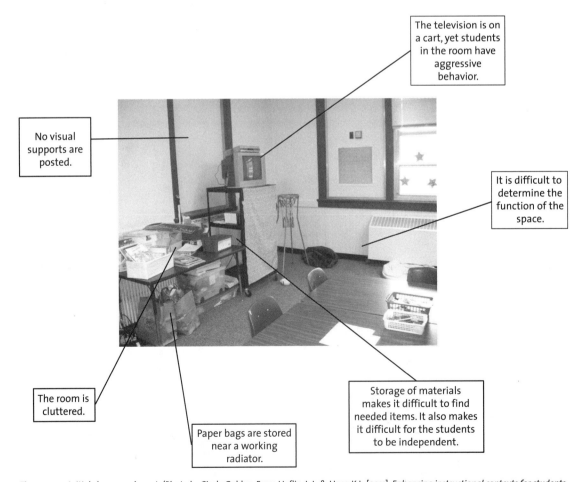

Figure 4.7. Initial classroom layout. (Photo by Cindy Golden. From Heflin, L.J., & Hess, K.L. [2011]. *Enhancing instructional contexts for students with autism spectrum disorders [EIC-ASD].* Retrieved from http://education.gsu.edu/autism/)

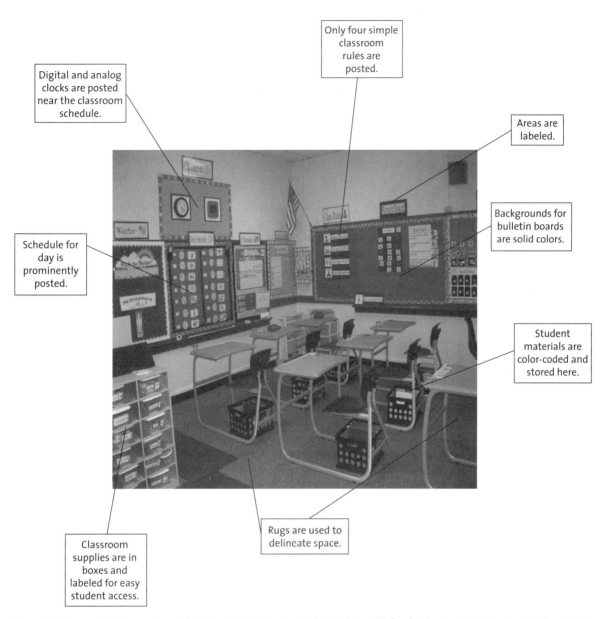

Digital and analog clocks are posted near the classroom schedule.

Only four simple classroom rules are posted.

Areas are labeled.

Backgrounds for bulletin boards are solid colors.

Schedule for day is prominently posted.

Student materials are color-coded and stored here.

Rugs are used to delineate space.

Classroom supplies are in boxes and labeled for easy student access.

Figure 4.8. Reorganized classroom layout. (Photo by Cindy Golden. From Heflin, L.J., & Hess, K.L. [2011]. *Enhancing instructional contexts for students with autism spectrum disorders [EIC-ASD].* Retrieved from http://education.gsu.edu/autism/)

As I told you earlier, I have taught in classrooms of many different shapes and sizes: a very small rectangle-shaped closet, a large square oversized room, a double-wide rectangle-shaped mobile unit, and an odd pie-shaped room with metal walls. Regardless of the setting, I always managed to deal with my classroom space with grace, making the most of what I had. You, too, need to make the most of what you've been given. Even an oddly shaped area can function as a classroom when planned and organized to make the most of every inch of available space.

Every classroom will be different and sometimes certain areas may serve double or triple duty. You also need to build on the room's strengths. If you have a metal wall, don't complain—buy magnets! If you have a fuzzy, carpet-textured wall, don't fuss about it—just try using Velcro. If you have a cement wall, then try fastening things with hot glue. If you have a very slick, smooth wall, try a waxer, which is a simple machine that puts a thin coat

Use this sheet as you work through the next sections of this chapter. It will help you organize your thoughts as you continue to plan for the arrangement of your classroom space.

ENVIRONMENTAL PLANNING WORKSHEET		
Areas	**Areas I need**	**Notes**
Individual work area		
Computer area		
Bookbag area		
Coat area		
Mailbox area		
Data area		
Behavior area		
Work centers/stations		
Leisure area		
Transition/waiting area		
Vocational area		
Cool-down area		
Classroom staff area		
Classroom supplies area		

Wall areas	**Areas I need**	**Notes**
Schedule		
Behavior and data		
Communication board		
Teaching boards		

Environmental Planning Worksheet

Figure 4.9. Environmental planning worksheet.

of wax onto laminated sheets of paper. You will show your professionalism if you go about developing the space you have been given to its potential with a smile on your face.

Here are 10 different areas that you may want to include in your classroom:

1. Individual academic area
2. Group work area
3. Book bag/coat area
4. Data-keeping area
5. Centers or work stations
6. Leisure area
7. Transition/waiting area
8. Vocational skills work area
9. Cool-down area
10. Staff work area

Individual Academic Area

Do you have any students who have a need to work in an individual space? Are they highly distractible? Do they exhibit significant behavioral issues and have a difficult time working in close proximity to other students? Are they academically advanced and require individualized academic plans? If any of your students fit any of these criteria, you may need to set up an individual work station in an area of the room.

Figure 4.10 shows an example of a study carrel that serves as a work station. This is arranged like an office and this particular student's home base is in a self-contained classroom, but the student attends class in an inclusive environment for all but two periods of the day. This student also checks in with this teacher in the morning and out in the afternoon so that the teacher can assist in his organization and monitor academic and behavioral progress during the week.

Figure 4.10. Study carrel that serves as a work station.

Study carrels are wonderful, but I know that they are typically difficult to access in a school because most teachers want at least one in their room. If you cannot find a carrel, you can certainly create an area with a desk and other furniture backed up beside it, such as bookcases or file cabinet. This area could hold a small clock, timer, lamp, data sheets, and basic supplies. I have also used a *clock in/clock out* sheet with students. This allowed practice for telling time and a way to practice a future vocational skill.

Group Work Area

Being in the field of school psychology for part of my career, I was lucky enough to get to run groups for several different areas of exceptionality. Having and managing groups of students with disabilities is a little more cumbersome than having the students do individual work, but it is extremely important. Early in my career I remember going into a classroom with a male teacher at the helm. He was widely known for his classroom management and the fact that *we never get office referrals or discipline issues coming from Mr. Jones' classroom.* Well, going into Mr. Jones' classroom, I saw why. All of the students were in study carrels against the wall. They had stacks of worksheet packets in a basket on one side of their desk. Mr. Jones had a desk at the front of the room and the paraprofessional had a desk at the back of the room. You could have heard a pin hit the carpeted floor. This is not teaching.

Groups are essential for teaching students how to get along with peers, how to comply with directives, how to communicate with adults and peers, and how to use appropriate social skills. You cannot do this at individual desks isolated from each other.

So, make a group area. Maybe your entire classroom is a group area! Maybe your desks are pushed up against each other, forming a small group. If so, it may be good to visit the individual work area section to determine if you have students who may need an individual space now and then.

A group area can definitely be multifunctional. It will typically include a table of some sort or desks pushed together to form a larger surface. This area will be used for social skills groups, leisure activities such as games and snacks, or other group art or holiday activities. One tip to using this area for multiple purposes is to use a visual support to show the activity that is going to occur at the table. For example, look at Figure 4.11.

Figure 4.11. Sample of a visual support to indicate the activity. (The Picture Communication Symbols © 1981–2011 by Mayer-Johnson LLC. All Rights Reserved Worldwide. Used with permission.)

This is an old cardboard box that I cut up and bent into a triangle shape. Taped together with duct tape and covered on two sides with stiff felt, this makes a great way to indicate the function of the group area. It is also cheap! If you are doing an art project, use the visual to indicate that project. If you are using it as a break time, then use the break symbol. This symbol used in Figure 4.11 is one of Mayer-Johnson's Boardmaker symbols (http://www. mayer-johnson.com). Visuals tend to *prime* or *prepare* the student for the activity so they will understand the expectations before beginning the group.

Book Bag/Coat Area

Book bag areas should typically be placed close to the door of the classroom. If traffic flow is a concern, locate the area across the room so there will be less traffic at the entry door. This area could contain cubbies or some type of crate system to serve as mailbox areas for communication folders and other things. There will be one idea for creating an inexpensive mailbox system later in the *Color Coding* section of this chapter (see Figure 4.26). It should also contain a place for coats, jackets, book bags, and lunches.

If teachers lack space and cannot place hooks in the wall, the back of a bookcase can be made into a color-coded place for the students to hang their coats. Placing color-coded baskets on top would further structure the area to allow for storage of all materials coming to and from home to be housed in one location.

If you have students at a lower developmental level who need a great deal of modeling, then why not use this area for teacher storage also? Classroom staff members can certainly model appropriate behavior in storing their coat, bags, etc.

Remember to respect your students. If you have older students, then clothes hooks should be high enough that their jackets and coats do not drag on the ground. Younger students should have lower hooks to increase the opportunity for independence.

Data-Keeping Areas

Data keeping is essential in classrooms for students with special needs. There are many ways to organize this area, so let me go over a few tips with you so that you will have choices in what works in your classroom.

This area may be on a wall or it may be on a shelf. Try placing a bulletin board above this to hang data-keeping clipboards. Look at Figure 4.12. See how this teacher covered the confidential information by using different colored construction paper? She placed these on the table area that she used as a data-keeping area.

The data-keeping area is most conveniently housed very near the teacher area. One of the easiest ways to organize this area is to hang clipboards on a wall with file folder crates below them—one for each student. This way, the data sheets can be removed daily from the clipboard and filed in the crate below.

Your data sheets can also be kept in three-ring binders on a shelf to create a data-keeping area. If you choose to keep data in a notebook then this is the perfect way to store them. Keep all of them in the same area so that you will always be able to quickly access them. Place hooks above this bookcase to hold stopwatches or counters for easy access.

You can also place acrylic pockets on a wall to create data-keeping areas. In these pockets, place data-keeping notebooks or folders with data sheets inside. Below this area you can place file crates to hold the filled data sheets. You will always be able to access data.

Centers or Work Stations

The idea of using work stations or centers has been around for years. Using an isolated area to house all the materials used for a particular task or activity is the overall focus of a

Figure 4.12. Example of a data-keeping area.

station. Students would then move from station to station, either as individuals or as small groups. This works so well in classrooms for students with whose needs vary. This also works well for students with autism spectrum disorders because the structure helps them to understand the expectations for that particular center.

There are many kinds of centers or work stations. Some common types are

✦ Art
✦ Music
✦ Sensory activities
✦ Academic subjects
✦ Leisure activities
✦ Computer
✦ Vocational activities
✦ Workboxes
✦ Functional activities

Work stations or centers work well in preschool classrooms and high school classrooms. They work well in self-contained special education classrooms and in inclusive regular education classrooms. You can include work stations in classrooms of 30 or in classrooms of three. They are versatile and can be implemented into any schedule.

Look at Figure 4.13 for an example of a music center. This is in a high school classroom of students with significant disabilities. There are visual supports included that will help the students be independent in completing the task of using the CD player. There is also a white board attached in case the teacher has to give specific choices for CDs to use.

There are no requirements to creating a work station or center, but there are a few tips that may help make it more successful for use with students with autism and other types of developmental disabilities. Here are a few:

✦ Include visual supports and a task analysis of the activity. This will encourage independent completion of the task.

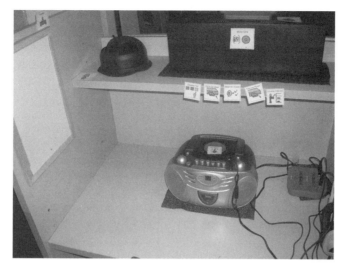

Figure 4.13.   Music center of a high school classroom of students with significant difficulties.

✦ Include a visual timer or egg timer so the student will understand the length of the time period he or she is to work at the center.

✦ Attach a data sheet at the center if data are to be kept on that task. This would go along with the scattering of data collection clipboards in certain subject areas of the classroom if you chose this arrangement.

✦ If you do not have a study carrel, arrange the furniture to create a semi-isolated area free from distraction.

✦ Create a classroom schedule that moves the students around from center to small group to large group to even individual one-to-one time with the teacher.

✦ Use a center for Discrete Trial Training in a one-to-one setting with the teacher.

✦ Use centers to do a round-robin approach to taking data on individualized education program (IEP) objectives. If you have more than one classroom staff member then the students would move around to each who would focus on probing of IEP objective data.

Remember, create the environment that works for your students, but use these ideas to help you think *outside the box* or even *inside the carrel!*

Leisure Area

A leisure or break area may or may not be an important part of your classroom. Your students may have break time in between academic work periods and you may need to set up an area of the classroom to use during this time.

What does this look like? Well, it may include a chair, a loveseat, a bean bag, or just an empty space with shelves of leisure activities such as blocks, books, small craft kits, magazines, puzzles, trains, and dolls. You can even throw in a small DVD player and a choice of videos. Make sure to always be respectful of the students regardless of their level of cognitive impairment. Try to use materials that are as age appropriate as possible.

A couple of things to remember are that these activities should never take up a large portion of the day. A very short break or a structured leisure activity time would be more than enough. The focus would be to include this as a means of implementing a structured behavioral intervention plan that calls for short periods of work followed by short breaks. Another focus would be to teach students who may eventually live their lives in a group home setting to use unstructured time in a positive way. Teaching students about choices they have for using leisure time is very important. These choices would include activities that fit into their particular interests.

This area could also be used as the natural environment teaching area. This area could be a place to practice the formally taught social skills in a more natural environment.

Transition/Waiting Area

The abilities to transition and to wait are two very important skills to teach students with autism spectrum disorders. A student's ability to access a less restrictive environment will be hindered if those skills are not developed. If a student has a difficult time waiting his turn then it will be difficult to function in a large group setting. If a student has a difficult time making the transition from one activity to another without exhibiting inappropriate behaviors, it will be more difficult to access a large group environment, one in which there is constant change. So, these skills must be taught and practiced.

How you teach and practice these is dependent upon the student's ability level. If the student is functioning at a high level and is an older child, there will not be a need for a separate transition area. These students just need individual strategies put into place for them. For example, these students may need something to fiddle with during times of transition; they may need a hint from the teacher that a transition is coming; or they may need a visual schedule that shows them a list of upcoming events or tasks.

Students who are functioning at a level where transition and waiting skills are significantly impacting their ability to learn may require external areas that are structured to teach them to wait. Look at Figure 4.14.

Figure 4.14 shows a waiting area at the door that is structured to teach waiting and even reinforce academic skills. During time of transition the students are to stand on the specific money increment as directed by teacher. These are placed at an appropriate distance apart in order to practice personal space. While they are waiting to leave the room, the group reviews the hallway expectations that are posted on the inside of the hallway door. This does not have to be coins but could be letters of the alphabet, numbers, photos of the

Figure 4.14. Waiting area structured to teach transition skills.

Figure 4.15. Waiting/transition area for more significant needs.

students, pictures of something you are covering in a certain subject, etc. Use this time to learn to wait and to reinforce skills.

Now for the next photo (Figure 4.15), let me set the scenario:

CASE IN POINT Danny was a student with autism in third grade, who was being served in a self-contained classroom because of the significance of his behaviors. Danny was  nonverbal and unable to focus on tasks for more than 3 minutes at a time. He did not understand the meaning of "Wait." The classroom staff had a difficult time attempting to transition Danny from one task to the next, and when attempting to begin a new task, it took several minutes to get him to begin the task. So the teacher had a plan. She created a wonderful waiting area for the students to use during times of transition, like a mini waiting room. She began taking Danny to this area between each of the scheduled task times to learn to wait. At first she had to stand in front of him, holding both of his hands, while he sat in his chair. She would say, "It's time to wait," and she would count. This went on for a few weeks until finally Danny began to grasp the concept and was able to go to his waiting chair and wait as the classroom staff prepared for the next activity. It was and still is a great success!

Here is a photo of the waiting area that the teacher created (Figure 4.15). Tennis balls were cut and placed on the legs of the chair for those with sensory issues. This area was such a simple concept yet yielded great results!

A deficit in transition or waiting skills is one of the things that sometimes keeps students with autism spectrum disorders from making progress in a more typical classroom setting, so make sure to structure your classroom to teach these skills.

Vocational Skills Work Area

The nature of a vocational skills area will be determined by both the level and age of your students. For older students, vocational skills can be center-based. They may include a computer to research various jobs' skills, an area to complete job applications, or a table to

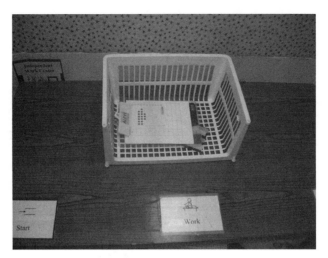

Figure 4.16. Example of a vocational skills work area.

complete job-related tasks such as filing papers, simple assembly tasks, and office tasks. For other students, this center may require a larger area.

Figure 4.16 shows a long table with easy access to work boxes and a picture jig for task completion prompts. The student accesses vocational work boxes that are placed on a bookcase next to the table.

Cool-Down Area

Some students with special needs have a difficult time monitoring and controlling their behavior. Sometimes it is beneficial to have an area of the classroom that provides a place for the student to cool down when he or she is frustrated or angry. I have seen some classrooms with small tents in a corner of the classroom. This provides an area for the students to decompress when upset.

This area could be a dual-purpose area and may contain a chair or even a bean bag in a corner of the room, separated from the distractions of the rest of the room. The area provides students a place away from excessive stimuli. This allows them an area where they can cool off or calm down. It should be a quiet area with minimal visual clutter.

An important item to include is a set of "Cool Down" steps placed on a poster somewhere in the area. It may also be important to include posters or social stories outlining the steps in how to appropriately express emotions. The area should contain no access to items that could cause harm. Carefully examine the area. Is there an electrical outlet, a window, or a bookcase that could be toppled? Then the space may *not* be appropriate to use as a cool-down area. You should also include a timer and a choice of sensory items to elicit the facilitation of independent, self-calming strategies. But do remember that this area should not be a seclusion area isolated from view of the classroom staff.

Classroom Staff Area

The classroom staff space is an important area, but it should not dominate the classroom. There are few things more discouraging than walking into a small classroom and discovering that the teacher desk and bookcases consume a third of the classroom.

Remember, the classroom is for the students. Sometimes in special education there are numerous staff members who work in a single classroom. There may be a teacher and at least one teacher's aide or paraprofessional. One classroom may not be able to support two or three large teacher desks. As top-notch teachers do not spend class time sitting at their desk, you may want to rethink the number of staff desks that you have in your classroom.

Your objective is *to interact with the students, not to teach from your desk*. You should never sit at your desk during an academic teaching time.

Now, scan the room. Is there a small area where a desk can be placed that can be shared by all the classroom staff? A staff desk? Sure, it would be nice to have room to provide each of your classroom staff members with his or her own desk, but this might create too much wasted space. With one classroom staff area, you can house not only the desk but also your file cabinets and bookcases. These bookcases could hold baskets for each staff member's personal items. You would also keep lesson plans, student portfolios, emergency plans, office supplies, and student files in this area. This area should be separated and blocked off from the students. Remember to always store items that students could access and would be potentially dangerous for them *in* your desk—*not on it*. This includes scissors, staplers, protractors, and other such items.

Although your desk is very personal, you may not have the space to decorate it with all the knick-knacks you've collected over the years such as photos of your family or pets and your collection of apple paperweights. Remember that this becomes visual clutter. One tip to remember when dealing with the management of all of the things teachers need to keep versus the visual clutter they may cause is to use solid-color fabric stapled onto a bookcase to create a curtain or visual barrier to the clutter. This works wonders!

Organizing Your Walls

It will not matter how uncluttered your room is and how organized the floor space is if you look up and the wall and bulletin boards are a visual mess. In keeping with our interior designer theme, this is when the designer would, of course, organize the walls with photos, pictures, and bulletin boards.

Areas of the classroom can be easily identified through the placement of wall items. But, excuse me a second while I clarify a few things:

✦ I'm not talking about visual clutter!

✦ I'm not talking about hanging 13 different posters of information that is meaningless to your students!

✦ I'm not talking about hanging all of the awards that you have been received during your teaching career!

✦ And I'm not talking about hanging 51 photos of your children on your vacation to Hawaii!

What I am talking about is allowing the walls to give you the space to place visual supports in order to further support your organized environment. Remember, the focus of the classroom should be on teaching students.

Wall space can further delineate the areas of your room by creating visual boundaries. When students go to that area, they should have visual clues as to the area's function. If there are bulletin boards in the areas discussed previously then use these to place information the students will need in that area.

Schedule Area

There are two types of schedule areas: the student schedule and the staff schedule. This is the basis for your entire day. A schedule should not be some abstract piece of information known only to the staff and not understood by the students. You should model for the students the importance of using a clock and the importance of using a written schedule. This is a life skill.

Try placing the schedule in a prominent place in the classroom and it would be optimal to place this board or poster near a clock.

Figure 4.17. Behavior area.

Behavior Area

The behavior area will be the area that displays the behavioral expectations and the reinforcement system used in your classroom (see Figure 4.17).

This could be accomplished by placing several poster board items on the wall or dividing or devoting a bulletin board for this purpose. All behavior items could be placed in this area so that they can be easily found if needed.

Communication Board

A communication board area is always important. There are many different functions for this area. You should think about what works best for your setting, but here are a few ideas:

✦ This wall area could be combined with a mailbox area. This would organize this one area for all communication going to the students.

✦ Try combining information that you would post for classroom staff on this same board. This way the teaching staff are able to model for the students the use of a communication board as a life skill.

✦ Place a bookcase in this area so that you can place assistive technology communication devices here for powering up with electricity. This way all things "communication" oriented will be housed in this area.

✦ Place items related to picture symbols in this area also. Each student may have certain picture symbols they use to communicate requests or needs.

✦ Posters of sign language used in the classroom may be helpful in this area to remind the staff and students of the correct signs to use.

Data-Keeping Area on Walls

Data keeping is a requirement of special education classrooms. So, if you have to do it, then create a way of organizing the task. This area could be organized by hanging several clipboards on the wall that hold student data, one clipboard per student. It could also be spread across several areas, and in each area that you teach certain skills, you could place a clipboard with all student data sheets for that particular task.

Teaching Boards

Bulletin boards can take hours to create or they can be overlooked altogether. Let's update our thinking on how to use bulletin boards.

There is no room for *fluff* in a classroom for students with special needs. This is the term used for bulletin boards that serve as decoration only. Yes, teddy bears are awfully cute and snowmen, reindeer, and leprechauns may be seasonally festive, but aren't they actually just visual clutter?

The OMAC system gives those old bulletin boards a new name and associated concept. The system refers to them as *teaching boards*. This helps define their purpose and function as well as eliminate the fluff.

There are a couple of different ways to do this. You can devote a bulletin board in each of your classroom zones to that subject: reading, math, vocational skills, social skills, and other areas. Use these boards to support the information the students will need in that particular area. For example, if it is a computer area then use the board to hold

✦ Behavioral expectations for working on the computer

✦ Choices they have on the computer

✦ A visual timer for students to structure their time on the computer

Just use simple visual supports that will be helpful to the students in the area.

Another way to use a teaching board is to make it interactive. Why only use a teaching board for calendar time?

Look at the example in Figure 4.18. This is an interactive board that is used in the morning during calendar time. A great thing is that the students can follow down the board using a notebook (designed by the teacher) that contains small versions of the items on the board.

How about a social skills board that could hold visual supports in this area and be something to teach from during the social skills daily lesson? Just think outside the box but don't waste this area of the room.

What if you don't have that many cork boards? If allowed, use a small amount of wall paint and paint a large square on the wall in a different color. You can now hang items in this square and it will appear to be a separate wall area that goes with the zone of the room. You may need to purchase cork squares or bulletin boards. Here's a good tip: thrift stores are great places to find old bulletin boards. If you still have chalkboards hanging in your classroom, try using those as a place to create a bulletin board. The background creates a great visual foundation. Chalk dust and felt erasers are a thing of the past, but many classrooms still have chalkboards on the wall even if they are no longer used. Look at Figure 4.19. Do you see how the background allows for the items placed on it to stand out? The smooth, dark, and matte finish creates a wonderful background.

In terms of "purposeful décor," consider using traffic signs to help arrange your classroom. Students with autism spectrum disorders do not generalize skills well, so this is a tremendous opportunity to use signs such as Stop, Yield, Danger, Phone, Bathroom, Enter, and Exit. Because these are typical symbols found in the real world, these signs help students reintegrate into society.

Figure 4.18. Interactive board used during calendar time.

Now that you have information and some ideas about several different areas you could put into your classroom, go ahead and sketch out your layout; this will include things you want to place on your walls. I have included a format that you can use (see Figure 4.20 and Appendix 4F). After you sketch it out and see that it makes sense, you can get a buddy and begin moving furniture around.

Step Six

You, as the designer, have cleaned, planned, bought items, moved furniture, and have even organized your walls. Now let's move on to the icing on the cake. This is when a designer would add the fluff with things such as decorative pillows, knick-knacks, and house plants to finish the room. You, on the other hand, do not need to worry about knick-knacks, but do have a couple of other areas to consider.

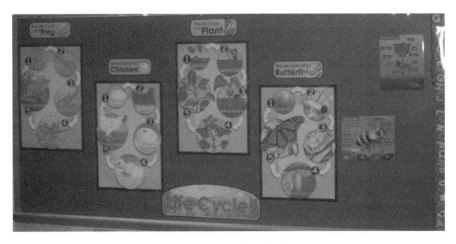

Figure 4.19. Chalkboard being used as a place to create bulletin board.

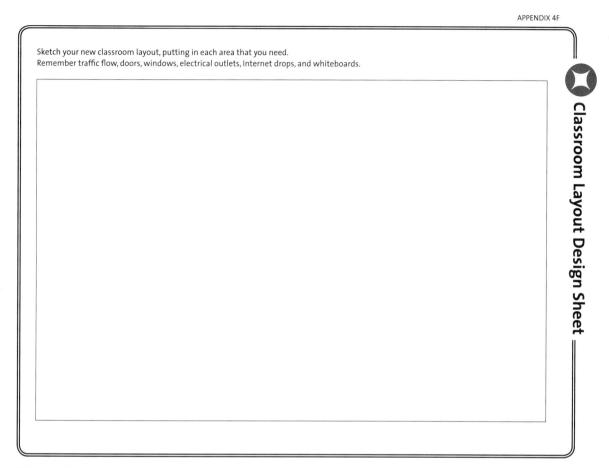

Figure 4.20. Planning sheet for environmental organization.

Color Coding

Designers love to add a little color and we are going to do just that. The OMAC system is steeped in simple organization techniques. One of the easiest and most important ways to organize is by using a color-coding system. When you are organizing the environment for students with autism or other developmental disabilities, it is important that the organizational system of the classroom be simple and easy to understand by both staff and students. The organizational system can employ the use of color, numbers, picture symbols, or names and is usually based on the developmental level of the students.

Typical high school classrooms have a coding system. When a high school student enters the biology classroom, he or she recognizes each area of the class and its function. The student understands this by reading labels, making use of unwritten social cues, and by using logic and memory to determine the routine and function of the space.

So, why should special education classrooms be any different? There may be those who say that over-coding a room lends itself to dependency upon visual supports and external cues. Remember that your focus is to structure and create an environment where the students can function independently. When a student with special needs enters your classroom, it is because he or she needs extra support not provided in a typical classroom. For a time, that student will need maximum support and structure. As the student is able to internalize those supports and become more independent, you can begin to move the visual coding system that you have chosen to one more typical of one used in a regular classroom setting. We as educators need to teach our students ways of organizing themselves for future success and this is one way to do so. But, do not forget that the coding of your classroom is as much for you and your classroom staff as it is for the student!

Ways to Code

If the student is unable to exhibit independent behavior in maneuvering the classroom, has low verbal skills, and is developmentally disabled and struggles in the ability to read, I recommend the use of a three-way coding system: color coding paired with the printed word and the student's photo is recommended for this student. Look at Figure 4.21.

This student may not be able to recognize her name yet but does know her photo. If the environment is coded in this way, the student has the opportunity to see her photo, color, and name together and, as she is able, will advance up the continuum of visual supports from the recognition of her photo, to her assigned color, on to the ability to recognize her written name. The photo is always paired with this strange mixture of letters that the student will eventually recognize as her name. The student is able to also access all of her items in this classroom if they are coded in this manner instead of a staff member getting them for her so she can strive toward independence.

You can code items and areas in the room by any combination of ways. If the student can read then certainly do not go back to using his or her photo, but if you will add a color along with the name it will make the room much more organized for the staff.

Here are some general tips that may be helpful in the creation of an organized environment:

✦ If you have five to eight students, it is easy to code each of the students by color. If you have more students, you can double up and have groups of two students per color.

✦ Use solid-color fabric and sew a small fabric covering for the student's desk or chair. This is an easy way to color code.

✦ Use different low-tack colored masking tape, which is available in many discount stores. The tape can be used to separate student areas.

✦ File folders and hanging file folders come in many different colors. Use these creatively.

Figure 4.21. Three-way coding system.

Figure 4.22. File folder holder created using a large cereal box.

✦ File folder holders are also very handy. They come in several different colors, but if you do not find what you need, try spray paint. If you want to try a less expensive way, then create your own (see Figure 4.22) using a large cereal box or laundry detergent box.

✦ Colored felt sheets are handy items also. These sheets of stiff, colored, adhesive felt can be used to easily create boards for adhering Velcro items.

✦ Paint various areas of the wall to serve as the background to each student's communication area.

✦ Try solid-color fabrics to use as the background for certain areas of a bulletin board. This will separate the area for each student or student pair.

✦ You will find many colors of plastic baskets and crates in dollar stores. These can be used to color code the student's area.

✦ If all else fails, try using spray paint or spray paint for plastic to paint items you cannot find in certain colors.

✦ Colored poster board, colored card stock, and construction paper should be staples in your classroom. They allow you to color code many of the items that the students use throughout the day.

✦ Use colored placemats to help students identify their places at the snack table. Do not call attention to the student, but if the student is functioning at a level that this will assist in their being more independent, then try it. Rolls of nonstick material come in a variety of different colors, and can be easily cut and used in many different ways (see Figure 4.23)

✦ Colored folders and clipboards will go a long way toward helping you organize both data and home communication folders. A little spray paint goes a long way in color-coding clipboards. Just spray the back and turn them around to protect any student-specific information that may be on the front.

✦ Round colored sticky dots are great for color coding areas. You can't find dots in the colors you need? Purchase the white ones and use markers to create your own.

✦ Did you know that you can use colored Styrofoam pool floaties in your classroom (see Figure 4.24)? They can be cut and split down the middle to place on the back of chairs to code them. They can also be spray glued and covered in felt to be placed on the side of desks and used for behavior plans. Just be creative in their use.

Figure 4.23. Rolls of nonstick material can be used as placemats.

✦ Try using colored duct tape or electrical tape to color code items such as small white boards.

✦ You may have trouble finding plastic milk crates in different colors so place a piece of construction paper on the inside to color code these items (see Figure 4.25).

✦ Last, but not least, try using the very large laundry detergent boxes for mail boxes (see Figure 4.26). They can be easily color coded by spray gluing colored felt or by spray painting. Use electrical tape in the same color and colored felt to create a mail box area for each student and one in which visual supports can be placed on the side with Velcro. This is very inexpensive and parents can save these for your classroom.

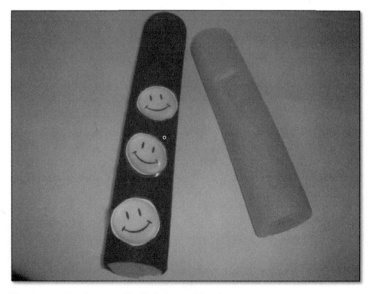

Figure 4.24. Styrofoam pool floaties being used to color-code classrooms.

Figure 4.25. Colored construction paper used to color-code plastic milk crates.

What to Code?

There is such an easy answer to this question: everything! You do need to determine if you are going to color code students and areas of the classroom. I would recommend that you do. Think about how easy it will be to have all of your math center items in blue: baskets, folders, markers, boxes of supplies, etc. When an item is found in the classroom that is blue, the teacher could easily ask a student to put this in the math center because of the way it is coded.

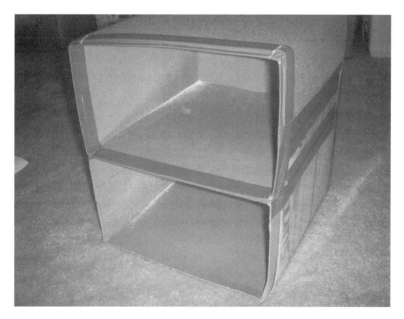

Figure 4.26. Large laundry detergent boxes being used as mail boxes.

What are some other items you could code?

✦ Use color to code each student's desk or study carrel.

✦ Code areas of the book bag area to assist students in organizing their own things.

✦ Use colored dots or chair covers to code specific chairs or places at the group table.

✦ Code crates that hold student's IEP materials you use to work on specific objectives.

✦ Color code all subject area books and materials to structure the environment, promoting independency in cleaning up the classroom.

✦ Create a mailbox area to hold student home-communication folders or returned worksheets.

✦ Code student notebooks that hold data, IEPs, work samples, etc.

Using color coding, along with other coding methods, is that added layer of organization that will help you organize both your staff *and* your students, but always move students toward less and less restriction as they are able.

Lighting

There is a lot to be said about lighting in a classroom environment. Many students with disabilities, including autism, have sensory issues and may become over stimulated by certain types of lighting. An over abundance of visual stimuli, which could include lighting, clutter, or volume of material, will be difficult for the student to filter.

Let me tell you a true story that I have encountered.

 **CASE IN POINT** Suzanne, the school counselor, loved going into Ms. Smith's classroom. It was a special education classroom with about 10 students, grades six through eight. The students had significant behavioral needs. The teacher struggled with the organization of her room; in other words, it was a cluttered mess, admittedly so. Upon entering the classroom, the counselor also commented to herself how dark the room was. Yes, there were incandescent bulbs in lamps sitting around the room and a small amount of light coming in the window, but Suzanne struggled to see as she entered. When Suzanne approaches the teacher about the lighting, Ms. Smith always states that the overhead lighting is too much for the students and she seemed to feel that it increased their negative behavior, so she turns most of them off. She states that there are lamps around the room and a window to provide extra natural lighting. Even with the lamps and the window with sunshine, the counselor still can't see. As she enters the brightly lit hallway and walks into the cafeteria for lunch duty she thinks about several questions: What do the students do at lunch? Do the students' inappropriate behaviors increase just because of the difference in visual stimuli? Are there data to back up the impact of the darkened classroom on behavior? And what will the students do as they transition back into the typical environment and on into life outside school?

Decreasing the visual stimuli in the room caused by an overabundance of buzzing, humming, and flickering fluorescent lights may in fact lessen distraction and the stress that an increased volume of sensory input may cause, but it does not mean that students should have classrooms that are significantly different from other parts of the building, with lighting that is insufficient for teaching. So, what should you do? Be aware of the fact that *yes, lighting may impact overload of sensory input,* but the room should be well lit and there should not be a significant difference in the lighting of the environment between different areas of the school building. Lighting is not an accommodation that can be taken from place to place like visual supports or ear plugs. Visuals can be taken from one environment to another to accommodate for the student's communication needs and ear plugs can be worn in lots of different places in the school to accommodate for an increased level of auditory input. A well-lit room is essential for teaching.

CONCLUSION

Stand and take a bow because you have just completed the first OMAC system component and are one step closer to a model classroom!

Your room is clean and clutter-free. You have designed the environment to meet your students' needs and you have created unique spaces in your classroom. You are now ready to continue on to the next component: the organization of communication and visual supports.

Organization of Communication and Supports

You have completed step one of the Organization and Management of a Classroom (OMAC) system. Your environment is clean, rearranged to meet the needs of your students, and organized. In other words, you have the foundation on which to build your classroom environment.

So now let's put the *icing on the cake* in the environment.

Reviewing where you've been and priming yourself for where you are going is a great technique used for students with autism spectrum disorders and I'm going to model this strategy for you. This will provide structure for this next chapter and the chapters to come.

WHERE I'VE BEEN

- ☑ I cleaned classroom.
- ☑ I organized classroom.
- ☑ I rearranged classroom.
- ☑ I structured traffic flow.
- ☑ I created areas in room.

WHERE I'M GOING

- ☐ I will determine which communication supports are needed.
- ☐ I will add communication supports to my classroom environment.
- ☐ I will add communication supports to my teaching.

Remember, when the students were diagnosed with autism spectrum disorders, one of the primary criteria used was to recognize a demonstrated difference in the area of communication. Everyone communicates: students who are neurotypical, students with developmental disabilities, and students with autism spectrum disorders. But even though everyone communicates, that does not mean that everyone communicates in the same way nor that each one can be understood by the other. So, in what ways do people communicate? People communicate through their behavior, interaction with others, words, and even their facial expressions and body language. Any difference in this communication from what is considered to be the norm may impact development of other areas.

Imagine, for a moment, that you are in the jungles of the Amazon. You are from the United States and have gone to the Amazon to assist a remote tribe of people. You have no information on the tribe, so you do not know the culture, societal expectations, or the language. This does not even take into account the difficulty you will have in other areas, but, for the time being, you should just be considering communication.

You have to rely on the spoken and written word only. How far would you get in maneuvering through the day?

You probably look strange to the native language speakers because you are babbling away, staring at people's faces to try to determine what they are saying. You are frantically moving your hands around attempting some sort of sign language. According to the looks on the faces of the tribe members you are probably not following any of their cultural expectations because you can't figure out what the expectations are and you are getting more frustrated by the minute and it is beginning to show.

You are trying to communicate but no one can understand you. You begin to realize that even though you know what you are saying and the tribe knows what they are saying this difference in communication will, in fact, impact your ability to progress in this environment. You have to find an equal ground and accommodate for this communication difference if you are ever to move forward.

WHICH COMMUNICATION SUPPORTS DO MY STUDENTS NEED?

You know that you need to put things in place to enhance the student's ability to communicate and to receive and understand the communication that is going on in the classroom, but how do you determine where to begin and what needs to be put into place? Which of the communication supports is the most appropriate to unlock the student's potential? Let me give you a place to start. If the student has a speech-language pathologist (SLP) who works with him or her then you need to begin there. The SLP has expertise in the area of communication and should be consulted first.

Think about each individual student when you are pondering each of these questions:

✦ Does the student have the ability to express his or her wants and needs in some way? How?

✦ Does the student have the ability to receptively understand one- or two-step verbal directions for an academic task?

✦ Does the student use verbal language, a communication device, picture symbols, or sign language to communicate in the classroom?

✦ If I were to verbally ask the student to get something located in the classroom, would he or she understand and be able to locate the item?

✦ Does the student need functional tasks (e.g., unpacking a book bag) broken into smaller steps for understanding to occur?

✦ Do visual pictures appear to increase the student's ability to understand?

✦ Do pictures or black-line drawings appear too abstract for the student and does he or she appears to require a photo or the actual object to understand?

✦ Does the student have the ability to communicate through using the written word (i.e., only needs words as reminders and does not require the use of picture symbols)?

These questions should have helped to guide your thinking about your students' communication needs. Now, look at the example that I created in Figure 5.1 (a blank version of this form is also included with this book as Appendix 5A).

You will notice that there were seven students in this particular class. In looking at the checklist, it appears that the only two students who are not in need of some type of auxiliary communication support are Chloe and Brenna. It appears they both are

Which of the following communication supports is needed by the students to function and progress in the classroom?

Student name	Communication support required by the student					
	Words	Sign language	Speech-generating device	Picture symbols	Photo symbols	Object symbols
Sally Mae					X	X
Lucinda Louise				X		
Chelsea Lynn		X	X	X		
Chloe Alysse	X					
Jeffery Ray				X	X	
Brenna Baxter	X					
Nate Goolsby			X	X		

Communication Support Needs

Figure 5.1. Completed Communication Support Needs form.

verbal and understand verbal language. It also seems that they can navigate the classroom environment and progress in the learning environment without the use of alternative forms of communication supports. Chelsea and Nate require a few more intensive supports. In addition to sign language, Chelsea also uses a speech-generating device (SGD) or augmentative communication device (ACD) and picture symbols. Nate also uses a SGD and picture symbols. It appears that Lucinda only uses or requires picture symbols for support with her communication. The two students who require the most intensive level of supports are Sally and Jeffery. Both require photos instead of black-line picture symbols and Sally is at a level that she will require the actual object to be shown for communication.

In this classroom the teacher will have a little work to do. Picture symbols will be needed in many places in the environment so that it is structured enough that the students can navigate independently. He or she will need to take photos of the students' environment and activities to support the communication needs of two of the students. It also shows the need to create a place to electrically charge the SGDs that some of the students use. So, you see, the knowledge you gain from the information on this checklist will directly impact the way the classroom is designed.

Let me take just a moment and touch on one topic that came to light in the previous paragraphs: the use of black-line picture symbols, photos, and objects. There is a continuum of abstractness with those three items (see Figure 5.2).

Do not assume that the student will always be successful with pictorial representations of objects. Some students, dependent upon their levels of cognitive and communication

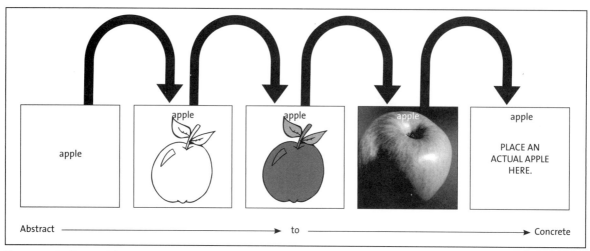

Figure 5.2. Continuum of abstractness with the use of black-line picture symbols, photos, and objects.

ability, may require a much more concrete example. Start the student where he or she is independent. If your students are not able to independently maneuver your classroom environment then you do not have enough or the correct kind of visual supports in your space. Your goal is to begin at the student's independent level and continue moving to more abstract models as they are able.

To organize you in your creation of communication supports that are needed in your classroom I am going to provide you with a checklist you can use as you read through the next section (Figure 5.3; a full-page version of this checklist is included as Appendix 5B). If you have a paraprofessional or teacher's aide who assists you in the classroom, you can provide this to them so that they can help you create the supports.

I want to give you two very helpful hints:

1. Do not ever just make one copy of a visual. If you do then you will finish it and within 1 or 2 weeks you will go to get the visual that you need and you will not be able to find it. Now you will have to remember what you did, find the picture symbols or photos, and go to a lot of trouble to recreate the wheel. Do I sound as if I have been there? Yes, I have. My advice is to create several. Not only create them but also store them in the organizational notebook that I am going to talk about in the next section (see Figure 5.4).

2. Team up with two or three teachers who need the same types of visuals. Form a small group of teachers in your school or even in a neighboring school who may be creating the same types of items. Try the strategy of divide and conquer! One person may make 10 or 12 of the same visuals and share with each other. Be creative in how you use your time!

COMMUNICATION SUPPORTS FOR THE CLASSROOM ENVIRONMENT

Before I begin giving you examples of ways to visually support the classroom environment, I would make one suggestion: Create a picture symbol book that will hold all of the extra symbols that you create. Let me explain: You will go to a lot of trouble creating lots of picture symbols. You will create them with a computer program, print them, cut them out, laminate them, cut them out again, and attach Velcro or magnetic tape. How many times

APPENDIX 5B

As you read through Chapter 5, use this list to check off things that you think will be needed in your classroom. Include the page that you found the information on so that you can refer back for specifics. There are blank lines for you to put other ideas of items you would like to create.

Item to be created	✓	Specific information on page
Picture support book		
Labeling areas and objects		
Labels for areas of the classroom		
Labels for classroom supplies		
Schedule		
Group schedule		
Individual student schedules		
PowerPoint or SMART Board schedule		
Behavioral expectations		
Add structure to the behavioral expectations for entire classroom		
Add structure to individual student's behavioral expectations		
Add structure to the behavioral expectations of different areas of the classroom		
Teaching		
Structure different group teaching activities		
Structure specific teaching activities for individual students		
Functional routines		
Create communication structure for the basic routines of the classroom		
Create communication structure for students to indicate wants and needs		

Communication Supports that Need to be Created

Figure 5.3. Communication supports that need to be created.

have I been in a classroom only to hear, "Does anyone know where the picture of the bathroom is?" You know that you have probably made 35 of the bathroom symbols over the past 3 months, but at that point in time when Jimmy really needs that symbol, no one can find even one of them. What I recommend is shown in Figure 5.4.

 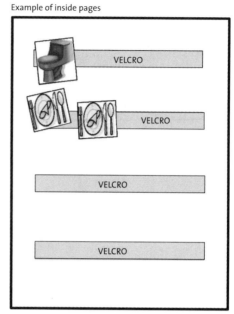

Figure 5.4. A picture symbol book showing the cover and inside pages.

Use a three-ring binder with a customizable cover and create a picture symbol book to hold extra picture symbols. On the inside pages create the example that I show in the figure. Place strips of Velcro on cardstock; punch holes and place in the notebook binder. As you create picture symbols, make extras and store on the Velcro strips. You will always be able to find the pictures and it is much more organized than throwing extra symbols in an envelope.

So, in this section I am providing numerous examples of things you can create in the classroom to support the student's communication. Here are the areas I will cover (Figure 5.5).

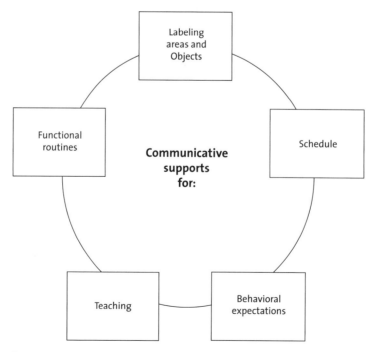

Figure 5.5. Communication support for labeling of classroom areas.

Communication Support for Labeling of Classroom Areas

Think about the signage used in our everyday lives. When you drive down the street you will see signs that serve as labels for buildings, areas, and objects, such as railroads, hospitals, libraries, and crosswalks. You will also see road signs indicating curves, crossroads, and stoplight ahead. They are all visual supports. You know the building is there but there is also a sign as an extra visual indicating its existence.

Think about it this way. Your 3-year-old is sitting in the back seat of your car while you drive to the local discount store. You pass a fast food restaurant and your child screams "french fries!" She isn't old enough to read and may not be old enough to recognize the building but she *does* recognize the big golden arches and the sign that indicates that there are french fries available to her in that place. That's visual support that labels an area simply enough for all to understand. We all use it.

One more way to describe our use of visual supports for labeling is to think about the large mega-discount stores. The layout is a big, square box. Traffic pattern is set with furniture, but what else do they have? Signage. They have signage that indicates areas of the store. Yes, when looking for a three-ring binder, you do know to look in the office-supply area, and you see aisles that have office supplies on the shelf, so you can deduce that a three-ring binder will be housed on those shelves. But, isn't it easier to just look around the space and see *Office Supplies* labeled on signs hanging above? Even you as an adult find it easier to maneuver the space when you have simple signs available that indicate where things are in the space instead of relying on memory and having to deduce from the materials housed in that spot. Well, the same thing goes with students with autism and other developmental disabilities.

Visual supports should be an accommodation for all students with autism spectrum disorders. I know you are probably thinking *My students do not require picture symbols or photos up around the room,* and you are absolutely correct. Visual supports do not only mean picture symbols; words are also considered to be visual supports. I know for my own organization in my laundry room and sewing area, I use a labeler to create small labels for all of my items. I have four laundry baskets for different types of clothing: colors, whites, towels, and dishcloths. Do I label them? Absolutely! If not, the members of my household would just throw the items to be washed anywhere and my life would be a little more stressed. Now at least they have visuals to assist, if they choose to use them.

Students with special needs come in all shapes and sizes. Some of the students may have verbal ability but some may not. Some students may possess the ability to read, but again some may not. Some may be able to follow verbal directions where as others may not. But, true to the nature of the disability, they *all* need some level of visual support now and will most likely need to learn a way of visually supporting themselves on into their independent life as adults.

Go to the front door of your classroom and look around. By now, you should see a clean room and clearly delineated areas with purposeful spaces and teaching boards. Have you put any labels around the room to indicate the function or name of the area? You know, if you do, this will not only provide a visual structure for you and your students, it will also create a wonderful way of structuring your lesson plans and make it simple for your paraprofessionals, substitutes who may work in your classroom, support personnel such as speech-language staff, and administrative staff who visit your environment.

Now on to what the visuals should look like, then where to put them. Look at Figure 5.6. The visual label for this area was created by using the following structure:

✦ Use simple lettering in solid black type—large lettering produced with a word processing program. If you cannot print banners, then increase the size and use several sheets of paper to print.

✦ Use white paper as the background.

Figure 5.6. Visual label for an area.

✦ Place on top of black construction paper so that it stands out, especially against white walls.

✦ Use font that is simple to read and display it in a horizontal fashion.

✦ Lastly, it also contains a picture symbol indicating a musical note.

Do you see how simple things make a big difference to students with special needs?

There are so many areas and objects you could label to create a more structured, communication-friendly space. Figures 5.7 and 5.8 show examples of labeled objects or areas.

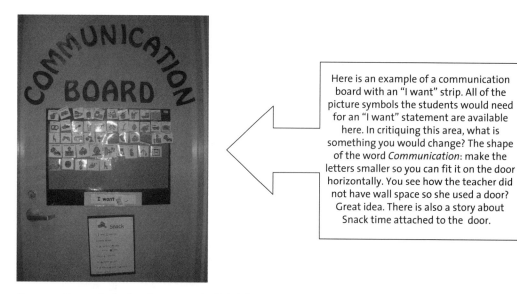

Here is an example of a communication board with an "I want" strip. All of the picture symbols the students would need for an "I want" statement are available here. In critiquing this area, what is something you would change? The shape of the word *Communication*: make the letters smaller so you can fit it on the door horizontally. You see how the teacher did not have wall space so she used a door? Great idea. There is also a story about Snack time attached to the door.

Figure 5.7. Communication board as an example of labeled area.

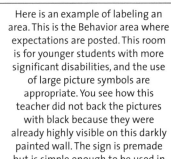

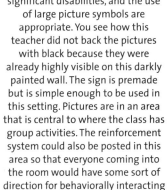

Here is an example of labeling an area. This is the Behavior area where expectations are posted. This room is for younger students with more significant disabilities, and the use of large picture symbols are appropriate. You see how this teacher did not back the pictures with black because they were already highly visible on this darkly painted wall. The sign is premade but is simple enough to be used in this setting. Pictures are in an area that is central to where the class has group activities. The reinforcement system could also be posted in this area so that everyone coming into the room would have some sort of direction for behaviorally interacting with the students.

Figure 5.8.   Labeling of Behavior area. (The Picture Communication Symbols © 1981–2011 by Mayer-Johnson LLC. All Rights Reserved Worldwide. Used with permission.)

Communication Support for Labeling of Classroom Objects

To create a setting that is structured enough for students to be independent in most aspects of the school day, it is very important to apply visual labels to as many objects in the room as is possible. You are probably thinking, *Now what am I going to label and why*? Imagine this:

CASE IN POINT   Ms. Johnson has a class of kindergarten students and three of the students have special needs. These three students are included in the classroom for two segments a day during centers and calendar. Ms. Johnson was finding that as she observed the students in the classroom, they seemed to struggle most at just maneuvering the classroom space. This came to light when she asked one of the students, Joseph, to get additional crayons and paper during a group activity. The child went to the supply area but came back empty handed. Ms. Johnson sent another student with Joseph but he too came back not being able to find the crayons. She went over to the supplies and found them easily but realized that it may be difficult for the students to find the materials in the classroom without adult assistance. She vowed to begin organizing and labeling the materials in plastic shoeboxes to make it easier for the entire classroom to be independent.

This same scenario could happen in elementary, middle, or high school. Now what to label? Ask yourself which materials or supplies are the students going to be using and could access independently? This could include basic supplies, books, videos, CDs, workbooks, math manipulatives, assigned work materials, puzzles, snacks, calculators, art supplies, recess equipment, timers, leisure materials, clipboards, or audio equipment.

When labeling objects in the classroom, you may want to use words only, picture symbols, a photo of the items, or even an item itself. It all depends upon the needs of the students. Figure 5.9 shows one way of labeling classroom objects.

Figure 5.9. Labeling of classroom objects. (Photo by Cindy Golden. From Heflin, L.J., & Hess, K.L. [2011]. *Enhancing instructional contexts for students with autism spectrum disorders [EIC-ASD].* Retrieved from http://education.gsu.edu/autism/)

The teacher in this classroom had students who did not require picture symbols or photos. The students were older elementary and were able to be independent in getting materials with this type of labeling system.

Now look at Figure 5.10.

These are manipulatives that are used for various tasks. The students require a picture symbol as a label. Another way of labeling this would be to place a photo of the objects on the front or hot glue one of the items on the box itself. If you have a student with significant needs you could give them one of the pieces and have them match it with the one on the box in order to independently get their own materials. After they had mastered that skill you could work toward labeling with a photo, then a picture symbol.

Figure 5.10. Manipulatives used for labeling.

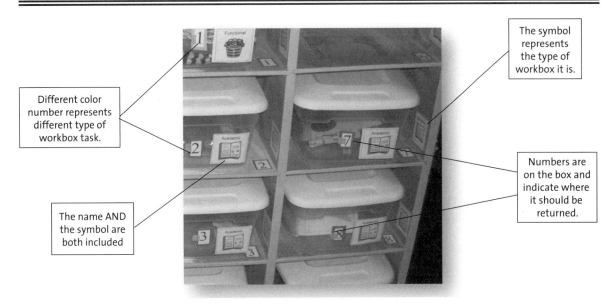

The symbol represents the type of workbox it is.

Different color number represents different type of workbox task.

Numbers are on the box and indicate where it should be returned.

The name AND the symbol are both included

Figure 5.11.   Example of labeling that also enables cleanup.

One of the best ways to label that creates an environment where the students can not only find the materials but also put them away and clean up the space is shown in Figure 5.11.

One of the most important things to remember is to label not only the item but also where it should be returned. Another way to assist students in how to clean up the space is to take a picture of what the space looks like when cleaned, enlarge it, glue onto card stock, laminate, and post in the area. Now the direction could include: "It's time to clean up; let's make it look just like this."

Another way to structure the environment so that students with special needs can be independent in using the space is to implement the use of *object placement jigs*. In other words, everything must have a home. These homes can be labeled by using words, picture symbols, or photos. These visuals are taped to the places the items are to live, so to speak, so the students will know where to return them. It is now not up to the teachers to make sure things gets back to their homes—it's up to the one who is using the object and, many times, that is the student.

So you have now labeled the areas and the supplies in the classroom. I will move on to provide you with ideas of ways to provide communicative support to your group and the students' individual schedules.

Communication Support for Classroom Schedules

A good schedule is the key to the success of an organized classroom. A schedule is like a roadmap: It keeps everyone moving forward and gives a clear direction as to how they are going to get there.

Have you ever been on a long trip with children in the back seat yelling "Where are we? When are we going to get there?" And are you one of those people on a long trip who just needs to see the map to actually monitor where they've been and where they are going? I certainly am. Well, a schedule is just like a map, but if one person in the car keeps the map and never lets anyone else know where they are going, where they've been, when they will get there, and what they will see as they travel, that person may just have a mutiny on his or her hands. And if the map is so complicated and difficult to understand, you may just throw it out the window. I am going to provide you with some tips and tricks to providing communication support to your classroom schedule.

For the classroom schedule to be useful to students with special needs, it needs to be concrete, easy to understand, and interactive. Some students can use a group schedule that is posted on a central bulletin board at the front of the classroom. Some students may need their own copy of that group schedule placed on their desk. Some students may require an individual schedule, one that is mobile and specific to their own class schedule. Other students may need an individual schedule that is extremely basic and may only consist of two steps. Let me get you started by providing some general information:

✦ Post a large classroom group schedule in a prominent place in the room. Preferably you should also place a clock nearby so you can model checking the time and referring to it as you look at the next activity on the schedule.

✦ Create a schedule that is as interactive as possible. It may be important to the students to either mark the task off as completed or remove it (if placed on with Velcro) and place in a *finished* box.

✦ Depending on the level of the students, it may be necessary to place not only the analog time on the schedule but also the digital time. Seeing the two types of time together will assist those students who are not able to read analog time and promote independence by creating a schedule all students can follow. What a great way to practice the generalization of telling time!

✦ Include picture symbols or event photos of the activity to enhance understanding of the tasks. Look at Figure 5.12.

If only the middle columns were included, would this be a good schedule? Yes, but it depends on the needs of the students. By looking at the schedule it appears to be designed for students with more significant needs. Now, thinking about that scenario, if you were to ask me that question again I would have to say *no*. Is a written list simple and concrete enough for the students to be independent? No. What about the students who do not read? They will be totally dependent on others in the environment. Will this do anything to promote skills the student needs to know as an adult? Probably not, because it is too difficult for them to use. However, with the clocks and the illustrations included, the schedule is much more concrete. The "finished" strip can be placed over the activities that are complete. To make the board interactive it is important that one of the students be the one to place the strip over the activity that has been completed. Refer to the clock to add an opportunity to reinforce your teaching the concept of time.

To make the transition of activities even more concrete you can make layered picture schedules. Use a black and white symbol as a base and have the colored symbol on the top (attach with Velcro) so the colored symbol can be removed and taken to the place the activity will be held and matched to a picture that is placed there. Outside the lunch room can be placed a small black and white picture the student can match when he or she gets to the lunch room. When the picture is removed from the schedule the black and white one remains so the student knows where to return it. This creates a great deal of structure for the student to begin understanding the schedule.

In my experience, some students with Asperger syndrome become rigid about the start and end time of activities. If this occurs you may want to remove the time aspect of the schedule and organize it as a sequence of events. Begin adding a class one at a time using the time of day, but teach the concept that time is not rigid and sometime things happen that may cause a shift in the schedule. Use this as a naturalistic teaching opportunity. You may also want to do this with students who are not yet ready to grasp the concept of time.

To teach flexibility or change, you may want to put a *?* on the schedule from time to time. This indicates an activity that is *unknown*. When it comes time for this activity, the teacher can decide what the activity will be, or the students can choose from a couple of activity options, or someone could pull a piece of paper, indicating an activity, from a box. This is a great way of using the schedule to teach a skill that is difficult for students with autism spectrum disorders.

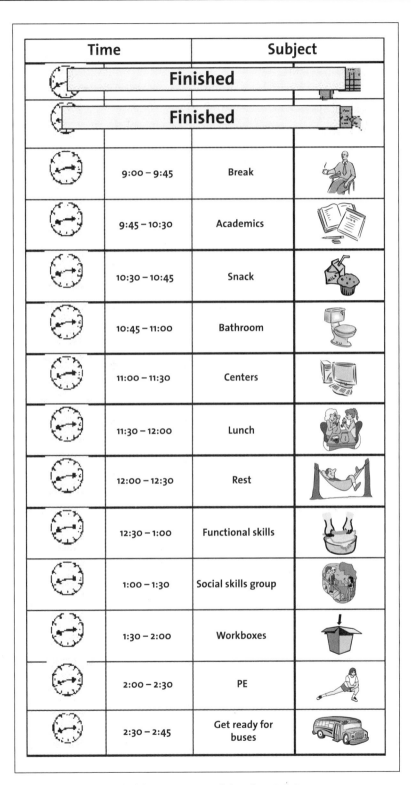

Time		Subject	
	Finished		
	Finished		
	9:00 – 9:45	Break	
	9:45 – 10:30	Academics	
	10:30 – 10:45	Snack	
	10:45 – 11:00	Bathroom	
	11:00 – 11:30	Centers	
	11:30 – 12:00	Lunch	
	12:00 – 12:30	Rest	
	12:30 – 1:00	Functional skills	
	1:00 – 1:30	Social skills group	
	1:30 – 2:00	Workboxes	
	2:00 – 2:30	PE	
	2:30 – 2:45	Get ready for buses	

Figure 5.12. A classroom schedule using picture symbols and event photos.

Examples of Schedules

Let's take a closer look and examine some examples of schedules used in today's class-rooms. Let's start simple and work from there. Look at Figure 5.13.

This schedule is very simple: it includes visual supports and analog time, it divides the day into morning and afternoon, and is in a pocket format so that *finished* cards can be placed over each activity of the day. This classroom is a self-contained primary classroom and, even though the student's work is individualized by levels, the overall subject area remains consistent.

Do you have an interactive white board in your classroom? Do you use it? Well, one of the best ways to use the interactive white boards included in many of today's classrooms is to create a classroom schedule and display on the board. This will allow the schedule to remain visible during the day. As its name implies the board is interactive and the students have the opportunity to use the interactive feature to mark off each activity as it is com-pleted. You can move the schedule out of the way as you use the board for other subjects. If you have white boards available you need to be creative in how they are used.

Okay, you may not have an interactive white board but do you have an LCD projec-tor that will allow you to project a Microsoft PowerPoint schedule from your computer onto the front screen? If so, you can create a schedule with Microsoft PowerPoint. This will also become somewhat interactive. Let me give you simple steps to the creation of this type of schedule (see Figure 5.14).

Now if you want to get super fancy you can also add voice-over. Purchase an inexpen-sive set of headphones with a microphone and add instructions to the activity slide. When the screen is touched or the mouse is clicked the students will hear your voice giving the name or instructions for the activity.

Now I am going to move into providing you with a few creative ways of designing schedules for individual students.

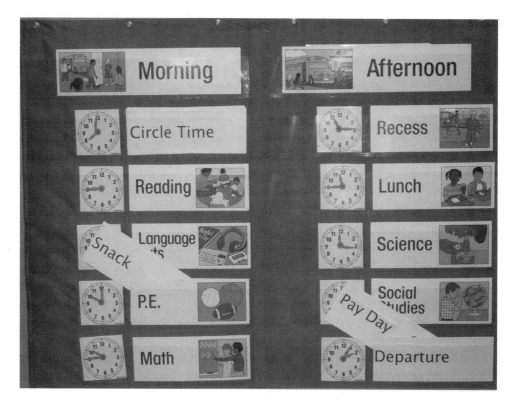

Figure 5.13. A simple schedule that includes visual supports and analog time.

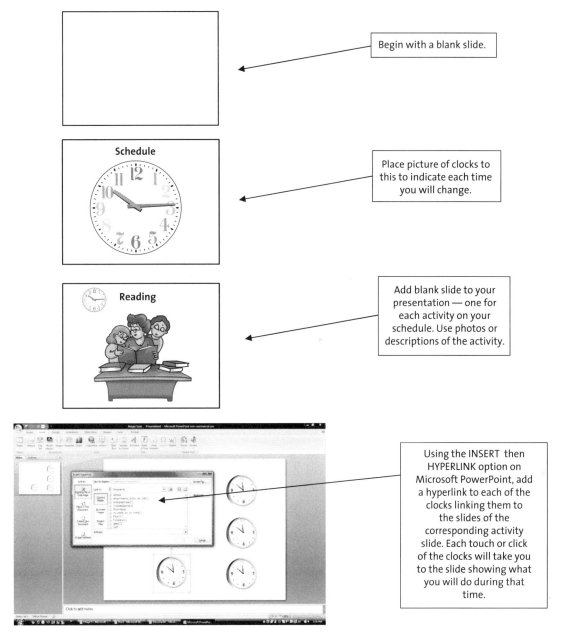

Figure 5.14. Microsoft PowerPoint schedule.

1. Let's go back to paper. You can certainly use a paper schedule and one will be provided to you with Chapter 6: Organization of Teaching Methods and Materials. You can also post on the student desk a strip of paper indicating the student's schedule (see Figure 5.15).

   As you see, the student can check this one off as the activities are completed. You can also do this divided out with an a.m. and a p.m. schedule.

2. You can also post strips with each child's schedules posted (Figure 5.16). A finished pocket is attached at the bottom so the students can place the pictures in the pocket as each activity is over. This is also a good example of the use of a *?* to teach flexibility and change.

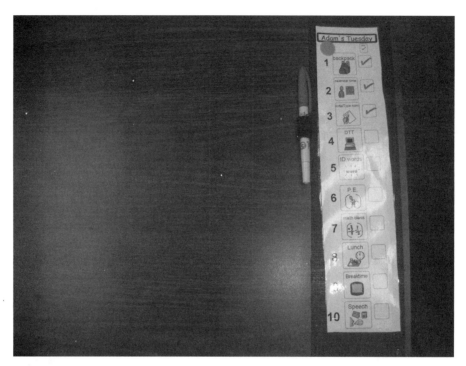

Figure 5.15. Strip of paper indicating schedule, posted on a child's desk. (The Picture Communication Symbols © 1981-2011 by Mayer-Johnson LLC. All Rights Reserved Worldwide. Used with permission.)

3. Do you teach multiple grades in your classroom and need to keep up with several different schedules? The students can do this by using schedules that are color coded by grade levels and other items in the classroom use this same color-coding system; for example, all items for third graders are green and all fourth grade items in the classroom are yellow.

4. What about using those very inexpensive plastic 4" by 6" photo albums? I find mine for a dollar at a local dollar store. They can be customized by taking the paper cover out of the plastic on the front cover and putting in a photo of the student. Each page can be one activity out of the student's day. They even have more expensive albums that have a recording capability. These are available online at http://www.attainment company.com.

5. I was also able to purchase business card holders for a dollar at the same local dollar store. It was very easy to create week-long schedules for individual students by using these. The students could take these with them helping even the ones with more significant needs to become more independent.

6. I have also been experimenting with the use of the very small keychain-size photo keepers. These are run by a battery and you can flip from photo to photo with a push of a button. Why not download photos of the student's schedule into these? The student can push a button to flip to the next activity. As new technologies become easier to use, think outside the box.

7. The last idea is using a touch-screen computer. If you have one available to the student then using the same Microsoft PowerPoint schedule described in Figure 5.13 you can create a schedule for an individual student. What about the new touch-screen computer notebooks that are lightweight and compact? They may be expensive now but as time goes on these would be a wonderful way of creating a schedule for individual students.

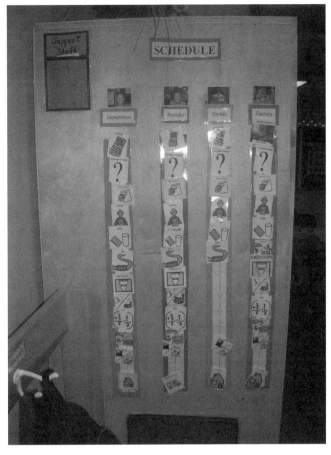

Figure 5.16. Strips posted with each child's schedule.

Communication Support for Behavioral Expectations

You know there is nothing that makes a teacher do a dance of joy more than a well-behaved classroom. Teachers love to teach, and if the behavior in the classroom is under teachable control, teachers can do what they do best. In this section, I am going to show you some of the ways you can support the communication of behavioral expectations in the classroom through the use of visually supported tools and interventions.

In terms of behavior you will want to find ways of

✦ Communicating the behavioral expectations of the classroom in general

✦ Communicating the behavioral expectations each student will have per their goals and objectives from the individualized education program (IEP) document

✦ Communicating the different behavioral expectations of each of the areas or activities in the classroom

So, keep in mind that you will need to find ways of making each of these objectives more concrete for the students. How can the students follow classroom behavior expectations if they do not understand them? If students with autism have learning differences in the area of social skills and have a difficult time understanding the abstractness of the social environment, how will they truly understand what it is that you are expecting? We need to level the playing field. You need to go back to the checklist from Figure 5.1 to determine how concrete you need to make the concepts.

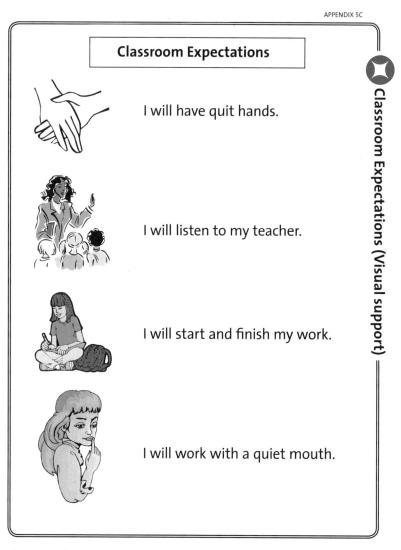

Classroom Expectations

I will have quit hands.

I will listen to my teacher.

I will start and finish my work.

I will work with a quiet mouth.

Classroom Expectations (Visual support)

Figure 5.17. Classroom expectations.

Communicating the Behavioral Expectations of the Classroom in General

Figure 5.17 shows how to simplify and visually support your list of behavioral expectations for the classroom.

This is available for you full-size as Appendix 5C if you choose to use this format. Do you see how it is clearly labeled as to where the behaviors are to be expected, clear positive concise directives personalizing it with "I will...," and a picture symbol is included. This is how to use communication supports to explain to the students what you mean in terms of behavioral expectations. It needs to make sense to the students. In addition to this you can add more structure by using the technique of placing a colored picture symbol over a black and white one. This way you can remove the colored symbol to use with individual students as reminders.

Now, look at Figure 5.18. This shows placement options for the behavioral expectations posters.

Do you see that this is located on the door going from the hallway back into the classroom? This will further assist to create environmental clues to what types of behaviors you expect upon entering the classroom, which further supports your communication of

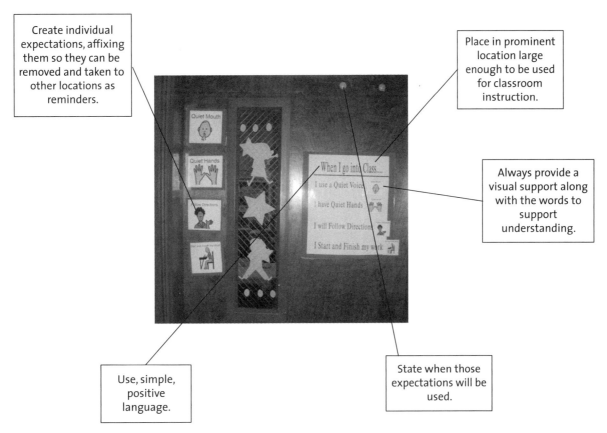

Create individual expectations, affixing them so they can be removed and taken to other locations as reminders.

Place in prominent location large enough to be used for classroom instruction.

Always provide a visual support along with the words to support understanding.

Use, simple, positive language.

State when those expectations will be used.

Figure 5.18. Placement options for the behavioral expectations poster. (The Picture Communication Symbols © 1981-2011 by Mayer-Johnson LLC. All Rights Reserved Worldwide. Used with permission.)

expectations. You would also post this (Figure 5.19A) inside the door so that you could discuss this with the students before entering the hallway and post the sign shown in Figure 5.19B outside the door to discuss before entering the classroom.

Another way to draw more attention to specific expectations is to use large picture symbols and increased font size on the statement. Again, you can use a photo of the students exhibiting this behavior and this would create a more concrete example. These are placed on posterboard and can be laminated to increase longevity. They can then be pulled out to do group lessons or as reminders for specific activities or for specific students.

Another method is to use one of the large white board paddles (see Figure 5.20). Affix a piece of Velcro on the paddle and use this to attach larger picture symbols for use with larger groups. This is great for holding up when the students are in the hallway, at recess, or in the lunchroom to remind them of what types of behaviors are expected in those locations. These paddles are available at http://www.schoolbox.com and other school supply stores.

Remember to also creatively use the technology that you have available to you in your classroom. Do you know how to use Windows Movie Maker? It is free to download from http://www.microsoft.com and is very easy to use. If you are not tech-savvy, try using Microsoft PowerPoint. With either of these you can create great displays for your behavioral expectations. Remember my tutorial on how to create a schedule using Microsoft Power-Point from Figure 5.14 of this chapter? Try using the same format to create a presentation for your behavioral expectations. Yes, it is a little more work, but when you have it completed, it is done for the year. You can put photos of the students in the presentation. You can auto run a Microsoft PowerPoint presentation and have voice-over. Use this in the

A

In the Hallway I Will .....

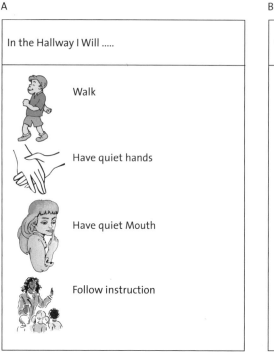

Walk

Have quiet hands

Have quiet Mouth

Follow instruction

B

When I Go Into Class .....

I use a quiet voice.

I have quiet hands

I will follow directions.

I will start and finish my work.

Figure 5.19. Environmental clues on behavioral expectations.

morning and before certain activities to formally teach and remind the students what is expected. This enhances the student's ability to understand your verbal communication of what you expect of his or her behavior in the classroom.

Some teachers wear a lanyard around their neck with a ring at the bottom that holds several picture symbols placed on laminated card stock. This way the teacher has the picture ready wherever the class may be at the time. This works well for community-based trips and going into the lunchroom or the library.

Figure 5.20. Large white board paddles used for mobile use of symbols. (The Picture Communication Symbols © 1981-2011 by Mayer-Johnson LLC. All Rights Reserved Worldwide. Used with permission.)

Communicating the Behavioral Expectations to Individual Students

For individual students who may need even more structure, you may find that they need the icons or photos placed on their desk. Make sure to use the same icons to represent the same expectation. If the student needs a photo of himself or herself exhibiting the behavior, then put it onto cardstock, laminate, and place on the student's desk. Always make the wording simple. All of these are created by using the Boardmaker picture symbols program, which is available at http://www.mayer-johnson.com (see Figure 5.21).

The behaviors listed in Figure 5.21 are specific to this student's behavioral goals and objectives from his IEP document. The teacher has to only come by the desk and touch one of the pictures to remind the student of the behavior to be exhibited.

Always communicate the expectations for the students by using simple, positive phrases as seen in Figure 5.22. Communicate by indicating the behavior you want them to demonstrate and not the behavior that is inappropriate. You would use these requests instead of saying *No hitting* or *No talking*. If you use the negative statements, then you actually waste your time teaching the student what not to do instead of teaching what to do.

If there are areas of the classroom or things that you do not want the students to have access to, you can use clear, universally known symbols that will make certain that these are off limits (see Figure 5.23). You can place this symbol over a photo of what the student is not to have access to. If computer use becomes an issue, as it does with some students, try covering the computer with a piece of black fabric and placing this sign over it when it should not be in use. You can also find this symbol in word processing programs and can place it on top of other photos or picture symbols by formatting it to be placed on top. These are great ways to support the communication you are using in order to limit student

Figure 5.21. Icons and photos placed on the student's desk for communicating behavioral expectations at an individual level. (The Picture Communication Symbols © 1981-2011 by Mayer-Johnson LLC. All Rights Reserved Worldwide. Used with permission.)

Figure 5.22.   Use of simple, positive phrases to communicate the expectations for the students.

access to certain areas and/or items in the classroom. This is just another way to make this communication more concrete.

Remember Figure 5.19? Look back at those signs and see how they created a very simple, concrete, visually supported way of communicating the expectations of the classroom to the students. What about those times when the students get angry and need to know the appropriate types of behaviors to demonstrate during those times of frustration? Look at Figure 5.24. I have provided a copy of each of these as Appendixes 5D and 5E for your use. Enlarge them for use as posters. They work great when used as group lessons.

Look at Figure 5.24A. This poster uses picture symbols to describe to the student what it feels like to be angry. This helps to create a more objective look at an emotion. The student can then move into the appropriate types of behavior to demonstrate when angry; in other words *When I get angry I should try to calm down by_____* (see Figure 5.24B). Together, these posters would be good to hang in an area where you place a basket of relaxation squeeze toys. What a great way of teaching the students to begin to recognize the need for calming strategies and the types of calming strategies to use.

Let's move on, in the same frame of mind but a different strategy. Appendix 5F includes cards that you can copy and place in a small photo album or small notebook to use in a

Figure 5.23.   Universally known symbol can be used.

group activity or to give students when they are angry to help them understand what they are to do. This would also make a good Microsoft PowerPoint slide show, complete with voice-over from you. Remember, always teach replacement behaviors that will include ways of calming down before the student gets angry. This is a good way of breaking down the concept of being angry into small, discrete concepts that are simply explained with picture symbols (created with Boardmaker).

We need to think about your students who are included in typical environments and may be outside your classroom. These students may not require the use of pictorial supports to enhance communication of behavioral expectations but they may need something. Try creating a list of reminders for things the students may need to remember. Place these on the front cover of their notebook or on the back. Three-ring binders with the front/back slip-in pockets work the best. The student may want to keep this in the inside front pocket of the notebook so it will not be seen by other students and that works well also.

Communicating the Behavioral Expectations of the Different Areas of the Classroom

Unless you have a room the size of a small gymnasium, you'll never have enough room for everything you want to do in your classroom. Some of the areas you have set up in your classroom to teach will just have to serve dual and sometimes triple functions. For example, your circle table will likely serve the following functions: snack, group art projects, group

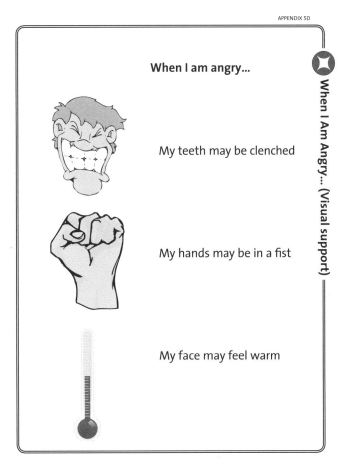

APPENDIX 5D

When I am angry...

My teeth may be clenched

My hands may be in a fist

My face may feel warm

When I Am Angry... (Visual support)

Figure 5.24. A, Use of picture symbols to describe what anger feels like. *(Continued).*

Figure 5.24. *(Continued)*

APPENDIX 5E

To calm down I can...

Close my eyes

Take five deep breaths

Ask to take a break

Ask to take a walk

Get a relaxation toy

To Calm Down I Can... (Visual support)

Figure 5.24. B, Use of picture symbols to describe what can be done to calm down.

game table, social skills activities, lunch or breakfast on special days, and holiday events. With each of these activities comes different behavioral expectations. For example, see Figure 5.25.

Do you see how one area can serve multiple functions, all carrying with them different expectations for the students? Because of this you may need to designate the function of the area by placing a visual support in the middle of the table. Remember reading about the unwritten rules of the school environment from Chapter 2 and how it is difficult for the students with autism to understand what is expected of them if not directly taught? If you provide a visual support for the activity, this will serve to *prime* the students for what is to come. Here are a couple of ways you can do this:

✦ Try putting a bucket or a basket in the middle of the table, and for each of the activities you are going to do in that location, place an object in the basket to signify the task. For example, place a book for reading, crayons for an art activity, a game for a social activity, or a box of crackers for snack, in the basket. This is just enough to signal certain behavioral expectations for this teaching activity.

✦ Using an old cardboard box, you can create a tripod stand that will serve as a visual support (refer back to Figure 4.11). This is an easy way to signal to the students what activity will be going on in any area of the room and a way to show the students that there may need to be a shift in behavior.

✦ I have also posted on the table itself a list of behavioral expectations for group work. Actually tape to the table the behaviors that are expected when working together. You can also post a social scenario that explains how the group should act or even

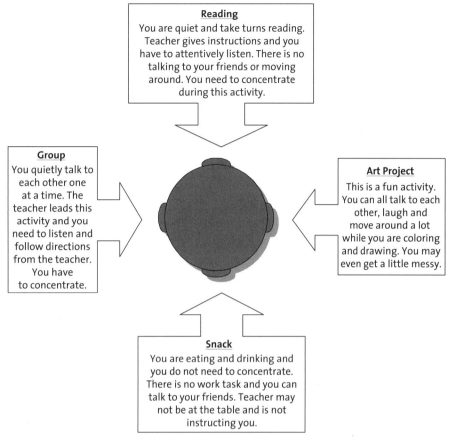

Figure 5.25. Different behavioral expectations of the same area.

conversation starters or communication scripts the students can use when communicating to friends in the group.

✦ You can also copy photos of how the group should look onto 8" by 11" card stock and laminate. These can be kept in a folder that is actually stored under the table and affixed to the table. You only have to reach under the table and pull out the photo card.

✦ Another way to store these is to create a pocket by sewing a piece of oilcloth and affixing it to the side of the table with Velcro. This will hold visuals that are placed on cardstock and laminated.

✦ You can also place the table close to a wall and hang a plastic document pocket on the wall to hold the visuals you will use to explain the behaviors you expect in that area.

✦ Writing a narrative scenario in a way the students can understand is also very helpful. Carol Gray's Social Stories (http://www.thegraycenter.org) are wonderful ways of supporting a student's communication in a way that makes it more personal and concrete. Figure 5.26 shows some simple narratives or scenarios that can be written to help personalize and make the expectations of different areas of the classroom more real for the students. All of these are available full-size in Appendixes 5G–J.

Figure 5.26A shows an example of how you can concretely support the break area. This would be for students who do not need pictorial supports and can be enlarged and hung in the break area, if you have one in your classroom. Figure 5.26B is something that you may read to the students, teaching them how to use transition time when they will be required to wait for the next activity. Figures 5.26C and D show concrete ways that you can structure a music area and the routine the students could use in the morning upon entry into the classroom. Figure 5.26D can be posted on the front of the classroom door or in the bookbag area.

Communication Support for Teaching

To support the communication of your teaching, one of the things you need to consider first is the need. You may have students who do not need a great deal of visual supports for teaching. If you have students who are functioning at a more independent level, these students may only require less intensive strategies. Let me give you a few ideas of ways that you can support students who go into typical classroom settings but need a little extra support in terms of communication:

1. Try providing the student with a copy of teacher notes on a chapter and provide these before discussing them in the classroom. This will *prime* the student before tackling the content as a group.

2. Before calling on the student to answer a question in a large group setting, let them know that you will call on them, and you may even want to let them know what question you will ask. This will allow the student to prepare. As the student becomes more able to verbally answer questions in a group, reduce the information that you provide. You may also want to set up a cuing technique with the student to let him or her know you may ask them a question. A touch on the desk is a good way to quietly cue the student that he or she may be required to answer a question aloud. Do not require the student to answer with long responses; begin by asking questions that can be answered in one-word responses.

3. When you are giving assignments, make sure to always write them down on the board. It may be easier for the student if you would set aside one section of a white board for homework assignments. Section this part off with colored electrical tape so that it stands out. The student will always know to copy these assignments from the board.

In Figure 5.27 I have provided you with an easy one-page assignment book for the students. This is included as Appendix 5K and can be copied front to back on card stock. It provides a simple visual for each day of the week. This helps structure the student. You could also cut and paste a copy of the school logo on the front before copying to make it more acceptable to older students.

Figure 5.28 shows an example of how to structure a workbox area the teacher uses to teach certain skills.

Notice in Figure 5.28 that the entire task is analyzed into six discrete steps and there is a clear directive for each step supported with a picture symbol. There are also colored mats, created by using the rolls of nonskid material that is available in most discount stores. Look at how the colors are used. The students will place the workboxes on the green, meaning they are ready to do; they will work on the yellow meaning they need to slow and be careful to complete the box to the best of their ability; and when they have finished they will place the finished box on the red mat.

Another very simple and inexpensive way to support the communication of the tasks involved in a readying area is to use a small white board. These are available at most discount and dollar stores and this one (see Figure 5.29) I purchased for a dollar.

There is a strip of Velcro placed on both sides of the board. On the left side are the steps to completing the activity in the independent reading area. As the student completes each step, he or she can move the task card to the right side, which indicates that it is finished. On the white board the teacher writes the specific book or pages in a book the

APPENDIX 5G

Waiting

I must learn to wait standing up and sitting down. We wait standing up in a line at the grocery store. We wait sitting down at the doctor's office. While I am waiting I can draw, read a book, or look at a magazine. Sometimes I take objects with me to help me wait. I can take puzzles, video games, or a favorite toy. I play with these while I wait , and when it is time to go, I put them away.

Waiting Story

A

APPENDIX 5H

Break Time

I use my break time to relax. It is fun to have time to do something that I enjoy. I can read a book, do a puzzle, listen to music, or draw. It is good to take a break from work. I take deep breaths and try to relax. I can also use my break time to visit with my classroom friends. We can talk about the things that we enjoy doing after school. We can talk about video games, watching TV, or playing sports. When my break time is over it will be time to work again.

Break Time Story

B

APPENDIX 5I

I like music

I get to listen to my music.

I am quiet.

I have quiet hands.

When time is finished....

I follow directions from my teacher.

I do another activity.

I Like Music (Visual support)

C

APPENDIX 5J

My morning routine

When I come in my classroom in the morning I am quiet.

My teacher will greet me and say "Good morning."

I look at her, smile, and say "Good morning."

I put my bookbag in its place.

I sit at my desk and listen for directions from my teacher.

I will have a great day.

My Morning Routine (Visual support)

D

Figure 5.26. A, Teaching students on how to use transition time when they will be required to wait for next activity. B, Example of how to support the break area for students who do not need pictorial supports. C, Concrete ways in which the music area can be structured. D, Routine that students can use in the morning when they enter the classroom.

APPENDIX 5K

Figure 5.27. One-page assignment book.

students are to complete. This again helps structure the communication of instructions for this particular activity.

As you think about your particular students and their needs, you may notice that the students are functioning at a communicative level where they need photographs of the steps involved in the task, instead of picture symbols or words. Figure 5.30 shows a micro-task analysis or schedule of a sorting coins workbox task. I define a micro-task as a visual sequence of very small discrete steps within a larger task.

Notice that there are also words for each task. As the students become able to bring their attention to the words that correspond with the photo, this creates a scenario that expands their learning and does not limit them by only providing one type of support. Organize this by copying onto cardstock and laminating the card and remember to always make more than one just in case you need one later.

Now, during certain teaching times it may be helpful to provide the students with a short story or scenario, much like Carol Gray's Social Stories that we discussed earlier, that will describe what the activity is all about and the behavior you expect during this time. Figure 5.31 shows one that could be used in the workbox area or during workbox time. This simplifies what is expected during this activity through the use of short, concise phrases and pictorial symbols. This is also provided to you as Appendix 5L.

There is another way to provide individual students with a strip of what they are to do during certain types of teaching activities. Look at Figure 5.32. Instead of giving the students a long set of verbal instructions for a task and expecting them to understand and remember each step, you can provide the students with a simple set of discrete steps that are easy to understand and to remember.

This is but a drop in the bucket of ways that you could provide communicative structure in your teaching. It should have provided you with a few ideas and guidelines that will help to get your creative juices flowing!

Figure 5.28.   Structuring of a workbox area used by the teacher to teach certain skills. (The Picture Communication Symbols © 1981-2011 by Mayer-Johnson LLC. All Rights Reserved Worldwide. Used with permission.)

Communication Support for Functional Routines

You are probably wondering what "functional routines" encompasses. Educators all know how important academic skills are; they all know how important it is for students to know how to read, write, and calculate. But with our students who have autism and those with other developmental disabilities, there are many other types of skills that they need to have the opportunity to practice to prepare themselves for the outside world.

Figure 5.29.   Whiteboard being used to support the communication of tasks. (The Picture Communication Symbols © 1981-2011 by Mayer-Johnson LLC. All Rights Reserved Worldwide. Used with permission.)

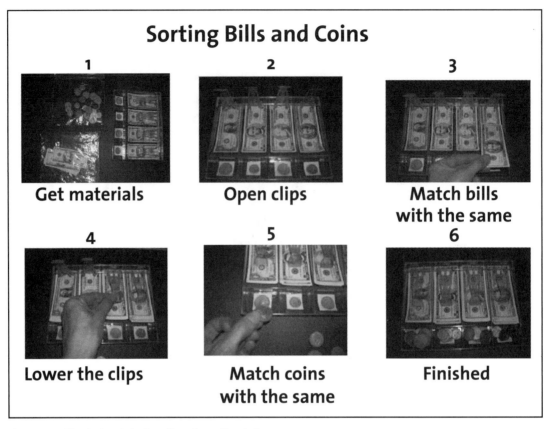

Figure 5.30. Micro-task analysis of a sorting coins workbox task.

Let's brainstorm a minute so that you will have a list of other types of functional routines a person is required to perform within a school setting. Some examples might include personal hygiene issues, getting lunches and taking care of yourself in terms of eating, maneuvering in classroom space, or asking for help. So, you know what I mean by functional tasks; now you need to begin thinking about how you can provide communicative structure and support to those tasks so that the students can independently complete them. Of course I will provide you with a few ideas to get you started.

I am going to present this section in chronological order beginning with the students coming in the door of your classroom. This is the way I want you to think of it; also, it will help organize your thoughts and planning. So, what do the students do first? Probably put away their bookbags. So, let's look at that first (see Figure 5.33).

Figure 5.33 shows a simple task-analyzed strip that provides the student with a structured format for an unstructured task. From the time the student enters the classroom door until he or she sits at his or her desk is somewhat unstructured. This will be the time that you can set the stage for the rest of the day. Post a visual support in your bookbag area so that the students will be able to understand this task and move toward completing it independently because what you do not want to do is create an environment where the students are waiting on a staff member to either physically or verbally prompt them in the routine. This works in a typical classroom or in a self-contained special education classroom. To promote independence (which is your goal), you must provide a transition support from your physical and verbal prompts.

At some point in the morning hours the student may need to find a place at a group activity table. Look at Figure 5.34.

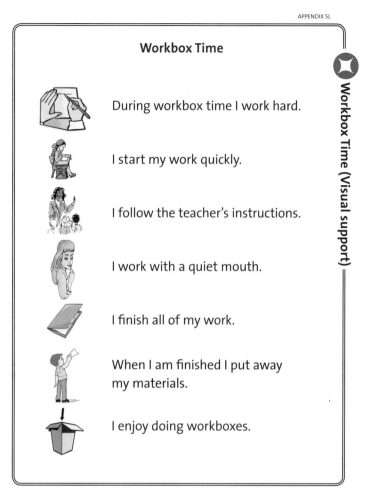

Figure 5.31. Workbox time (visual support).

This is another functional skill the students need to know how to do and do independently. This is in a younger classroom and the teacher has identified where each student is supposed to sit at a group table by not only color coding the students but also with their name. Some students may require a photo at their spot at the table. You may consider making a colored slip on a cover for the back of the chair—complete with photo hooked

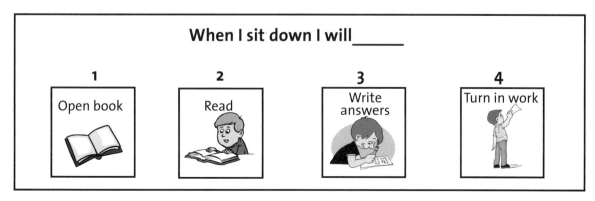

Figure 5.32. Strip using pictorial symbols and concise phrases to communicate a task.

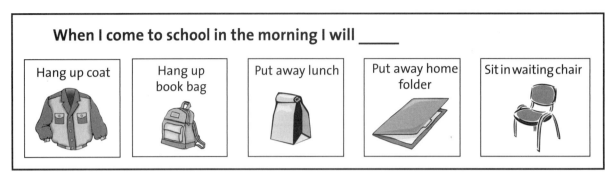

When I come to school in the morning I will _____

| Hang up coat | Hang up book bag | Put away lunch | Put away home folder | Sit in waiting chair |

Figure 5.33. Simple task-analyzed strip providing the student with a structured format for an unstructured task.

onto the back. Whatever you use, it is important to indicate this in some way, so that the student will independently come to the area and sit in the correct place. The key word is *independently*.

It's lunchtime! This is definitely an area of functional activities that you want the students to have the ability to do. These are life skills. Teach them early and practice to mastery. The communication that goes on from the time the students leave, moving toward the lunchroom, until the time they return to the classroom is massive. Teachers and staff members do not realize how much they verbally prompt the students; it would be better to provide them with a visual cuing system of things to remember instead of repeating verbal directions 351 times within a 30-minute period of time! Look at Figure 5.35.

Figure 5.35 shows a middle school student with significant needs at the lunchroom table. The student not only ate what was on her plate but also picked off of everyone's plate around her. When she was finished with her food, she thought she was to leave—and

Figure 5.34. Group activity table.

Figure 5.35. Middle school student with significant needs at the lunchroom table. (The Picture Communication Symbols © 1981-2011 by Mayer-Johnson LLC. All Rights Reserved Worldwide. Used with permission.)

at that moment! The teacher was constantly prompting the student, so along came the visual schedule and placemat. The student was now to eat only what was on her particular placemat and the student was prompted to do the tasks listed at the top of the placemat. This lends itself to encouraging independency on a functional task. The visual schedule is provided for you as Appendix 5M. You may want to copy it and place it on a 9" by 12" sheet of colored construction paper to color code each student. You may also need to put the student's photo on the back, further structuring the task. Use this as needed with your particular students.

Every student needs to have the ability to communicate his or her wants and needs. Some students may have the ability to use words to express wants and needs. Some may use sign language and others a voice output device or SGD. Other students may use picture symbols.

Figure 5.36 shows you a couple of ways to make picture symbols easy to access. If the students are to communicate using a method other than words, then it is imperative to make sure that the method is accessible. If their SGD is sitting on a shelf with a dead battery, it is not useful. If the student is able to use a few manual signs to communicate but you are the only one in the classroom who understands the sign, it is not useful. And if the student uses picture symbols to communicate but they cannot find the ones they need then, it is not useful. Let's remedy that problem; look at Figure 5.36.

One last idea is to use communication rings or communication wallets. These can be made out of inexpensive wallet-type business card holders with plastic sleeves. You can make communication rings by laminating picture symbol cards, punching a hole in them, and using a hook to place them on a key ring that is hooked onto the student's pocket. This allows for the picture symbols to be accessible whether the student is in the classroom, the hallway, the lunchroom, or the bus.

Be creative with your students and structure the classroom with the appropriate level of communicative supports that will foster independence in all types of tasks.

Now, remember at the beginning of this chapter I said that the visuals were going to add the icing to your environmental cake? Well, you have iced your cake! Look around your classroom through the eyes of your students. Do you feel that it makes more sense to them? It should. Communication is such a vital part of the teaching day. It is essential that

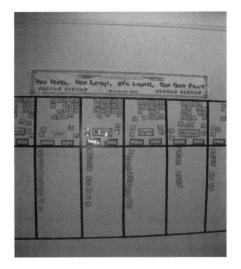

Here is an example of a communication board using a metal wall. Each child had a strip with To Do and Finished. This served as not only the student's schedule but also the communication board. It provided the students with picture symbols for requesting objects and activities. As you can see extra symbols were kept above. Each child's name was also color-coded. This way each time the students needed a picture symbol to request something in the classroom, it was easily available to them.

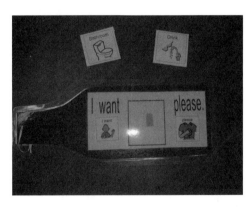

This is a portable request board. This was used by a teacher who had students just walk out the door when they wanted water or to use the restroom. Through observing the eloping behavior, the staff determined that the student had no way to verbally request the desire to do either. This was designed and hung by the door along with the communication symbols. The student now uses this and hands it to a staff member to request the need for water or to use the restroom.

Figure 5.36. Examples of ways to make picture symbols easy to access. (The Picture Communication Symbols © 1981-2011 by Mayer-Johnson LLC. All Rights Reserved Worldwide. Used with permission.)

you establish a good communication system if you are to establish an environment where the student is going to flourish. You as the teacher should also be feeling a weight come off your shoulders in terms of managing the space. These weights will continue to come off as you become more in control of your classroom space and your teaching day.

Organization of Teaching Methods and Materials

Y ou can be proud because you have completed the first two components of the Organization and Management of a Classroom (OMAC) system. You are really getting started in the creation of a well-run classroom.

I want you to begin thinking about *teaching*. You may say, "I have been thinking about teaching while organizing the other areas," and that is true, but this chapter focuses on the organization of teaching materials, teaching schedule, and teaching methods. Regardless of the type of student needs that you address each day—autism, intellectual disabilities, emotional/behavioral disorders, each of your classrooms will have a few common issues that I will discuss. I will assist you in thinking logically about how to organize the area of teaching so that you are able to meet the needs of all of your students. So let's get started.

Like a good teacher I am going to take just a minute to reflect on your progress in order to get your engine revved up for this next race. First, look back at your environmental layout. It should now make sense. Your classroom should be sectioned off into discrete areas for teaching. Each area should have definite boundaries, and your environment should be organized, clean, and clutter-free. You should also have a schedule around which classroom life will revolve.

Secondly, your room should contain numerous visual and communicative supports. The space should be visually organized, labeled, and color coded, and the students should have a communication system in place that will enhance their ability to be independent within the classroom.

Regardless of the types of student needs you encounter on a daily basis, there are four steps involved in the organization of teaching. You will be required to:

1. Determine the student's needs.
2. Determine the subjects and schedule.
3. Determine the methods you will use to teach each subject.
4. Determine the materials you will need to teach.

It does not matter the setting in which you teach. You could be teaching all subject areas to the same group of students all day in a self-contained classroom; you could be teaching one subject area to several different small groups of students in a resource classroom; or you may be teaching just a couple of students with special needs in a regular education inclusive environment. Regardless of the setting or the number of students, it will be easier to organize the teaching part of your day if you follow these four steps. So, let's begin.

STEP ONE: DETERMINE
THE STUDENT'S NEEDS

You are probably saying to yourself that step number one is pretty obvious, and you are correct. But when you are planning the teaching aspect of your day, it is vital that you review all of the needs of the students.

If you are a special education teacher with a multigrade classroom, you may be fortunate enough to have the same students this year that you did last year. This will certainly help you in knowing the students and you could just skip right over this next step. But, it may be that you are the case holder for a student and you are unfamiliar with the student's abilities and/or needs. In this case, completing this next step may be very helpful to you in moving forward. Either way I am going to provide you with a simple form that may serve to help you organize your thoughts in planning. Figure 6.1 shows an example of the *Organization of Student Needs Worksheet.* (This is also available as Appendix 6A so you can include it in the Organizational Notebook described in Chapter 3.)

In looking at each of the columns, you may find that you will not be able to provide information for each area until you work through the next step, which is to determine the subjects you will teach and the schedule you will use to teach each subject. But let's look at the form in more detail and fill in what you can.

✦ *Who:* Fill in each student's name, using one page per child.

✦ *What:* List the subject areas that are required for the student. You will need to review the child's individualized education program (IEP; see Figure 6.2) for information about areas that may be required. This may also include a class in social skills, vocational skills, speech-language, and so forth.

APPENDIX 6A

WHO	WHAT	WHERE	WHEN	HOW
Ann Smith	Math	Resource room	8:00–8:30	Small group
	Writing	Regular classroom	9:00–9:45	Large group with paraprofessional support
	Reading	Resource room	2:00–2:45	One-to-one instruction

Organization of Student Needs Worksheet

Figure 6.1. Sample Organization of Student Needs worksheet.

Special education program/services				
	Frequency	Duration	Location	Initiation date
Math	5 x week	50 mins	Resource	1/05/09
English/language arts	5 x week	50 mins	Co-taught	1/05/09
Science	5 x week	50 mins	Co-taught	1/05/09
Reading	5 x week	50 mins	Resource	1/05/09
Social skills	3 x week	30 mins	Self-contained	1/05/09

Related services				
	Frequency	Duration	Location	Initiation date
Speech/language	1 x week	45 mins	Speech room	1/05/09
Occupational therapy	2 x week	30 mins	Resource	1/05/09
Adapted PE	1 x week	30 mins	Reg. PE	1/05/09

Figure 6.2. Sample of Individualized education program (IEP) template. (*Source:* New York School System.)

✦ *Where:* There are several environments within the school where students can receive their instruction. Students in special education classes may have instruction in a small-group resource setting, a small-group self-contained setting, a co-taught inclusive education environment, or a regular classroom. Make sure to review the IEP (see Figure 6.2) for information about the setting in which the student will be served for certain academic areas.

✦ *When:* This is where you would draft the child's schedule. This is the one column where you may have to delay putting in all of the information until after you have worked through the next step, "Determining Subjects and Schedule." Complete the column with the information you have at the moment, and after Step 2 you can go back and finish this column.

✦ *How:* This column is for deciding which method you will use to teach the child—will it be to include them in a large group setting; will they be in a small group setting; or will the student require one-to-one instruction?

In Figure 6.2 you will see a sample of part of an IEP template developed by the state of New York. This is a wonderfully simple, yet complete IEP template. I referenced Figure 6.2 previously, so let's look at the Programs and Service sections in the figure to show you how the IEP will determine details of the student's schedule.

Figure 6.2 shows an example of the information that a student's IEP may give you. In looking at this part of the student's IEP, I have pulled out two of the columns from the *Organization of Student Needs Worksheet* to show you how you can include this information to help organize yourself (see Figure 6.3).

From Figure 6.3 you can see how complicated that one student's schedule could be. If you do not organize yourself early, you will be stressed and you will be the one doing all of the work instead of the student. I want you to get a handle on the organization of the student's day so that you can pass on this organization to the students and create a way for them to manage as much of the logistics as possible. Once this is organized you will know that you have

✦ Followed the specific needs of the student

✦ Followed the requirements of the student's IEP

✦ Created a way of knowing where each student on your case load is at all times

✦ Created a way of providing a schedule for a substitute

✦ Created a way to show not only the student's parents but also school administrators that you are a top-notch teacher who runs an organized, well-managed classroom!

What	Where
Math	Mr. Ted's **resource** class
Science	Ms. Watson's **co-taught** class
Social studies	Mr. Zane's **regular ed** class
Language arts	Mr. Lou's **co-taught** class
Reading	Mr. Golden's **resource** class
Speech/Language	Ms. Angie's **speech** room
Occupational therapy	Ms. Smith's lang art **resource** class
Social skills	Ms. Jones' **self-contained** class
Adapted PE	**Regular** PE class
Music/art/specials	**Regular** class

Figure 6.3. One student's schedule pulled out from the IEP.

STEP TWO: DETERMINE THE SUBJECTS AND SCHEDULE

Let's think for a minute about how to schedule your teaching day. You began organizing your environment; you created a schedule of the day, because the entire structure of the classroom revolves around that schedule. Now your schedule must be refined and a little more individualized by subject areas, so in this section we will discuss how to determine the subject areas you will teach.

We will discuss a few different scenarios. First, this scheduling process may be easy for you because in your school you may have a person who is the *scheduler,* for lack of a better term, and your schedule may be outside your control. That could be good or it could be bad, but you need to take that schedule and move forward. For example, if you are teaching in a regular education inclusive environment, the schedule will follow the grade-based schedule and is most likely broken into subject areas. If you are in a pull-out resource setting, your day may also be divided into set subject areas. Your students may be in middle or high school and the day may be broken into periods based on a bell schedule so that you will not have much control. That is okay; you will just use that as your format and move on. However, if you do have more control, you will need to consider how long the students are with you during the day and break the day down accordingly. You need to determine how much of the day you devote to the areas based on the needs of your students.

You may be a:

CASE IN POINT   Regular education teacher who teaches a third grade classroom. You will probably teach every subject unless you are departmentalized and share subject areas with other third grade classrooms. You may have students with disabilities come in and out of your classroom dependent upon the needs of the student. You may also have paraprofessionals and/or special education co-teachers coming in and out of your classroom. So your schedule and the subject areas are easy—you teach everything! Is this you?

Or you may be a:

CASE IN POINT   Special education *resource teacher* who teaches a few different subject areas to several grades of students with disabilities. You will have smaller class numbers and will focus on the IEP objectives provided for each student. You may even serve as a special education co-teacher going into a regular education setting to assist in teaching students with disabilities who are included in the regular education setting. If you are in this case, your schedule may or may not be provided to you. You may have more flexibility in scheduling. So, determine if this is you.

Or you may be a:

CASE IN POINT   Teacher in a *self-contained* setting. If you are in this type of environment, you will probably teach most subject areas to several different grade and ability levels. You will probably have a great deal of flexibility in the development of your schedule, and it will be very important that you review each student's IEP to determine how to group the subject areas together in your schedule. Even though you have the most flexibility, you may have the most difficult job as some of your students will probably be accessing resource settings and inclusive education settings. You will need to be very detailed in your scheduling.

If none of these is you, then you may be a combination of all three!

Now that you know who you are, you need to determine the subject areas you will teach so that you can create your schedule. Using the schedule you created in Step 1, you can probably determine the subject areas you will teach during the day. We will discuss the method in which you will teach these subjects in Step 3 because you could be teaching some areas as a small group, some as a large group, or some subjects on a one-to-one basis.

While I am on the topic of *subject areas,* allow me to digress to provide you with information about the sometimes *forgotten subject areas* that are vital to the education of students on the autism spectrum and to those with other types of developmental disabilities. Regardless of the classroom setting, you want to consider working these additional subjects into your schedule, dependent upon the needs and IEP objectives of the students. These skill areas are part of best practice as they help provide the student with skills they need to learn in order to strengthen less developed areas. Consider building a time during the day when you can teach transition/learning to wait, communication skills, functional skills, vocational skills, social skills, and leisure skills/using unstructured time. Students with developmental disabilities of all types, including autism spectrum disorders (ASDs), could benefit from instruction in these areas. Whether you teach a pull-out resource classroom or a regular education inclusive classroom, you may want to consider building activities from these subject areas into your schedule for these students based on their needs. Review the students' IEPs. Are there goals and objectives for social skills? Vocational goals? Maybe goals on learning to wait or for transitioning from activity to activity? Let's discuss each of these areas in a little more detail:

1. Transition/waiting/learning to wait: One of the areas that students with ASDs struggle with is transition or learning to wait. Whether it is caused by difficulty reading social cues, anxiety in not knowing what is going to happen next, or differences in communication, many students struggle in this area. According to talks I've had with parents of students with special needs about the struggles their child has in the home setting or out in the community, one of the most important is the student's inability to wait. But, if you think about it, we as adults use our own transition and waiting skills numerous times during the day! Think about the most recent time you had to wait out in the community: Were you in line at the bank, waiting for a table at a restaurant, waiting in the waiting room at a doctor's office, waiting at a red light, or waiting in line at a grocery store? It's annoying! But, even though it is an annoying part of everyday life, it is inescapable. It is a life skill that will become a survival skill for students with disabilities. Is the inability to wait or transition holding your students back from accessing a less restrictive environment in the school setting? If so, then you need to make the time to teach these skills to your students. Students with ASDs do not learn through osmosis. They need direct instruction to learn the steps involved in transition and waiting.

    Will this be a separate subject area? No. It will be built into your day, but if you are not aware of it and its need, then it will be forgotten.

2. Communication skills: This is one of the criteria for the diagnosis of an ASD. This includes both verbal and nonverbal communication. Everyone communicates. Think about a baby. At 3 weeks of age, that baby certainly does not speak, but does that baby communicate? Absolutely. Just ask a new mother if her baby is able to tell her when he or she is hungry! Your students will communicate their wants and needs regardless of the level of their verbal ability. As you know, communication and behavior go hand in hand, and behavior is a mode of communication. Regardless of the setting in which the student is placed, communication skills must be addressed. You may say, "The students are already receiving speech-language services by the speech-language pathologist," and that is great! But communication does not stop there. For students with ASDs, the ability to communicate to express needs or desires is vitally important to the student moving forward.

    Will this be a separate subject area? No, But if you do not think of it as a subject area you teach, then it, too, will be forgotten.

3. Functional skills: Functional skills are the everyday skills necessary to independently function in society. These may involve caring for personal hygiene needs, demonstrating the skills to independently maneuver through the classroom or school setting, or independently completing other age-appropriate tasks required for the school setting.

    Will this be a separate subject area? Yes and no. You should immerse your teaching of these into the everyday routine, but it would be wonderful if you could have a separate time of the day to focus on certain functional skills.

4. Vocational skills: Vocational skills are skills that would be related to a future vocation. Our students with developmental disabilities sometimes require direct instruction for skills that other students may learn indirectly. What are these skills? They may include tasks as simple as sorting, matching, assembling, packaging, or filing. They may also include skills such as basic computer tasks, keeping an agenda or calendar, following multiple step instructions, accepting constructive criticism, time management, and completing applications.

    Will this be a separate subject area? Yes and no. Again, you should immerse your teaching of these into the everyday routine, but it would be wonderful if you could have a separate time of the day to focus on certain vocational skills.

5. Social skills: The inability to use age-appropriate social skills is one of the diagnostic criteria for ASDs. These skills are vital if students are to make friends, participate in environments with typical same-age peers, and progress toward functioning independently in society. From my own experience, this appears to be one of the areas that is most concerning to parents as they come to IEP meetings. It is vitally important that this is included as one of the subject areas that is taught during the school day.

   Will this be a separate subject area? Yes and no. You should always immerse your teaching of social skills into the everyday routine, but, again, it would be great if you could separate the formal teaching of social skills from the generalized practice of social skills in different types of environments.

6. Leisure skills/unstructured time: Unstructured time is difficult for students with autism and other developmental disabilities. It is difficult to predict what will happen next during unstructured time, especially if you are a student who has a difficult time understanding nonverbal or verbal communication!

   Students typically have no problems finding things to do during a break. But students with ASDs tend to struggle with determining what to do during leisure time. Several people in a group home setting for adults with disabilities have told me the one area that bothers them the most is that the clients living there seem to just sit in front of the television a great deal of the time. Even if the opportunity exists to do other types of leisure activities, unless directed, the clients do not seem to understand how to *structure their unstructured time*. Leisure skills need to be taught and should include both group and individual activities. Knowing how to use this time is a life skill that needs to be taught and should be a teaching focus.

   Will this be a separate subject area? Again, yes and no. You should immerse your teaching of these into the everyday routine, but it would be wonderful if you could have a separate time of the day to focus on certain skills such as making choices of things to do and how to play games with peers.

Now, take the time to look back at the schedule you created in Chapter 4, *Organization of the Classroom Environment.* Does it need a little refinement? Maybe a little more detail? Provided as Appendix 6B and shown in Figure 6.4 is a classroom schedule template that you may want to use to create a little more detail for individual students.

This template can be used for a large group schedule or for an individual student. The example is specific to the student's needs from our earlier example. Try laminating this schedule, three-hole punch, and place in a notebook for the student to use. As each class is completed, the student will use a dry-erase marker to place a check mark in the column to the right. This will assist the student in becoming more independent.

If you turn back to Figure 5.15, you can see another example of a student schedule. This schedule is simpler than the one in Figure 6.4. This would be more appropriate for a student who is functioning at a lower level and needs more structure. After determining the subject area needs of the student, you would create the schedule, laminate, and fasten to the student desk with Velcro. Using a wipe-off marker, the student could be independent in following his or her own schedule of activities. Notice this schedule is divided by the morning and afternoon activities. This is also because of a need for more structure by the student.

Let's look at one more example of a student schedule that is more detailed based on information gathered about the specific needs of the student. Let me ask you a question. Do you carry some type of calendar? I do, and I would be lost without one. I carry one everywhere, and in addition to calendar information it also contains information about other things that I may need during the day. Well, if that works for me, then why wouldn't it work for our students?

Look at Figure 6.5. This schedule is easy to create by copying the template that is provided for you as Appendix 6C onto cardstock and printing on both sides of the cardstock.

CLASSROOM SCHEDULE		
Time	**Activity**	**✓**
7:30–8:00	Homeroom (Ms. Watson)	
8:00–8:30	Speech (Ms. Angie) Monday Music (Ms. Williams)	
8:30–9:10	Reading (Mr. Golden)	
9:10–10:00	Math (Mr. Ted)	
10:00–11:00	Science (Ms. Watson)	
11:00–11:30	Lunch	
11:30–12:50	Social studies (Mr. Zane)	
12:50–1:30	PE (Ms. Johnson)	
1:30–2:20	Language arts (Mr. Lon)	
2:20–2:50	Social skills (Ms. Jones)	
3:00	Dismissal	

Classroom Schedule

Figure 6.4. Completed classroom schedule.

Personalize it by placing a photo of the school mascot, school building, or classmates on the front cover before copying.

Copy the student's schedule in the booklet and this will create a small, age-appropriate schedule that is easy for the student to manage and will provide enough information to enhance his or her ability to be independent in maneuvering the class schedule.

STEP THREE: DETERMINE THE METHODS YOU WILL USE TO TEACH EACH SUBJECT

This section is not going to be one in which I provide instruction in how to use a certain method in the classroom. That is for another book at another time. What I am going to discuss in this section is how to take you from Step 2 to Step 4. Step 2 helped you to determine what you are going to teach in terms of subject areas and how to create your schedule. Step 4 is going to discuss how to arrange each of the teaching areas of the classroom in terms of materials and basic organizational ideas. So how do you get from one step to the other? Because you know the student's needs, it is how you determine the method or the way in which you will use to teach the student that will get you to the next step. The term *method* is to be used loosely in this section and basically means *how and in what type of setting a teacher teaches a student.* That's what I'm going to discuss in this section.

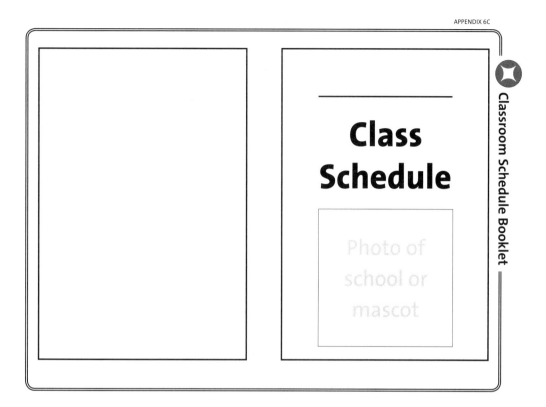

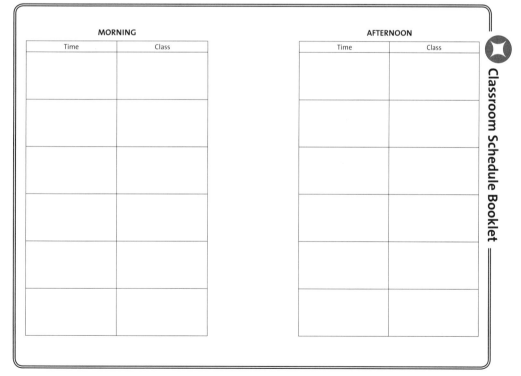

Figure 6.5. Classroom schedule booklet.

To determine the method or setting that you will use to teach your students, there are three questions you will need to ask yourself:

1. What level of academic content will the student be doing?
2. What types of communication support will be needed to teach the student?
3. How much behavioral reinforcement is required for attention and completion of tasks?

Level of Academic Content

When you are determining the most appropriate methods to use when teaching students with disabilities, it is important to determine the level of academic ability the students possess. Several questions come to mind:

✦ Is the student academically functioning at or above grade level?

✦ Is the student academically functioning at or below grade level?

✦ Does the student have areas of significant concern but other areas of strength?

✦ Do the needs of the student appear to be focused on pre-readiness skills?

✦ Does the student appear to require a functional skills curriculum?

There are so many things that you need to consider when planning the methods and settings you will use to teach your students. For example, if the student is functioning at a pre-readiness level but is in the fourth grade, then he or she may work well if presented with some of the academic material in a work station or work center format. If the student is in the 10th grade and has some significant social skills differences but is highly gifted in the area of math, you may want to consider individualizing the student's instruction in math using the computer so that he or she is able to progress as far as his or her ability allows.

Do you see how knowledge about the level of academic functioning can assist you in planning the methods and settings to use? Now, the IEP committee will determine the appropriate placement for the students, but once the student is in that placement, there are still options to be considered. I will describe each of these options in the upcoming sections to give you a general idea of the options you need to consider.

Communication Supports

As you recall, Chapter 5 was all about communication and the use of visual supports. I promise that I am not going to repeat myself in this section. What I am going to do is to help you understand how knowing what each child requires, in terms of communication supports, can help you determine how to teach the student. Some of the students may not require any communicative supports and may have the ability to function independently in a large group setting. But some students may demonstrate a need for supports in this area. Let's review the types of communication supports you may use with your students.

Think about what your students require to be independent.

✦ Verbal directives: Some students need only the spoken word. They understand and can follow typical verbal directions.

✦ Written word: Some students with ASDs may be functioning at a higher academic level, may be hyper verbal, and may appear to have no need for communicative supports. They may still require the use of visual supports and these supports may be in the form of words.

✦ Picture symbols/augmentative communication/sign language: Sometimes students with autism and other types of developmental disabilities require an alternate form of communication. For students who are not verbal, sign language is, at times, needed for the student to understand instructions. The use of picture symbols paired with the spoken word will be needed for some students to encourage verbalization and comprehension of receptive language.

✦ Physical prompts: This is the most restrictive accommodation or modification used to communicate with students. Some students may not possess the ability to understand the meaning of the picture symbols and may require a great deal of physical prompts. These communication supports may include physically modeling, or using a touch, a point, or a gesture.

Do your students require any of these modifications or accommodations? If so, you will want to take this into account when determining the methods with which they will be taught.

Behavioral Reinforcement

For students with autism and other types of developmental disabilities to access the curriculum, they must exhibit the ability to attend, focus, and follow directions. It does not matter how advanced a student is academically if he or she is not able to focus and follow directions. Determining the level of need the students exhibit in the area of behavioral reinforcement is important in making recommendations as to the setting and method that will be used to teach them. This is not a book on the specifics of behavior, but I do need for you to understand and take into account two things:

1. The type of behavioral reinforcement that is needed for the student to remain focused and follow directions
2. The schedule of reinforcement that is needed for the student to focus and follow directions

Knowing these about your students will help you to determine if they will be able to access instruction in a large group, small group, or on a more individual basis. Let me touch on these two areas.

Types of Reinforcement

There are typically three types of reinforcement:

1. Verbal: These students require that occasional "great job" or pat on the back. They may be intrinsically motivated to do their best. It is important to reinforce them just as you do with all your students. These students will be able to access instruction in most any type of setting.
2. Verbal and tangible: Students who require something more than intrinsic rewards may need a combination of verbal and tangible reinforcements. The tangible reinforcements may be earning time to do a favored activity, or it may be earning objects or even edibles. These students can also access instruction in most settings but will require more adult involvement.
3. Tangible reinforcement: This is the most challenging. Some students may require a great deal of tangible reinforcement, possibly several times a work session. This is a significant data-keeping opportunity and will prove important when you are creating an environment that promotes success. This student will be more likely to need a small group or individual type of setting.

Schedule of Reinforcement

Students, depending upon their needs, will require a variety of reinforcement schedules. Some students need a verbal "nice working" a couple of times during a class period. Some students will require a pat on the back or a "high five" several times during the class period. And some students will require that you keep a timer and reinforce a strict schedule using tangible reinforcers, such as tokens or coins. This schedule of reinforcement is much more intense and requires a higher level of adult attention. You see how knowing what the students require in terms of reinforcement and the reinforcement schedule can assist you in making a decision about the method and setting in which to teach them.

Instructional Methods/Settings

Now using the information you have gathered from answering the three initial questions, you should be able to decide on the most appropriate method or setting through which to teach your students. Let's go over some of your options: There are large groups, small groups, individual instruction, centers or work stations, and community-based instruction. Within each of these broad-based methods or settings, there will be several different discrete methods, such as

✦ Discrete Trial Training (method in which a task is broken into smaller discrete steps and the student, through the use of repeated drill and reinforcement, practices each discrete step to mastery)

✦ Errorless teaching (method where the student is prompted so that he or she always responds correctly)

✦ Three-step prompting (a prompting method where the student is given three prompts [tell-show-do] to guide them to completion)

This book is not going to give specific instruction for each of these methods as it is a book to teach you how to organize and structure your classroom. Each of these well-known strategies for teaching students with ASDs is worth the added investigation on your part, but what I am going to focus on is really a combination of methods and settings.

How do you typically teach your students? You probably use the three methods mentioned previously at the same time! But there are some students whose needs require a more intensive setting and way of teaching, and you need to determine that so that you will be organized in your teaching. You know the students' needs; you know the different ways you can choose to structure their teaching and learning; so let me now describe each of the methods or settings and let you decide which one would be the most appropriate for your student.

Look at these examples of the methods (Figure 6.6) in which the subject areas are taught.

You see it depends on the different levels and skills of the specific students. If you have had the students a year or so then you will know exactly how they need to be taught, but if not, you will need to decide based on the information you have gathered through review of the IEP and other student records.

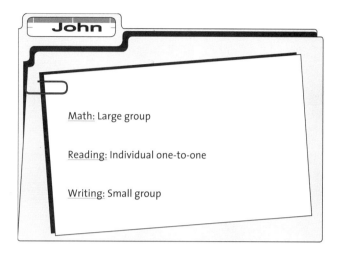

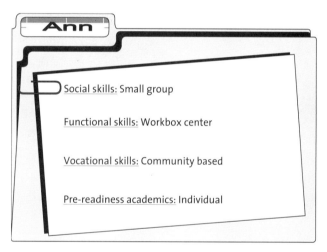

Figure 6.6. Examples of instructional methods in which the subject areas are taught.

Do you remember this?

CASE IN POINT Students sitting at desks all neatly in rows; teacher at the chalkboard with her back turned to the class; while writing on the chalkboard the teacher was hoping, just hoping, that all of the students behind her were not only paying attention but also were grasping the concepts being presented.

Well, that was the large group setting of yesteryear and certainly not the large group of today's modern classroom.

A large group in today's school environment is typically in an inclusive education setting where the subject matter is given to the group as a whole. The group may break up into smaller groups or pairs with the teacher making rounds, providing as much small group or one-to-one instruction as is possible, but the instruction is typically given in a group of about 18 to 25 students.

Some of the skills that are helpful for the students to have in order to access the instruction in this type of setting are the ability to

✦ Use joint attention skills

✦ Communicate wants and needs

✦ Independently maneuver the classroom environment

✦ Focus in groups with other distractions

✦ Follow directions

These skills are important in helping students with disabilities access instruction in a large group environment. These large group environments may include art, music, homeroom, lunch, recess, physical education, or any of the academic subjects.

You can see from this list that if your student needs to access a large group environment for social skills development but his or her academic ability is significantly delayed, there are other options of large group environments that he or she could access: homeroom, art, music, lunch, PE, and so forth. You need to be creative.

Remember that accommodations also come into play. You should not push a student into an environment where progress is not going to be made. But if, with accommodations, the student is able to successfully access a large group environment and make progress, then why not try it? Here are a few types of accommodations that may get you thinking about the needs of specific students:

✦ Have peer helper sit close to the student.

✦ Have student come in a few minutes early to get settled.

✦ Meet with teacher at the end of the day to debrief.

✦ Audiotape the class.

✦ Get copy of teacher notes or outline of the class.

✦ Get set of textbooks to keep at home.

✦ Reduce the quantity of the work.

✦ Allow alternate methods of testing and for projects.

✦ Use agenda to manage due dates of assignments.

✦ Use visual supports for expectations of the classroom.

With just one or two of these accommodations, the student may be able to access some time in a large group environment.

Small groups typically have between five and 10 students. Small groups are great for several different reasons.

✦ Help to increase student focus and attention

✦ Provide additional academic support from teacher

✦ Promote social skill development with peers

✦ Help to increase joint attention to tasks

✦ Help enhance speech and language

Small groups are great for control of the environment. The student may require a great deal of prompts for behavior, for attention or focus, or to communicate effectively. Smaller groups are great for that purpose. You can do any subject in a small group setting. It depends on the needs of the student as to your choosing this teaching method or setting.

Individualized instruction is also a great method for teaching students and is solely dependent upon their needs. There are pros and cons to using this type of teaching method or setting. Let me outline those for you so that you will have information from which to decide whether this is the most appropriate method to use for a certain student in a specific subject area.

PROS

- ✪ Teaching methods specific to the student can be used.
- ✪ If the student has significant behavioral needs, they can be addressed during instruction.
- ✪ If the student is much more advanced in a certain subject area, he or she can progress at his or her own speed.
- ✪ This will provide additional attention to the specific IEP goals for a student.
- ✪ Specific prompts for communication may be enhanced.

CONS

- ✪ Does not promote social skills development with peers.
- ✪ Isolates the student from the opportunity to learn from others.
- ✪ Isolates the student from hearing and practicing appropriate communication skills.
- ✪ Lessens the opportunity for the student to generalize skills learned in isolation.
- ✪ Student has the potential to become dependent upon adult prompting.

Individualized instruction can be used for students with significant issues in the area of academics, communication, or behavior. It can also be used for students who are much more advanced in certain areas than the other students in the group. A more academically advanced student may have significant issues in another area, such as behavior management, that warrant receiving services in a small group setting. This allows the student to continue making progress academically while addressing other issues critical to his or her overall achievement.

Remember that it is typically best practice for students to work with a variety of different adults in order to not become dependent on one person and to enhance their ability to generalize the skills they learn to several different people. Sometimes helpers or assistants who are specifically assigned to work with one student are called "Velcro paraprofessionals" or "Velcro assistants" because they appear to be fastened to the student at the hip. A student who has been assigned the same assistant all year may become rigid and limited in his or her ability to think outside his or her interaction with that one person. Here is a scenario that will help explain this issue:

CASE IN POINT Molly is a third grade student with autism and intellectual disabilities. She  struggles in most academic and functional skill areas. Ms. Roberts is her assigned paraprofessional and has worked with Molly exclusively for the past 5 months. Ms. Roberts has been assigned to assist Molly even though there are other staff members available in the classroom. Indeed, Ms. Roberts has helped Molly make a great deal of progress this year and, according to Ms. Roberts, Molly now has the ability to recognize a list of sight words, write her first and last name, and independently put on her jacket. No one else in the classroom, including the teacher, can elicit the same behavioral responses from Molly. Is this functional? Probably not, unless Ms. Roberts intends to follow Molly to the fourth, fifth, and sixth grades and beyond.

The answer to Molly's issue is to make sure that she has the opportunity to work with different people in different areas. Ms. Roberts may work with Molly on Tuesday and Thursday; Ms. Smith on Monday and Wednesday; and Mr. Jones on Friday. As the students learn skills, it is also important to have them share those skills outside the classroom. Have Molly walk down to the bookkeeper and show him or her how she can add one-digit numbers or count to 50. Share learned skills with lots of different people, in lots of different environments, and in lots of different ways. This is the way to generalize skills.

Centers or work stations have been used in classrooms for years. They are typically used in the primary elementary grades or in special education self-contained settings. Centers can be described as a finite space in the classroom where materials for a specific task are kept and the students go to this area to complete these tasks. You would typically divide the workstations or centers by subject areas. This is also where your workbox tasks could be stored.

With whom would you use work stations or centers? I can safely say anyone at any level. Workstations or centers can be used with

- Elementary school
- Preschool
- Middle school
- Below grade level
- High school
- Above grade level
- Functional skills
- Academic skills
- Vocational skills
- Pre-readiness skills

Would you like some ideas of work stations that you could implement in your classroom? Table 6.1 shows just a few.

Now, let me digress for just a few seconds and get a little more specific about workbox tasks within workstations. If you look back to Figure 5.28 (page 91), you see one example of how work tasks can be organized. Do you see how this center is based on the completion of workbox tasks? The center is organized and visually supported in such a way that will enhance the student's ability to complete the task independently. This structure was created by using green-yellow-red colors of nonskid fabric. This reminds the child that the boxes are placed on the green when they are ready to complete; they are moved to yellow while

Table 6.1. Ideas for workstations

Workstation	Description
Art	Provide art materials and "how to draw" books
Leisure	Provide a choice of different age appropriate activities like puzzles, magazines, books, toys
Sensory	Provide a box of sensory items such as crafts with playdough, glue, and fingerpaint or include water or sand play activities.
Reading	This could serve as a supplementary task to small group reading assignments
Workbox	Workboxes can be grouped into three main categories: academic, functional, and vocational skills
Math	Try using tasks in this center to supplement and reinforce the tasks completed as a larger group
Computer	There are several ways to use this center: creative writing tasks, research, programs in basic readiness skills, or as an independent way to challenge students with above level academic ability
Vocational	This center could include short online vocational videos featuring different careers along with self-contained tasks relating to certain vocations

they are working on them; and then moved to red when the workbox task is complete. The task analysis at the top of the table shows a step-by-step schedule of tasks to complete at the workstation.

This station is based on tasks that are functional in nature. These workbox tasks are simple and include a *work jig*. For example, a work jig could be a simple visual that structures the task by showing the student the three pieces that would go into a resealable baggie. The student could be independent in completing this task because of the supports that are included.

There are numerous teaching objectives that can be practiced in the field. I have coined the term *community-based field experiences (CBFE)* as the community setting in which the student is able to practice skills taught in isolation. Students with autism and other types of developmental disabilities may grasp a task better if they experience it in a natural environment. Natural environment teaching or NET, is a method in which the student is provided with time in an environment that is more natural to the task being taught in order to practice the skills taught in isolation.

What kind of tasks could you teach using a NET method? Here are just a few examples:

✦ How to take turns in a game

✦ How to make a new friend

✦ How to start a conversation at the lunchroom table

✦ How to greet people

✦ How to ask for help in class

You see, NET is just moving away from the desk where drill and practice is the method into generalizing and implementing the skills you are teaching into a real life setting.

Are you using a community setting to teach certain tasks now? What types of tasks? Let me provide you with a few examples to get you thinking about ways in which you could add this to your continuum of teaching options. Table 6.2 lists some tasks that you may want to teach in the community.

Remember that CBFE does not mean that the student has to get on a bus and travel to a store, even though that would be a wonderful opportunity. How about school-based field experiences? Some of the larger high schools are run like small cities. There are numerous types of departments within the school, departments the students can access to enlarge their world and practice other skills (e.g., custodial department, lunchroom, athletic department,

Table 6.2. Topics for community-based instruction

Topic	Location
Eating out in a restaurant and different jobs	Restaurant
Waiting in line	Bank, restaurant, store and so forth.
Taking care of your health	Doctor's office
Buying toiletries/grooming products	Department store
Getting a manicure and caring for hygiene	Salon
Banking	Bank
What police do	Police station
Who to call in an emergency	911 center, police, fire department
How to mail a letter, buying stamps	Post office
Washing clothes in a Laundromat	Laundromat
Buying clothing for different seasons	Department store
Caring for plants	Plant nursery
Importance of medication safety	Pharmacy
What happens at a hospital	Hospital
What are office jobs like	Office building

media center, landscaping, print shop, music department). Think outside the box—*or outside the classroom*.

STEP FOUR: DETERMINE THE MATERIALS YOU WILL NEED TO TEACH

Now I know that as you look around your room, you are seeing a very neat, clean, organized environment, right? As you walk over and open the doors of your storage cabinet and peek in, you may be surprised that everything does not fall out on the floor. As you begin looking through some of the materials you have stored you may be amazed that you can find them! Your environment is organized. That is the prerequisite step to this last section.

I talked about the methods and ways you can group students in order to teach the subject areas that the students require. In this last section I will discuss the materials that will be required to teach. I will also provide you with ways in which you can organize those materials.

Large and Small Group Work Area

Large group areas are typically a collection of individual student desks or a set of tables with chairs. Small group work areas can be made up of a round or kidney-shaped table; a group of tables; or, if the students are young, it can be carpet squares on the floor. Here are some strategies for organizing materials for these work areas:

✦ Use plastic wall pockets that are available at office or discount stores to place on the wall behind the teacher desk. These pockets will hold materials needed during calendar time or large group activities. Make sure they are labeled by subject area.

✦ Hang clipboards on the wall or on a bookcase in the area you will be working so that data sheets will be within easy reach for data keeping.

✦ Materials can be kept in rolling cart drawers so they can be transported from area to area. You can use an entire rolling cart per subject area or just one drawer per subject area.

✦ Portable plastic bins with handles that hold cleaning supplies are great for portable access to materials teachers need in small groups. These are typically available at discount stores in the laundry department.

✦ Small group areas may require a more defined space. Use colored masking tape to define individual student spaces. Use this on the floor or on a table if several students will use one table area.

✦ If you are doing small-group work with students who are able to read and understand the written word, post rules and expectations for group work directly on the table. Use this to teach expectations before beginning the activity.

✦ Place the small group table by the wall or bulletin board so you can post behavioral expectations and a social story for teaching.

Figure 6.7 shows a few photos to help give you some ideas on how to organize your large- and small-group work areas.

Individual Student Work Areas

As I talked about in Step Three, there may be students who need individual work areas in order to stay focused and to maintain appropriate classroom behavior. There are many things to remember in setting up an individual academic work area and I am going to provide you with a few photos and some tips for the organization of these areas. I do want to bring up one point: Being in special education for as long as I have, I have been involved

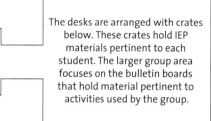

The desks are arranged with crates below. These crates hold IEP materials pertinent to each student. The larger group area focuses on the bulletin boards that hold material pertinent to activities used by the group.

The furniture is strategically placed in the room to create small nooks and areas to hold centers and individual student areas.

Figure 6.7. Organizing large- and small-group work areas.

with and have observed many classrooms. One of the things that I think is important to bring up for this area is that if a student is to begin accessing classes in a more inclusive regular education setting, then it is important to begin practicing the skills they need to get there. So, if the student work area is where the student is to do academic tasks, then have another area for the student to access break activities. In other words, if a student is to take a few minutes' break and do a puzzle or listen to music as part of his or her behavioral reinforcement system, then create another place for that to happen so the student understands that the work area is for work. Expectations for that area are set, and each time the student goes into that area, the student is to work. This will help you as you organize this area.

I have provided you with a few ideas on how to organize these individual work areas. Look through these knowing that you will need to pick and choose according to the level and nature of your students. This will just get your creative juices flowing:

✦ Pouches placed over the back of the student desk chair will house clipboards in which to keep data. These can be easily created by someone who sews or can be found online.

✦ Use plastic crates to hold all of the materials needed for each student and place these in the student work area. You can color code these crates for individual students, label with student name using card stock or purchase different colored crates for easy identification. Use these crates to hold individual student data sheets, work materials specific to the student's IEP goals and objectives, and items related to the behavior reinforcement system that is used with that particular student.

✦ Crates also work for to-do and finished work. Teach the students to place finished work in the correct spot. Students with ASDs, in particular, need to know expectations, so having

This is a way to isolate one desk because of the distractibility of the student. This is a floor mat and works well to prevent distractions from other activities in the room. Student's activities are still visible to classroom staff.

Using 2"-by-4" pieces of wood and plywood sheets, along with paint, this teacher was able to create separate work areas for each student. Cover the plywood with felt to create a Velcro board or paint with chalkboard or magnetic paint to create additional ways to organize.

Figure 6.8.   Use of carrels for creating individual work areas.

one crate for the work that is to be done on one side of the desk and one crate for the work that is completed on the other side of the desk will help structure work expectations.

✦ Carrels are great for creating individual student work areas. If you do not have access to study carrels, make your own from plywood and pieces of 2" by 4" wood (see photo ideas in the Figure 6.8).

✦ If you are using a Discrete Trial Training method with a particular student, it is important to have materials within reach because of the fast-paced nature of the teaching method.

✦ Individual student work areas need to be free from as many distractions as is possible. To lessen distractions for students who are highly distractible, locate the area in a corner of the room, blocked off by furniture but still in view of the teacher.

✦ Remember to use the walls as storage. Try to paint a wall or the back of a bookcase with magnetic paint or cover with felt to use as a Velcro board to create yet another surface you can access for one-to-one student work.

Figure 6.8 shows a few photos to help give you some ideas on organizing your individual student work areas

Work Centers or Work Stations

Centers or stations have been used in classrooms for many years. They can be used in any classroom, for any age, and at any level. In addition to creating consistency and organization for the students, centers are also an avenue to organizing yourself. These areas should be a way of triggering different sets of expectations for the students. They can serve as a gear shift to think about math or writing or reading or even leisure skills. Here are a few ideas about how to organize work stations or centers. Remember, modify according to the level of your students because these modifications may be at too low of a level for your particular students, but it will help you think about how you could implement this method of teaching into your setting:

✦ Study carrels make great centers because they minimize distractions. But if you do not have study carrels, try backing a small table to the wall and placing a bookcase on the side to store the materials needed for that center.

✦ Try using the tri-fold cardboard display boards to create a center. Use one for each activity because they can easily be stored by folding them flat. These are great for displaying the visuals needed for the activity, such as visual schedules of the steps involved in the activity or pockets for worksheets.

✦ Place a table in front of a bulletin board that can be used as a teaching board. This board could hold the expectations for the area or large posters of information the student will need for the activity.

✦ For easy access you can hang clipboards in this area with data sheets used for work completion. You can even get the students involved in checking off things they have accomplished in the center.

✦ Create a social story of behavioral expectations for the center and post nearby. Make sure to also post a visual schedule of instructional steps the student will need to follow for the activity.

✦ Color code the centers to help the students know what items go in what center. You can do this by placing a colored piece of carpet in that area, placing the same color on the bulletin board, putting a fabric cover on the chair, and even keeping the same color for the baskets that hold the materials. This will enhance the student's ability to clean up the classroom and return materials to their proper places in the room.

✦ Work boxes that are so typical in many of the self-contained special education classrooms should be set up as a work station. This way the organization in the station will promote independence on the part of the student. They should get their own boxes, complete them, and put them back.

Centers can be arranged by subject areas and can include places to do assignments in writing, reading, or math. The centers could also include subjects such as social studies, science, spelling, computers, workboxes, vocational skills, functional skills, art, music, leisure, or sensory areas. I have listed a few ideas in several different areas, so take a look at some of these and start thinking about the types of centers your students require.

Computer Center

✦ Organize the computer center with CD holders and all the materials the students will need to be independent. You may need to label the cover of the CD with the student's photo.

✦ Post visual directions for each step of the task and a visual story outlining expectations for this particular center.

✦ Post a photo of what the cleaned up area should look like.

✦ Keep a visual timer in the area so the students will be able to plan their computer activity and for easy transition to another task after completion.

✦ Use touch screens for those who are not able to use a computer mouse.

✦ Upload student photos to the desktop and create a link to these photos so that when the students click on the photo it will take them to the task you have outlined for them to do.

Vocational Skills Center

+ Create a vocational skills area complete with a long table and bookcase on each end to house the tasks. The table should have visuals to help the student with the work sequence.

+ Working from left to right, the table should contain a box or crate of "work to do" and another for "finished work."

+ A bulletin board area or an area with visual supports may be located above the work table. These supports can be a large poster-sized social story of what types of jobs vocational tasks lead to.

+ Post photos of someone dressed appropriately for the world of work. Also post behavioral expectations for the job setting.

+ Clock in and out! Post a time sheet that will help the student to understand that many jobs require that you sign in and out.

Functional Skills Center

+ These tasks can be stored in bags, boxes, bins, or drawers. Place them on a bookcase near the area for easy access. There are many types of bags: try using hanging library bags that are available from either your media center or online. These bags are typically used for holding books and will hang from a small rod placed inside the shelf of a bookcase or on premade holders also available online.

+ Consider hanging a small piece of pegboard on the wall or on the back of a bookshelf near the area. Hooks on which to store bags of tasks can be placed on this pegboard and will help you store the materials. Pegboard is easily accessible at home improvement stores.

Leisure Skills Center

+ Post posters or photos of things people do for leisure.

+ Use age-appropriate materials but simplify their use by using visual symbols or breaking down the task. Remember that these are skills the students may carry throughout life as leisure activities.

+ Make sure to include a social story of behavioral expectations for this area also.

+ This center should look like a leisure area and not a work area. If you have the room, place the materials on a bookshelf close by.

+ Use bins to organize all materials so they can be easily accessed, and place photos on the bins of the materials that go in each one.

+ Ideas of activities to have in this center include puzzles, card games, electronic games, art projects, listening to music, and magazines or books to read.

Workbox Center

+ Workbox tasks do not always have to be kept in plastic shoe boxes; they can be kept in hanging plastic bags, in baskets, or in the drawers of rolling carts.

+ Make sure that boxes are numbered for easy organization and reference.

+ Place photos of the contents of the box on the box.

✦ The bookcases that are usually found in preschool rooms are great for storing the work-boxes. They have individual slots to hold plastic boxes.

✦ To organize the schedule, try a piece of posterboard with pocket charts. Each student will have a name card that will be placed in the pocket corresponding to the workbox number they are to do that day. The student then moves his or her card to the next workbox for work the following day.

✦ Bookcases holding the workboxes could also have a check-off sheet attached.

Sensory Center

✦ Sensory centers can be stocked with the materials your students enjoy: workout machine, long ribbons, weighted items, pillow, rice or bean bins, lotion, fingerpaint, or squishy toys. Think outside the box—the items do not have to be expensive or made primarily for sensory issues; they can be items available at department stores that will provide sensory input. Check with your occupational therapist for more ideas.

✦ For organization, the items should always be placed in bins.

✦ Include a social story to teach students how and why they are to use sensory items.

✦ The students need to know why sensory items are used: for calming purposes or to invigorate their senses. This can be part of the student learning to self-modulate his or her own emotional state—knowing what types of activities they could use to calm themselves when needed.

Figure 6.9 features a couple of photos that show specific ideas that you could incorporate into the organization of your centers.

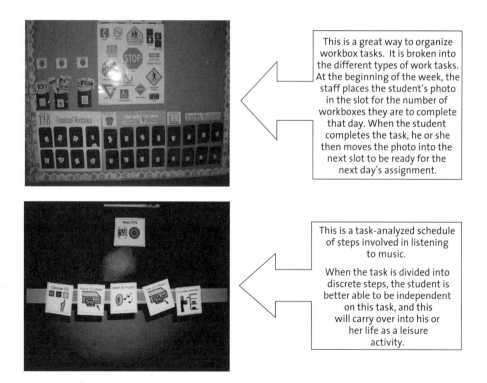

This is a great way to organize workbox tasks. It is broken into the different types of work tasks. At the beginning of the week, the staff places the student's photo in the slot for the number of workboxes they are to complete that day. When the student completes the task, he or she then moves the photo into the next slot to be ready for the next day's assignment.

This is a task-analyzed schedule of steps involved in listening to music.

When the task is divided into discrete steps, the student is better able to be independent on this task, and this will carry over into his or her life as a leisure activity.

Figure 6.9. Specific ideas to incorporate into organization of centers. (The Picture Communication Symbols © 1981–2011 by Mayer-Johnson LLC. All Rights Reserved Worldwide. Used with permission.)

The checkered flag is flying—you have completed another level of the OMAC system. Ready for another pat on the back? Go ahead, because three of the most important areas of organizing your classroom are finished! Good for you. Are you finished? No. But hang in there because it will be worth it, I promise. If you are ready, we will dive into the organization of behavior.

Organization of Behavior Management

You are halfway finished with the implementation of all of the areas of the Organization and Management of a Classroom (OMAC) system. I am certain that your classroom is looking great. After working so hard, you need a break, so, let's begin this chapter with a brainstorming activity.

Quickly name everything that you have to do in your classroom in the area of behavior for students with special needs. Figure 7.1 shows tasks that most special education teachers will have to complete at some point in their career, so the results of this brainstorming activity are going to help set the agenda for this chapter.

This chapter will be about you, not the students. It is solely about the organization of the behavior areas of your classroom: tips and tricks to the organization of all the tasks mentioned in Figure 7.1. This chapter contains suggestions and helpful resources to help you begin to organize everything in your classroom that deals with behavior. It will thoroughly address the creation of a positive behavior climate in your classroom, one that addresses the unique needs of students with autism as well as those with other types of learning differences.

Now, let's start the brainstorming activity. Look back at Figure 7.1. You will notice that, by the shape of the communication bubbles, I have categorized the tasks into three different groupings. These tasks are basically building blocks for behavior management in all types of special education classrooms. When organized into three tiers, these tasks are what make up the systems of positive behavior support (Crone & Horner, 2003). Now, depending

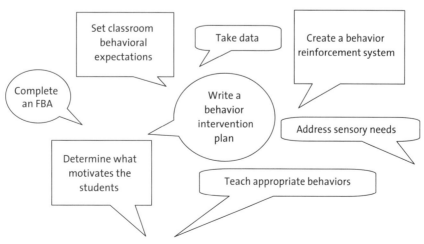

Figure 7.1. Behavioral tasks required of special education teachers. (*Key:* FBA, Functional behavior assessment)

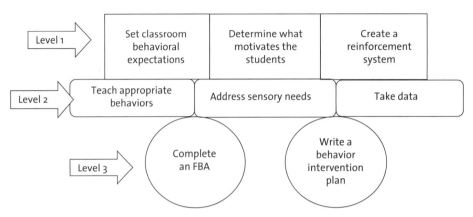

Figure 7.2. Management of behavior in a classroom. (*Key:* FBA, functional behavior assessment.)

upon the specific needs of the students you teach, you may use every task; but, again, you may only need to use a few. In this chapter, I will discuss the tasks in more detail so that you will have good ideas of ways to organize any task in the behavior area.

Look at Figure 7.2. Does it remind you of something?

Strangely enough, it resembles a wagon. Metaphorically speaking, the management of behavior in a classroom is also a wagon of sorts. Let me explain with a story:

CASE IN POINT   Ms. Smith is a teacher with 15 years of experience in the field of special educa-

tion, specifically in teaching middle school students with autism and other types of learning differences. Ms. Smith has a doctorate in special education. If you were to see Ms. Smith's lesson plans, you would note that they are impeccable. She knows how to teach and uses the latest and greatest practices to teach her students how to read, write, and progress in the area of math. But, if you were to sit in Ms. Smith's classroom, you would see that much of the academic time is wasted because she struggles with gaining control of the overall management of student behavior. The climate is tense and chaotic: there are no behavioral expectations posted, the students are not positively reinforced for appropriate behavior, no data are being taken on the frequency of inappropriate behaviors in the classroom so that appropriate interventions can be implemented, and some of the students with autism have sensory needs that are not being addressed. Ms. Smith is frustrated and for good reason.

The behavioral climate in the classroom sets the stage for learning. The overall behavioral management of the classroom has affected the time Ms. Smith spends on teaching academics. It does not matter that she is a master at teaching; she is not able to teach. The implementation and organization of everything related to behavior management is what carries the rest. The progress of everything else that happens in the classroom is related to the teacher's ability to manage the setting. The tasks related to the overall management are listed in Figures 7.1 and 7.2. Does that make sense? If the behavior wagon stops, so does the teaching.

Remember the rubric system that was used in a couple of the first chapters? Let's now do a rubric to help organize yourself in the area of behavior. You need to identify what you are already doing and what you need to do. In Figure 7.2, I placed levels on each tier of the

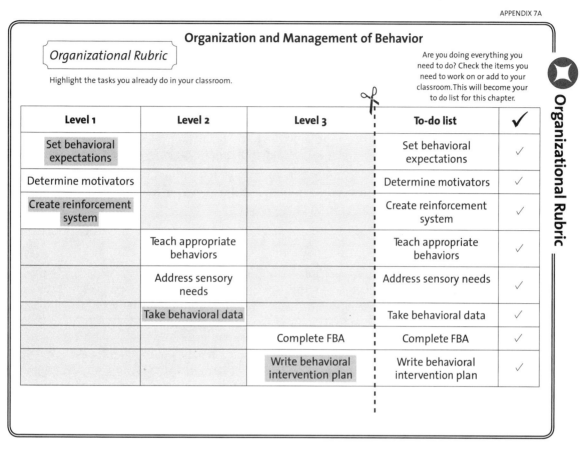

Organization and Management of Behavior

Organizational Rubric

Highlight the tasks you already do in your classroom.

Are you doing everything you need to do? Check the items you need to work on or add to your classroom. This will become your to do list for this chapter.

Level 1	Level 2	Level 3	To-do list	✓
Set behavioral expectations			Set behavioral expectations	✓
Determine motivators			Determine motivators	✓
Create reinforcement system			Create reinforcement system	✓
	Teach appropriate behaviors		Teach appropriate behaviors	✓
	Address sensory needs		Address sensory needs	✓
	Take behavioral data		Take behavioral data	✓
		Complete FBA	Complete FBA	✓
		Write behavioral intervention plan	Write behavioral intervention plan	✓

Organizational Rubric

Figure 7.3. Organizational rubric. (*Key:* FBA, functional behavior assessment)

tasks involved in creating an organized behavior system in the classroom. These levels are loosely layered according to intensity, but some are certainly interchangeable. This creates an organization I will follow in my discussion of each task.

The rubric that I included as Appendix 7A (a blank, full-size version) is one that will help you organize and create a to-do list that you can follow in this chapter. Look at Figures 7.3 and 7.4 as I discuss two different examples of how these rubrics may be completed.

CASE IN POINT Figure 7.3 shows Mr. Jones' responses. Mr. Jones teaches 12 students, all with significant needs. There are several students with autism in the group. In completing the rubric, Mr. Jones first highlighted, on the left hand side of the rubric, all of the items that he feels he has employed in his classroom. In reading through the rubric list, he realizes that he has not addressed several of the items. He has not determined what truly motivates the students, he does not have a system in place to teach appropriate behaviors, he is not addressing the students' sensory needs in the classroom, and he has not used functional behavior assessments (FBAs) to determine specific information about the students' behaviors. In reflecting on what he is using, he understands that there are behavioral expectations posted in the classroom, he has created some semblance of a reinforcement system, he takes some behavioral data, and he has written behavioral intervention plans (BIPs) for some of the students' individualized education programs (IEPs). Mr. Jones now realizes that if he were to determine what motivates the students, then his reinforcement system would need to be updated. He also realizes that if he begins a more structured way of teaching appropriate behaviors that he expects in the classroom, he may want to update his posting of those expectations. Mr. Jones looks at the way he is taking behavioral data. He only takes data for a few of the students, but he begins to wonder if it is really answering the questions and helping to determine progress. He would like to look at the data sheets he uses again in addition to completing FBAs for the students with BIPs in their IEPs. So, in reflecting on the entire classroom behavioral system, Mr. Jones has determined that he needs to check off every area, as he will need to implement those not currently being used or update the ones he is now using in the classroom.

Now, we can move on to our second example of a completed rubric (see Figure 7.4): Mrs. Watson's inclusive education setting.

CASE IN POINT   Mrs. Watson is a special educator who co-teaches with other teachers. She has a

couple of students with autism in several of her classes. The students come into the classroom independently without paraprofessional support and are included in every way. They are able to perform all of the academic tasks with little to no accommodations, but accommodations and support are needed in the area of social interaction.

Mrs. Watson completes the rubric and feels that she is currently implementing three of the tasks. She has highlighted those tasks on the left hand side of the rubric. She has posted behavioral expectations and has also given the students a copy to place in their notebooks. This is especially helpful to the students with autism. She has also created a reinforcement system but does not assess what motivates the students. If she begins to determine what the students' motivators are then she may need to update the reinforcement system so that it would have more meaning to the students. Mrs. Watson decides to check off: determine motivators, teach appropriate behaviors, and update the reinforcement system that she uses in the classroom. She has not highlighted nor has she checked off the need to take behavioral data, write behavior intervention plans, or do FBAs as the students who are included in her classroom do not have significant behavioral issues.

The students with autism all have significant sensory needs and Mrs. Watson feels that she has addressed those needs appropriately. What she would like to do is begin teaching appropriate behaviors in the area of social interaction. She knows that the students struggle in understanding how to make friends, enter and exit social situations, and carry on conversations with others. Mrs. Watson would like to begin doing some social modeling, peer mentoring, or even begin using visuals as reminders of the steps involved to several types of social interaction, so this is checked on her to-do list.

Do you see how this rubric can be used? It is just a way for you to organize your thoughts in this area. I am going to go through each of the levels and provide you with much more detailed information about each of these tasks.

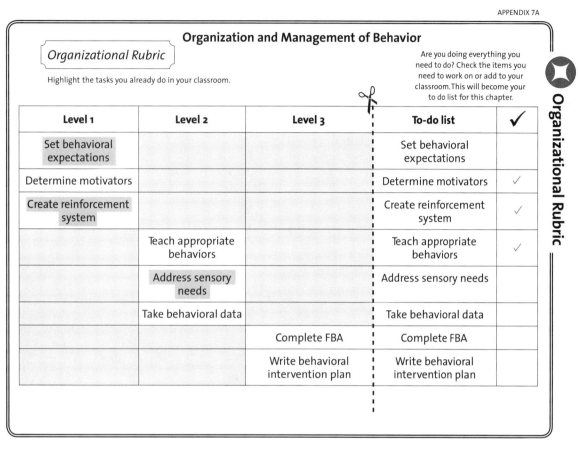

Figure 7.4. Organizational rubric. (*Key*: FBA, functional behavior assessment)

LEVEL ONE

The tasks from Level One are those that are used in every classroom, whether it is a regular education classroom or a special education classroom. It could be in elementary school, middle school, or high school. In fact, they are even used in the business world. The tasks are

1. Set classroom *behavioral expectations*.
2. Determine what *motivates* the students.
3. Create a *reinforcement system*.

Every setting has *behavioral expectations*. Some are written down in an employment contract or posted on an office bulletin board, some are taught by parents to a child going into a church service, and some are taught by friends at school. Others, as you read in Chapter 2 (Research Basis for the OMAC System), are unwritten rules to be learned from the observation of others.

Everyone is *motivated* by something. Sometimes it is a paycheck and other times it's a toy. Sometimes it may be food, a day off, or just receiving attention from others.

And every task has a *reinforcement system* based on predetermined motivators and behavioral expectations. This reinforcement system may entail the use of tangibles such as money, food, or objects. Some reinforcement systems use positive statements such as a pat on the back or time away from the task. And other reinforcement systems make use of more intrinsic motivators such as the feeling of accomplishment after completing a hard task, much like the one you will feel when you complete every layer of the OMAC system.

So, what are some of the ways to implement these tasks? I am going to provide several suggestions and helpful resources that will assist you in organizing and implementing the tasks from this first level.

Behavioral Expectations

What types of things affect behavior? There are several global issues that can affect the behavior of all persons, such as health, emotions, ability, senses, motivation, and communication. These things affect my and most likely your behavior. The behavior of students with special needs is also affected by these issues in addition to others. By the nature of the disability, the behaviors of students with autism spectrum disorders are influenced by several more specific issues. Remember that these same areas could affect the behavior of almost any students. Students with autism could have differences in:

✦ Reaction to sensory input: Personal space issues, making eye contact, and tactile defensiveness or touching others can all come into play in social situations. A student may exhibit inappropriate behaviors when the reaction to these types of stimuli is extreme. These behaviors may be caused by another person standing or sitting too close, touching or hugging, or requiring that the student with autism maintain eye contact, even when it is uncomfortable.

✦ Theory of mind: This is the student's ability to understand the thinking of others. Understanding the thinking of others or having the ability to look at a situation from another person's perspective will undoubtedly affect their behavior particularly in social situations with peers in a school setting.

✦ Cognitive ability: Students with autism have a wide range of cognitive ability and this in itself can affect the student's ability to understand behavioral expectations and independently problem-solve in social situations.

✦ Need for predictability: Change can be difficult and bring on feelings of stress and anxiety, and the preemptive anxiety that may accompany not knowing when change may occur may elicit inappropriate behaviors.

✦ Social motivation: Sometimes a student with autism may pull away and not have the motivation to interact with other students. If they are required to interact with others in some sort of group setting or project, students may have difficulty behaving appropriately.

✦ Comprehension of oral language: A decreased ability to understand oral language of both adults and peers can cause behavioral difficulties by a student misunderstanding what was said.

✦ Reading nonverbal social cues from others: Peers and adults in the school setting all use nonverbal social cues to communicate. Moving away, turning their head, or changing the subject may all be ways of ending a conversation with someone. Students with autism may not pick up on these cues and their continuation of an interaction may seem provocative to other students.

✦ Verbal expression: The anxiety that can be caused when a student is unable to express his or her wants and needs can provoke inappropriate behaviors.

✦ Executive functioning: This is the student's ability to problem-solve and this can affect a student's ability to interact with others. Social situations and the unpredictable nature of another person's behavior, particularly the behavior of children, require one to problem-solve on a constant basis.

How to Write Behavioral Expectations

Now, taking this deeper understanding of students with autism and other special needs, I want you to remember three words: *simple, simple, simple.* Keep those three words in mind as you create the behavioral expectations for your classroom. I do not mean to create behavior expectations that are not age appropriate; I just mean *simple*. To further assist you, here are four OMAC tips for writing behavioral expectations:

1. Keep it short.
2. Keep it concise.
3. Keep it positive.
4. Use a visual.

First let's discuss the phrase *classroom rules* versus *behavioral expectations*. According to the Merriam-Webster dictionary, the word *rule* has to do with *authority* or *control*. A synonym would be *law*. There is somewhat of a negative connotation to the word. According to this same source, the word *expect* is to *look forward to, anticipate, or hope* and a synonym would be *wait for*. Doesn't this have a much more positive connotation?

Wouldn't you rather hear, "my expectation is for you to complete your classwork" rather than "the rule is all classwork is to be completed on time." To use the phrase *behavioral expectations* denotes what you expect, what you are hoping for, and what you anticipate seeing. That in itself shows how to write the expectation. I am going to provide a few examples for each of the four OMAC tips:

1. Keep it short: Instead of "Please do not talk out during classroom group discussions," use "Raise your hand." Instead of "Always follow all instructions given by the teacher and adults at school," use "Follow directions."

2. Keep it concise: Do you know what an *alpha command* is? An alpha command is one that is concise and to the point. An example of an alpha command is "Walk please." The opposite type of command is called a *beta command* and it is vague and the directive is unclear, such as using the word, "stop." It's difficult for the student to know exactly what to stop doing. Being concise alludes to the fact that many times we use phrases that are more abstract than a student with an autism spectrum disorder is able to understand. Use concrete language that is easily understood by students with special needs. Even if the student with autism is extremely bright and verbal, he or she may still have a difficult time understanding a behavioral expectation that is abstract. For example, instead of "Always respect the materials of others," use "Ask to borrow." Instead of "Always try to do your best and work to your potential," use "Start and finish your work."

3. Keep it positive: Again, this is very basic and self-explanatory, but look at these real-life examples of some I have seen in classrooms: "Do not hit"; "No yelling"; "Do not talk out"; "No running." Instead of those, why not try using these: "Quiet hands"; "Quiet voice"; "Raise your hand"; "Walk."

4. Use a visual: Chapter 4 included several examples of how to use visuals. These visuals were created using Mayer-Johnson's Boardmaker computer program, which creates picture icons for simple words and phrases. Posted behavioral expectations can have visuals not only next to them but an extra set of removable visuals also can be offered to use as needed to teach social skills related to the expectations. This brings in the consistency students with autism need and helps with generalization of those skills to other settings.

How Many Behavioral Expectations Should I Write?

In this case, *less is more.* Look at the example in Figure 7.5.

In looking at this photo, there are visuals included (Great!) and the wording is short and simple (Wonderful!), but, needless to say, there are too many behavioral expectations on this poster. There are 16 class rules, and that is too many for a typical adult to remember and follow, much less a student with special needs. If you look closely you will see that this

Figure 7.5. A visual showing too many behavioral expectations. (The Picture Communication Symbols © 1981-2011 by Mayer-Johnson LLC. All Rights Reserved Worldwide. Used with permission.)

could be described as more of a list of social skills than a list of behavioral expectations. As an alternative, consider a list trimmed to just the following set of rules:

When I go into class…

✦ I use a quiet voice.

✦ I have quiet hands.

✦ I will follow directions.

✦ I start and finish my work.

This encompasses most of the rules listed in the photo and also follows the four OMAC tips for writing behavioral expectations as they are short, concise, positive, and can have a visual included. They even use the pronoun *I*, which brings a more personal aspect to the posted expectations.

If you could group the expectations together from Figure 7.5, you could create a list of four or five expectations that will encompass most everything that you want to occur in the classroom.

Examples of Different Kinds of Behavioral Expectations

I am going to give you a couple of different tips for creating behavioral expectations for a group and for an individual student. You may be the teacher in a self-contained setting with students who have significant needs, or you may be a co-teacher in a high school math class. Glean from these suggestions things that you could incorporate into your setting for the needs of your students. These examples may also spark your creative thinking about the needs in your own setting.

Figure 7.6. A visual showing concise list of behavioral expectations for the hallway. (The Picture Communication Symbols © 1981-2011 by Mayer-Johnson LLC. All Rights Reserved Worldwide. Used with permission.)

Post Behavioral Expectations on the Wall

Several classrooms that I have observed use this next type of system. If you will look back at the list of four expectations described in the previous section, you will notice that the posting shows the behaviors that are expected to be exhibited in the classroom setting. This is posted on the door to the classroom and serves as a great way to teach appropriate social skills while students are standing at the door before entering the classroom. It will help the student pull out the different file in their brains that contains a different set of expectations for the classroom setting. As you can see, Figure 7.6 shows behavioral expectations for the hallway. This is hung inside the classroom and the students practice these before moving outside the classroom. This is a good approach to teaching appropriate behavior for the hallway setting.

Also look at Figure 7.6 and notice

✦ Use of simple, direct language
✦ Positive language indicating what was expected
✦ Use of visual symbols giving a clue to the expectation
✦ White paper with a simple black font is posted on black paper to form a background that makes it easier to notice
✦ Big, bold, and neat for clear understanding

Post Expectations on Student's Desk

Post expectations related to the specific needs or goals of the student on his or her desk. This way, you can walk by the desk and point to the card while putting a token of approval in a container, which directly relates back to the token economy used for the student.

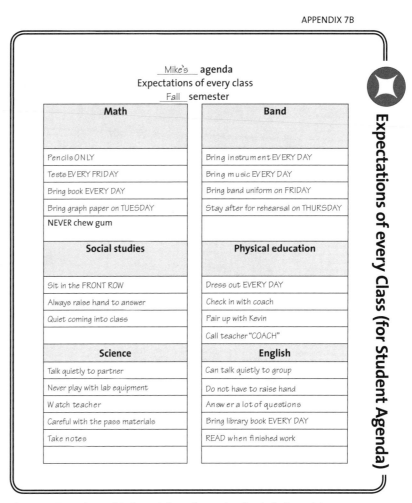

Figure 7.7. Example completed expectations of every class (for student agenda).

Post Specific Expectations for a Student in His or Her Agenda.

Figure 7.7 shows a completed example of a template that I have provided you as Appendix 7B. The student could include copies of the behavioral expectations of each setting in his or her agenda or notebook as a quiet reminder of how to succeed in each of his classes. This will promote not only success but also independence and teaches a life skill that this student with autism may use on into college and the world of work.

Determine Motivators

The assessment of motivation provides great information from which to build a system of reinforcement. This system does not have to be a token economy built on the receipt of tangible reinforcers; it could be built on a pat on the back, saying "great job!", time away from a task, a short walk down the hall, time spent with you, playing with a particular toy or object, time spent in a swing, time spent listening to music, or the receipt of a token to be spent at a school store or classroom treasure box. All of this is based on the needs of your particular classroom and the needs of your particular students.

Let me describe a situation:

CASE IN POINT John is a nonverbal student with cognitive impairments and is in a special education classroom. He has begun to exhibit problem behaviors, including screaming and aggression toward himself. Mrs. Gates, the teacher, has implemented the use of a reinforcement system and it appears to be working except during the morning. She completed a time sampling data sheet and has determined that the highest frequency of self-injurious behaviors and screaming was occurring between 10:00 and 10:30. During that time, John is engaged in workbox activities. Mrs. Gates is somewhat confused because John is also asked to do the same type of activities at 1:00 but with no problem behaviors. She uses the same reinforcement system during both times of the day, using access to a favorite toy as the reinforcer. The teacher begins to wonder if something else were occurring in the morning that would affect his behavior. Through closer observation she notices that during that time one of the other students who is diabetic would get a few crackers to eat for regulation of blood sugar. Mrs. Gates then realizes that John's motivation for food was much stronger during that midmorning work period than the motivation for a favorite toy. She changed the reinforcement object to a snack and the problem behaviors dramatically decreased.

The motivation for John was different during his morning workbox period than it was after lunch. If you have determined what is motivating for a student and have built the way you interact with him or her based on that information, be aware that the student may become satiated or change likes.

What motivates your students? Could it be attention from you, a snack or other type of edible reinforcer, watching a video, holding a favored action figure, or even taking a walk? Sometimes it can be difficult to determine what types of things to build into the reinforcement system you use. You do not have to implement a formal type of reinforcement system to make use of information on the student's specific motivators; it will help in your daily interaction with the students.

Appendix 7C is a template for a forced choice motivation screening rubric. This is an informal, brief type of rubric that uses a forced choice format to help you to think about the types of things that motivate your student. This rubric should be used with students, who are younger nonverbal, and/or functioning at a decreased level of cognitive ability. It will begin to give you an idea of the kind of things that motivate the student.

This screening rubric is not a formal assessment of motivation. There are formal assessments you can use, and if you have a school psychologist serving your school, he or she may be able to provide you with a more formal assessment tool. This is an informal rubric, and if you will look it divides motivation into five broad areas:

1. Attention: The students may be seeking attention from you or someone else in the classroom. This is a very easy motivational item to provide and can easily be generalized to a real-life setting. These are more intrinsic motivators and could include sitting beside the teacher at lunch, a pat on the back, verbal praise, or spending one-to-one time just talking.

2. Tangible: This is acquiring something and could involve the receipt of a token to be exchanged for something else later. This could also involve the use of something edible or getting to hold a favored object or toy.

3. Escape: Is a particular student motivated by taking a break? I know that I am. To enhance the work that the students are able to produce, it may be very reinforcing

Circle or highlight the one that describes something that, if he or she is given the opportunity, best fits the student's interest.

	ATTENTION	TANGIBLE	ESCAPE	ACTIVITY	SENSORY
When given a break the student will choose to	Interact with someone	Get a toy or ask for food	Get alone by him or herself	Draw or play with puzzles	Rock in rocking chair
If there is a lull in activity in the classroom the student will	Talk to someone in the room	Get some type of object to play with	Cover his or her head with a jacket	Ask for the computer	Get up and walk around
The student will complete a task if he or she is promised	A chance to eat lunch with the teacher	A glass of juice when the task is complete	A chance to get out of the next work task	A chance to play computer games	A walk outside
The student's favorite thing to do appears to be	Sit beside the teacher or friend	Eat a snack	Sit alone in the corner of the room	Do puzzles, listen to music, or another activity	Spin an object
The student shows excitement when	Teacher verbally praises him or her	Given a chance to get favorite book	Given a chance to get in a tent	Given a chance to watch a video	Allowed time to spin certain objects
The student may act out if	You attend to another student	He or she is refused an object or food	Given a task he or she perceives as difficult to complete	He or she is asked to stop engaging in a certain activity	He or she is asked to sit for long periods of time
If engaging in an inappropriate behavior, the student will stop if	The teacher touches his or her shoulder	Given a certain object or snack	Allowed to take a break	Teacher puts on a video	A weighted vest is placed on him or her
The student would work best	For time with the teacher	To get something	To get out of doing something	To get to play	To get to go outside and run around
*Total	1	0	0	2	4

Date: January 12, 2010
Student Name: Ida Bloombeng

Brief Motivation Screening Rubric

* The total from page 1 should give you an idea of which of the areas may be the most reinforcing to the student.

Figure 7.8. Brief motivation screening rubric.

for the students to complete a task or two knowing that if they do they will receive a break. Giving a student who has difficulty with beginning a task they perceive as difficult a choice in activities is also included in this area. If presented with a difficult task the student may be given the choice to "do this one first or last." This allows the student to escape the task for a few minutes only to be required to complete it later. This control may be much more motivating than to reinforce with something else.

4. Activity: This area could coincide with the tangible reinforcement area but more typically involves actually doing something. Drawing, putting puzzles together, playing with a toy, or watching a movie can be very motivating for some children.

5. Sensory: These are very common in students with autism spectrum disorders, but other students may also be motivated by these activities. Taking a walk, chewing gum, listening to music, or swinging are various types of sensory activities that may be motivating to some students.

Let's look at a completed motivation rubric (see Figure 7.8).

You will notice that the rubric is formatted so it forces the teacher to make a choice of provided items. It appears that Ida tends to be motivated by sensory activities such as walking around the room or walking outside, she has a hard time sitting for long periods of time, and she enjoys going outside. She appears to be more motivated by these types of activities than by one-to-one attention, gaining access to tangible items, or escaping a task. This is an overall screening of motivating items or activities that can be used by the teacher with a reinforcement system. It is also just great information to have in everyday interactions with Ida and may even assist the parents in the home.

Reinforcement Systems

Positive Classroom Climate

Creating a positive classroom climate is important to the advancement of student progress, regardless of types of the students you teach. A positive reinforcing environment is important to all of us. Think about the world of work. Have you ever worked with someone who you felt was always looking for something you were doing wrong and was very quick to point out the mistakes but slow in pointing out the successes? Working in an atmosphere such as this one can wear you down and drain your confidence, and it is the same way with students.

Using reinforcement in the classroom is much more than the creation of a formal system. You all know that a token economy system is a reinforcement system. But did you know that there are many other types of reinforcement systems, both formal and informal, that can be used in the classroom? Teachers reinforce students on a daily basis by their actions and by their words.

Before I get started with types of formal reinforcement systems, there are a few things I would like for you to know about the creation of a reinforcing classroom climate. I want you to begin to notice three things about yourself:

1. What is the ratio of positive to negative comments I make to the students in the classroom?
2. What is the rate at which I make positive comments?
3. Do I make more positive comments to one student over another?

Have you ever counted the number of positive to negative statements you make to your students each day? I'm challenging you to do this. Put a sticky pad of paper in your pocket. Draw two columns on the first page of the paper. Now each time you make a positive comment, make tick mark in the positive column. Each time you make negative comment, place a tick mark in the other column. Notice the ratio of negative to positive comments you make in your classroom. You may not notice many of the comments you make. If you want a more accurate count, ask a co-teacher to assist you in keeping a count. The number of positive comments should be significantly higher than negative ones, and positive comments should not be based solely on students performing academic tasks correctly. Try positively commenting on sitting quietly, staying on task, coming to class on time, or completing the entire assignment.

I recently observed in an elementary school classroom and this is what I saw:

CASE IN POINT   Ms. Cantor was sitting at a table with five young students, working on a group reading assignment. Most of the time, Alan, the young man I was observing, was not following along with the group, not answering appropriately, squirming in his chair, talking to himself, and drawing on his worksheet. Even though Alan was exhibiting numerous inappropriate behaviors, if you looked more closely there were fleeting moments of attentiveness. In listening to what he mumbled to himself, I noticed he was actually answering the questions posed to the group. Alan was able to exhibit appropriate behavior but for fleeting periods of time. Most of the other students were exhibiting behaviors that were appropriate and commendable during longer periods of time. During the first 10 minutes of the observation, Ms. Cantor's rate of positive to negative comments to anyone in the entire group was 1 positive to 17 negative comments. The rate of these comments was about 1 every 45 seconds and 16 of the 17 comments were directed to Alan.

I was flabbergasted at the data results from my observation. As you noticed, I stopped taking data on the student's behavior and began taking data on the teacher. One of my first recommendations was for the teacher to begin giving positive comments to the other students in the group! Offer praise like, "Great job answering, Sally!"; "Tommy, you are sitting up nice and straight!"; or "Nice job raising your hand, Ricky!"

Add a token system and pass out tokens or points. In watching the teacher's interaction with other students and the other students behaviors, Alan may begin to realize that if he exhibits appropriate behaviors as indicated by the posters and earlier teaching from classroom lessons, he may receive additional attention and reinforcement. During my observation he received a great deal of attention for demonstrating a lot of inappropriate behaviors and the teacher played right into his hands.

Reinforcement System Examples

I am going to discuss the use of reinforcement systems with students with autism and other learning differences. Let's first review the types of things that need to be included in any type of system used for students with autism. You know that such students thrive with the use of visuals, concise language, concrete expectations, and predictability and structure. Given all of these things, I am going to provide for you a few concrete examples of reinforcement systems appropriate for a group.

Group Reinforcement Systems

Do you have several students with significant behavioral needs? Do you have several students who need some type of reinforcement system to enhance their ability to meet behavioral expectations? Do you feel that with a whole group reinforcement system the students would work together to help each other better demonstrate behavior expectations in the classroom?

If you answered yes to any of these questions, then you may need to put some type of whole group reinforcement system into place. Always push your students toward using as many intrinsic rewards as possible as it is more applicable to where you will want them to be as adults.

Here are a couple of ideas you want wish to try or modify to fit the needs of your specific students:

Stars have been used for years but are still appropriate. This works well with small groups, possibly in pull-out resource settings. Students with autism would benefit from this type of reinforcement system as it has clear expectations and visual cues. This type of chart also works well for students with more significant needs and those needing additional visual supports. Use one chart per child and use each of the columns for different behavioral expectations, placing icons that represent expectations at the top of each column (See Figure 7.9).

There are several ways to use this chart, and a blank template is provided as Appendix 7D for your use. Figure 7.10 shows another example of something that works well for a group and is concrete enough for students with autism. You certainly do not have to use an edible reinforcer such as pizza, but you can use a photo of other types of items or activities: extra recess time, extra computer time, choice from coupon book (refer to Appendix 7E for a template for this), and so forth. The main idea is to create a visual that shows both the black and white and colored versions so that the students will see how much is left to earn, post the visual as a reminder, and create concrete expectation of the behavior that earns the reinforcer. The example from Figure 7.10 shows that the completion of homework earns a piece of the pizza, but it could certainly be any or all of the behavioral expectations of your classroom setting. This is a group system and the group of students work together to earn the reinforcer. Effectiveness will depend upon the nature of your group of students: either

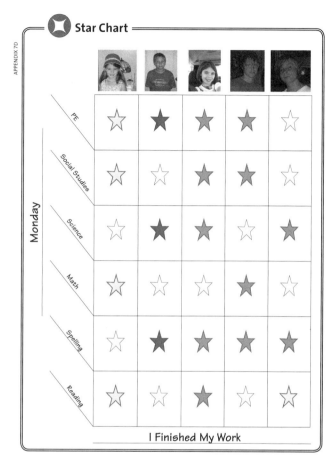

Figure 7.9. Example of star chart.

the students will learn ways of working together and encouraging each other, which is great for the students with special needs, or it will create a social situation with intense peer pressure that may not work for your particular group of students. I have witnessed students with autism being mentored by other students within the classroom and the student with autism assisting other students to meet the expectation. Use your judgment and be creative. If the students are not able to delay receipt of the reinforcer then make sure to create the pizza with fewer slices.

When using a coupon book, the students would each get to choose the reward they prefer. This provides choice and control for students who need that built in to the reinforcement system. This is also important as the motivating activity or item for a student with autism may be much different than that for the other students in the classroom. Going out to recess may not be as motivating as reading a particular comic book or playing a certain computer game. A coupon book template is included as Appendix 7E and can be modified to fit the particular needs of your classroom.

Token systems are also very useful types of reinforcement systems, in which points awarded for positive behavior can be accumulated and redeemed for some sort of reward. Modify the system to meet the needs of the students. If the students understand the exchange of coins and the value and use of money, a simple banking system would be a good way to both teach academic skills and reinforce behavioral expectations. You can also use blank checks and a simple checkbook register, both available in Appendix 7F. The students can earn money for each behavioral expectation met. They can spend this currency on reinforcing items within the classroom such as computer time, homework pass, work task pass,

Figure 7.10. Example of group reinforcement chart.

or ice cream at lunch. This is a great way to learn functional skills and basic math academic skills, and to incorporate these into a reinforcement system within the classroom setting.

There are all kinds of token systems from very simple (using dry beans as the token) to more elaborate (store-bought tokens). Use your imagination and base your system on the specific needs of your students.

Individual Reinforcement Systems

Sometimes you will have students who may need individual reinforcement systems. They may be included in regular education classrooms and may need that extra little something to take with them to help them stay motivated and on track in demonstrating appropriate behaviors.

Here are a couple of ideas you may want to use or build on in helping to reinforce individual students.

✦ Puzzle piece tokens are a great idea to use for students who enjoy art (see Figure 7.11). This design is colored by the student, laminated, and cut into several pieces, depending upon the student's needs. The students can earn pieces of the puzzle as expectations are met. After completing the puzzle they can earn time to draw, color, or do an art project. This also works for other types of reinforcement objects or activities. Figure 7.12 shows a version I used with adults at a training.

✦ You can see that I used something motivating to an adult and I put a photo of the actual drink on the card. You can see how important it is to have the black-and-white image because it shows how much is left to earn. This is especially important for students who think in more concrete terms such as students with autism. Use cardstock, a laminator, and Velcro to create this type of system. If the student goes into an inclusive environment, the student can still earn pieces of the puzzle to bring back to his or her home base and place on the puzzle template. For the reinforcer, use the information from your motivator screening to determine if you should use photos of edibles, activities, objects, or people.

Figure 7.11. Puzzle pieces used as individual reinforcement system.

✦ Point sheets are great because they can be modified for use with individual students or with groups. These point sheets can be in the form of punch cards, point sheets with numeric points, or point sheets with money increments.

Figure 7.13 shows an example of a point sheet that is more general in nature. It is simple to complete and an example of the completed one is shown. A blank template is included as Appendix 7G. Copy the point sheet front and back. On the back is a place for teacher comments. On the front the teacher gives one point for each expectation that is demonstrated in each class. The score is a ratio of demonstrated over possible

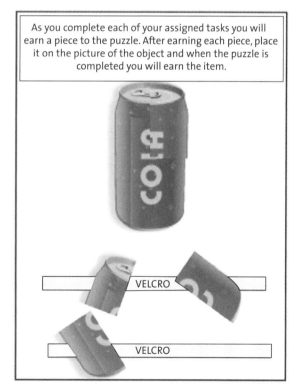

As you complete each of your assigned tasks you will earn a piece to the puzzle. After earning each piece, place it on the picture of the object and when the puzzle is completed you will earn the item.

Figure 7.12. Example of an individual reinforcement system.

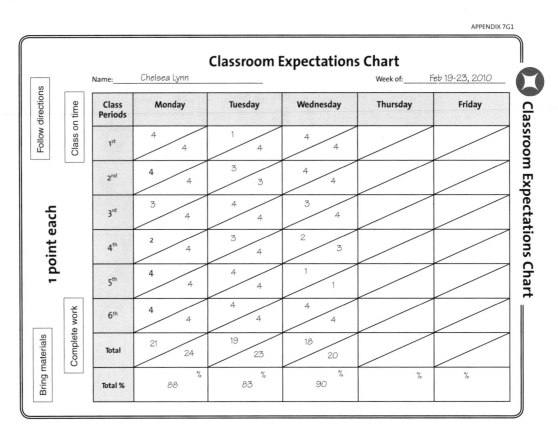

Classroom Expectations Chart

Name: Chelsea Lynn   Week of: Feb 19-23, 2010

Follow directions · Class on time · 1 point each · Complete work · Bring materials

Class Periods	Monday	Tuesday	Wednesday	Thursday	Friday
1st	4 / 4	1 / 4	4 / 4		
2nd	4 / 4	3 / 3	4 / 4		
3rd	3 / 4	4 / 4	3 / 4		
4th	2 / 4	3 / 4	2 / 3		
5th	4 / 4	4 / 4	1 / 1		
6th	4 / 4	4 / 4	4 / 4		
Total	21 / 24	19 / 23	18 / 20		
Total %	88 %	83 %	90 %	%	%

Classroom Expectations Chart

Comments

Class Periods	Monday	Tuesday	Wednesday	Thursday	Friday
1st		Talks a lot during class			
2nd	Fabulous job today				
3rd		Good report			
4th	Late to class I didn't finish work		We did no work in class - had a special speaker		
5th			Had school assembly today		
6th					

Classroom Expectations Chart

Figure 7.13. Completed classroom expectations chart.

points, as in some classes there may not be the opportunity to demonstrate some of the expectations. A total and a percentage are derived from the total points. This is an easy way to determine overall mastery level of behavioral expectations.

✦ Figure 7.14 shows a type of punch card. A blank template is included as Appendix 7H. Instructions are to copy front and back blank template on card stock, fill in the four behavioral expectations the student is working on, cut out around the card, and have the student take it from class to class. The numbers have a key with the corresponding classes on the back side. Teachers can hole punch, initial, or stamp if the behavioral expectations are met during that class period. Teachers can use special punches that are easily accessible at craft stores in the scrapbook section. Students return the card at the end of the day for the case-holding teacher to determine percentage. On the back, the teacher can determine a percentage for each expectation. Goals are set and can correspond to IEP goal mastery levels. If you divide the day into 10 segments, the percentage is easy to figure (e.g., three punches = 30%). This system is concrete and easily understood by the students. You can also use this same type of system and modify to fit the needs of your students.

✦ Do you have a student who is having significant behavioral issues on the bus? You may need to try implementing some type of system to reinforce appropriate behavior on the bus. Remember the Styrofoam pool tubes from Chapter 4 (Figure 4.24)? You can carefully cut it down one side and slip it over the seat in front of the child. It typically slips only the top of a chair or seat dependent upon the width of the seat. Cover it with spray glue, then stiff felt. Use tokens backed with Velcro. If there is a monitor or another adult on the bus they can either add tokens to the strip or praise the child and allow the child to get a token or smiley face and add to the strip. At the end of the ride they are rewarded with something from the bus driver's treasure box.

✦ Here is another idea for the bus. The sheet in Figure 7.15 was created for a child with autism who had a difficult time riding the bus. I have included the blank template as Appendix 7I for your use. The sheet was completed specific to the child's bus route. Place photos or landmarks the students will see on the bus ride. As they pass each landmark the student can place a check in the box.

This does not have to be based on trinkets from the bus driver but could play into a reinforcement system that is used at home for earning things such as computer game time or watching television.

LEVEL TWO

All of the tasks for Level Two are those that may be used in regular education inclusive environments, pull-out special education resource environments, and/or special education self-contained environments. The tasks are 1) teach appropriate behaviors, 2) address sensory needs, and 3) collect data. Let's get right to work.

Ways to Teach Appropriate Behaviors

I am going to discuss what types of behaviors to teach and how to teach appropriate behaviors. This area should have a great deal of importance placed on it if you have students with autism or students who struggle with demonstrating appropriate behavior. This may be students with emotional needs, students with intellectual disabilities, or those who need additional support in the area of social skill attainment.

What to Teach

To be diagnosed with autism, a child must have a significant difference in the ability to communicate and socially interact with other same-age peers. There should be a great deal

Punch Card

Complete all assignments

10 9 8 7 6 5 4 3 2 1

Remain on task and participate

1 2 3 4 5 6 7 8 9 10

Cindy Lou
Student Name
March 3, 2010
Date

You can
do it!

Get to class on time

10 9 8 7 6 5 4 3 2 1

Bring all materials to class

1 2 3 4 5 6 7 8 9 10

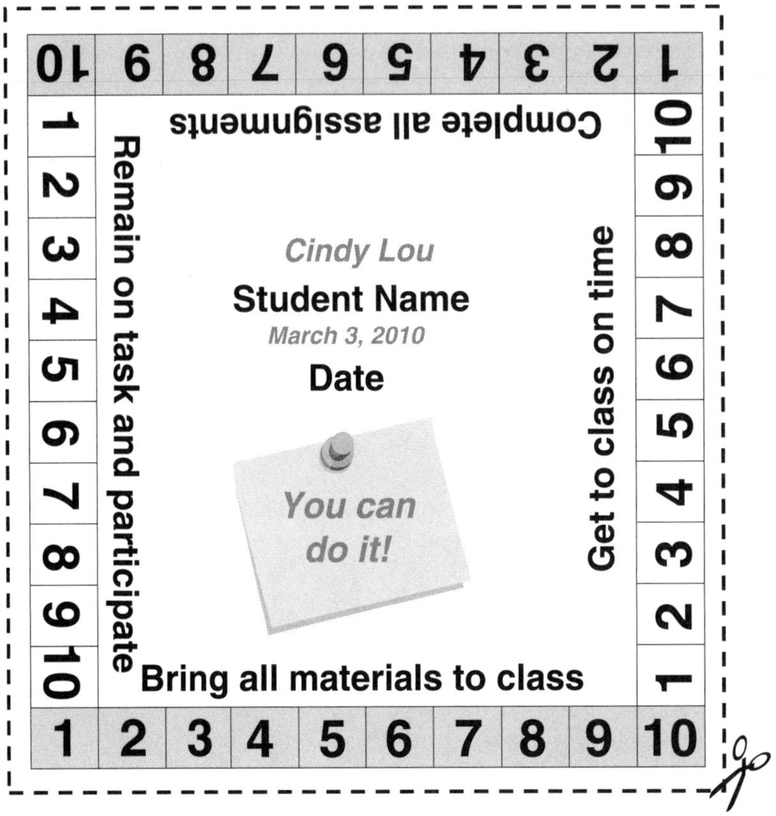

Print on card stock. Cut out around the square. Write four expectations around the edges. If the behavioral expectation is met, the student is to get a punch or stamp or teacher initial for each class period. Turn it in at the end of the day.

Key

Expectations	Daily percentage	Goal

1 – Homeroom	2 – Math
3 – Band	4 – English
5 – Social studies	6 – Lunch
7 – Art	8 – Science
9 – Reading	10 – Study skills

Figure 7.14.   Punch card.

of importance placed on the enhancement of social skills in the school environment. What more perfect opportunity is there to teach social expectations than in a classroom with other same-age peers?

My definition of social skills is *a set of acceptable skills or behaviors that one is expected to use in order to interact and communicate with others in a social setting.*

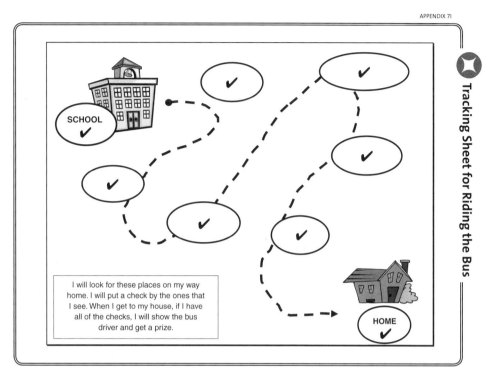

Figure 7.15. Completed tracking sheet for riding the bus.

Think about this: *What skills will my students need to be able to demonstrate if they are going to function independently in school and in society?*

Social skills can typically be broken into several different global areas. These could include friends, emotions, personal hygiene, conflict, conversation, manners, and nonverbal cues. You can see how skills in these areas may be difficult for students with autism and students with other types of special needs to attain. They will need direct teaching, modeling, and practice to attain a mastery level of these skills.

Look at Figure 7.16. It shows a list of social skills. This list is not exhaustive, but it will give you a great start. Keep the list as a fluid document and add to it as you encounter other social skill needs that may apply to your students.

Remember that each social skill means something different dependent upon the culture of the student. If the student is Native American, the culture in which he or she lives may dictate a difference in eye contact and personal space from a child who is of European descent. A student from a Chinese culture may communicate differently with his or her elders from a student who is African American.

How to Teach

Finding the time to teach social skills is a chore. You may be lucky enough to have a subject entitled Social Skills or Study Skills and time is built into the students' schedule each day for that class. You may have a self-contained classroom where you have control of the schedule and have set aside 20 to 30 minutes each morning to teach social skills as a morning group. Or you may be a teacher whose daily schedule is so packed with academic subject matter that you do not have a spare moment to let go to cram in another subject area. Because we know the importance of teaching social skills to students with disabilities, particularly those with autism, it is important that you find some time and some way to teach the skills necessary to function in school and in society. Let me give you a few tips that may help you.

Friends

• How to choose a friend	• How to support a friend
• How to make a friend	• Personal boundaries
• How to keep a friend	• Peer pressure
• Relationships with opposite sex	• How to break off a bad relationship
• Caring and thoughtfulness	• Unsafe people to avoid
• How to listen to others	• Sharing
• Taking turns	• How to spend time with a friend

Emotions

• How to appropriately show emotions	• Being a good loser/winner
• Being sensitive to others	• Matching appropriate emotion to the situation
• Dealing with anger	• Being told "no"
• Dealing with sadness	• Coping with sensory differences
• Recognizing emotions in others	• Coping with stress/anxiety
• Understanding your own personal disability	• Taking responsibility for actions
• Calm-down strategies	• How to stay emotionally healthy

Personal hygiene

• Daily hygiene	• Puberty
• Choosing appropriate clothes	• Maintaining healthy weight
• Looking your best	• Taking care of health needs
• Doctors/dentists and medication	• Good eating habits

Nonverbal behavior

• Personal space	• Facial expressions
• Eye contact	• Reading nonverbal cues

Conversation

• Appropriate topics	• How to listen
• Beginning conversation	• Showing interests in topics of others
• Ending conversation	• Using humor/telling jokes
• Sharing personal information	• Turn taking
• Using appropriate voice tone	• Apologizing
• How to introduce yourself	• Giving compliments

Manners

• Politeness	• Using appropriate manners in public
• Interacting with those who are different	• Being tactful in conversation
• Interacting with adults	• Sharing
• Helping others	• Accepting compliments and criticism

Conflict

• How to avoid conflict with others	• How to be assertive
• Basic safety skills	• How to compromise
• How to deal with bullying	• How to deal with rejection
• What to do in an emergency	• Saying no to drugs and alcohol

Miscellaneous skills

• Learning to wait	• Exhibiting an appropriate work ethic
• Being flexible	• Community rules and laws
• Appropriate behaviors for different settings	• Choosing appropriate leisure activities
• Planning for the future	• Caring for pets

Figure 7.16.   List of social skills topics.

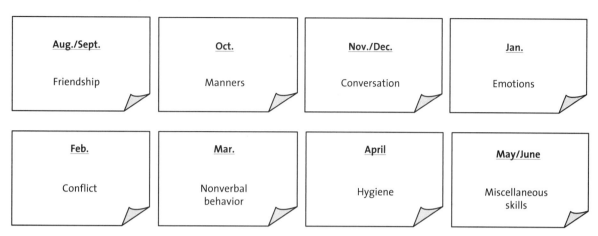

Figure 7.17. Social skills annual schedule.

✦ Divide the year into different social skills topics. For example, look at the schedule in Figure 7.17.

Put up a social skills bulletin board and change it each month as the topic of focus changes. List new subskills each month and incorporate skills into subject area lessons—for example, in science you may bring in a 5-minute lesson on *taking care of your health*; *appropriate conversation* may be a good topic within an English/language arts lesson; and *community rules and expectations* may be a good topic for a social studies lesson.

✦ Natural environment teaching: Natural environment teaching (NET) is teaching skills in a naturally occurring environment. What better way to teach social skills than in the environment in which they occur? Lunch rooms, hallways, media centers, and gymnasiums all become classrooms for teaching social skills. You can set up scenarios or use a naturally occurring situation to teach using appropriate manners, taking turns, making friends, personal hygiene, and how to be a good loser. The best way to use NET is as practice after a direct teaching lesson has occurred. It is difficult to initially teach a skill in the heat of a situation but to practice a skill already taught works wonders in a natural environment.

✦ The location on the outside of the door becomes a great place to teach a lesson on hallway expectations versus classroom expectations (see also Figure 5.19). Take 90 seconds while standing at the classroom door to discuss the behaviors that are expected of students upon entering the classroom. Post these expectations on the outside of the door. On the inside of the door there can be posted a list of behaviors that are expected of the students outside the classroom setting.

Figure 7.18 represents a list of social skills students could practice while in the hallway. This will be a great help to students with autism as it helps them to shift gears and know what types of skills to use in the hallway. Posting these on the inside of the classroom door and reviewing these will help to grab another social skills teaching opportunity where you did not think that you had one.

Remember, direct teaching is necessary for building a solid foundation of social skills mastery in students with autism and other types of special needs. If you can, try using some of these types of activities to teach social skills development:

✦ Using videos for social skills training is a great way to create a typical model. Model Me Kids (http://www.modelmekids.com) produces wonderful video clips in the social skills area.

I will remember to

1. Smile at my friends
2. Stay an arm's distance apart while walking
3. Watch my teacher
4. Hold the door for people behind me
5. Talk with a quiet voice
6. Wait my turn

Figure 7.18. List of social skills to practice in the hallway.

✦ As you create each social skills lesson, place it in a social skills lesson book. This way you are not reinventing the wheel each year. Include a cover, place the list of social skills from Figure 7.16 as the table of contents, fill the binder with tabbed index dividers, and place all of the materials that you find to teach each particular skill in the binder behind a tab.

✦ There are several types of social skills programs on the market and each one has its own unique niche. Check out these.

- ✪ Jed Baker's *Social Skills Picture Books* (http://www.jedbaker.com)
- ✪ Carol Gray's Social Stories (http://www.thegraycenter.org)
- ✪ Darlene Mannix's *Social Skills Activities for Special Children*
- ✪ Ruth Weltmann Begun's *Ready-to-Use Social Skills Lessons and Activities*
- ✪ *Social Skills Improvement System Classroom Intervention Program* by Stephen Elliot and Frank Gresham

✦ Use a variety of different media to teach social skills. Here are a few ideas:

- ✪ Microsoft PowerPoint slide shows: These are a great way to put photos of the students in different social situations. If you are using a SMART Board or a Promethean Board in your classroom, the PowerPoint slide show can make use of the touch-screen tool.

- ✪ Online story creation sites (e.g., http://www.tikatok.com): This will allow you to create a book personalized with photos. Create a book about behaviors the students should exhibit in the lunch room. If you have already obtained permission to take photos from the parents/guardians of your students, use a digital camera to take photos of the students and place them into the book. You can purchase it as an e-book and save to your computer or use in a digital format on a SMART Board.

- ✪ Online video clips from cartoons and TV shows: Old comedies such as the Three Stooges are great ways to bring humor into social skills lessons. Be creative and think outside the box.

- ✪ Reworking of store-bought books to personalize: Use a preprinted book that teaches a good social lesson and appropriate behaviors. Place a photo of a student from your classroom over the photo of a child in the book for an instant social lesson.

 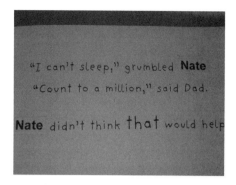

The character's head was replaced by a photo of a student to make it personal.
Page where the student's name replaces the character.

Figure 7.19. Personalization of store-bought books.

See Figure 7.19 for an example. This book is a great one about getting back to sleep and hearing sounds in the night. It is called *Wide Awake Jake* by Rachel Elliott and is just an example of how to personalize a story book. Try to find books on topics such as dealing with fear on the first day at school, how to make friends, or other topics appropriate for school.

With a digital camera, word processor, scissors, and a little glue, the ideas are endless; just use your creativity and imagination.

Address Sensory Needs

Many students with autism have atypical reactions to sensory stimuli. In fact, many other students with and without learning differences also have atypical reactions to sensory stimuli. I am overly sensitive to certain sensory stimuli: too many people all talking at once; a chaotic, unorganized environment; and a scratchy, irritating piece of clothing all distract me and are very stressful. You may find that you also have issues with certain sensory stimulation.

The deciding factor between just being minor issues and something that needs to be addressed is when there is an overreaction or underreaction to sensory stimuli that interferes with the student's ability to function in the school environment.

Types of Sensory Needs

There are all types of sensory issues that are troublesome to many students—students with autism, students with attention-deficit/hyperactivity disorder (ADHD), students with sensory processing disorder/sensory integration disorder, and even neurotypical students. Students can exhibit an overreaction or underreaction to auditory, visual, or tactile stimuli. It is important to proactively meet the student's sensory needs and begin to recognize the antecedent behaviors that will point to an inappropriate reaction to sensory stimuli.

I have put together a general list of different sensory issues (see Figure 7.20). This will give you an idea of things to be watchful of and help guide you in thinking of ways to assist the students in this area.

The Sensory Questionnaire from Figure 7.20 is a general checklist of symptoms of and activities for sensory issues. Read through the arrow boxes and ask yourself, *are any of my students sensitive to touch? Do they play too rough? Are they overly bothered by certain everyday smells?* This will guide you in determining if they are in need of some type of

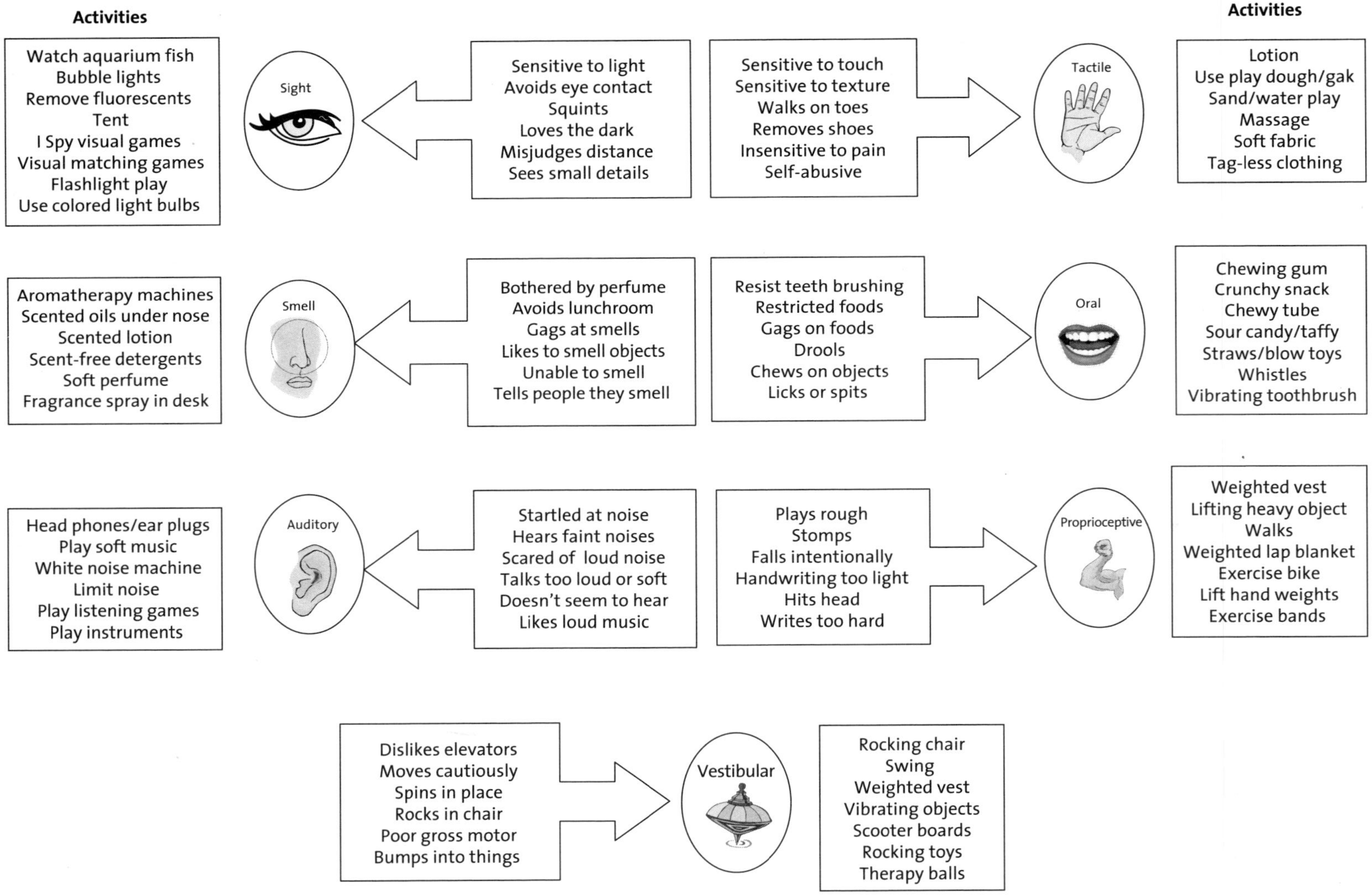

Figure 7.20. Sensory questionnaire.

Activities

Sight
- Sensitive to light
- Avoids eye contact
- Squints
- Loves the dark
- Misjudges distance
- Sees small details

Watch aquarium fish
Bubble lights
Remove fluorescents
Tent
I Spy visual games
Visual matching games
Flashlight play
Use colored light bulbs

Tactile
- Sensitive to touch
- Sensitive to texture
- Walks on toes
- Removes shoes
- Insensitive to pain
- Self-abusive

Lotion
Use play dough/gak
Sand/water play
Massage
Soft fabric
Tag-less clothing

Smell
- Bothered by perfume
- Avoids lunchroom
- Gags at smells
- Likes to smell objects
- Unable to smell
- Tells people they smell

Aromatherapy machines
Scented oils under nose
Scented lotion
Scent-free detergents
Soft perfume
Fragrance spray in desk

Oral
- Resist teeth brushing
- Restricted foods
- Gags on foods
- Drools
- Chews on objects
- Licks or spits

Chewing gum
Crunchy snack
Chewy tube
Sour candy/taffy
Straws/blow toys
Whistles
Vibrating toothbrush

Auditory
- Startled at noise
- Hears faint noises
- Scared of loud noise
- Talks too loud or soft
- Doesn't seem to hear
- Likes loud music

Head phones/ear plugs
Play soft music
White noise machine
Limit noise
Play listening games
Play instruments

Proprioceptive
- Plays rough
- Stomps
- Falls intentionally
- Handwriting too light
- Hits head
- Writes too hard

Weighted vest
Lifting heavy object
Walks
Weighted lap blanket
Exercise bike
Lift hand weights
Exercise bands

Vestibular
- Dislikes elevators
- Moves cautiously
- Spins in place
- Rocks in chair
- Poor gross motor
- Bumps into things

Rocking chair
Swing
Weighted vest
Vibrating objects
Scooter boards
Rocking toys
Therapy balls

146

sensory intervention. Maybe they need to stimulate their vestibular system by swinging; calm their auditory system by wearing earplugs; or they need for you to provide an accommodation for their need to seek oral stimulation by allowing them a crunchy snack several times a day. This questionnaire will guide you, but remember this is only a guide. If you should suspect significant sensory regulation issues in your students, you should contact the occupational therapist who serves your school.

Ways to Address Sensory Needs

There are several ways to use sensory activities as a way of enhancing appropriate student behavior. You can

+ Provide a sensory break when needed
+ Build a noncontingent sensory diet into the student's day
+ Provide optional sensory items or activities as a way of self-regulation

A *sensory break* can be used if you begin to notice the student becoming agitated, tense, distracted, or lethargic. You, as the teacher, can build sensory breaks into the schedule. Activities may include walking, exercises, swinging, playing in rice/beans/sand, water play, dance, exercise bike, or trampoline. Remember, it is best to use these items noncontingently so as to not reinforce negative behaviors. An example would be if the student was frustrated and throwing desk items on the floor and the teacher quickly gave the student a sensory toy. This act may inadvertently reinforce the aggressive behavior. So be careful how the items are used. It is good if you as the teacher begin to understand the preemptive behaviors well enough to know when the student needs a sensory break or use of a sensory object (e.g., weighted vest, crunchy snack, walk, drink of water).

A *sensory diet* is the use of several types of sensory activities and objects that are built into the student's day not contingent upon their behavior. These are activities that are scheduled, just as a class would be. For an example of a sensory diet, see Figure 7.21.

You will notice on Figure 7.21 that the student has a choice of three activities listed. The schedule is set for four times during the day for up to 15-minute blocks of time. This amount of time was set to encompass the entire transition, choice by the student, and the implementation of the sensory activity. Several different types of activities are included on this chart—some that will help the students calm their sensory system and some that will help energize them. Be creative and accommodate the needs of your particular students.

Providing optional *sensory items or activities as a means of self-regulation* is a great way to teach students to manage their own needs. We all have ways of relieving stress or frustration: some adults chew gum, some drink a cup of coffee, and others get up and take a walk. Using sensory items to encourage relaxation during times of stress is an appropriate life skill. Sensory items, which do not need to be expensive, may include hand weights, headphones, crayons, music, plastic pots, weighted blankets, sidewalk chalk, soft fabric, squish balls, therapy, or lotion.

Back in Chapter 5 (Figure 5.24, or Appendix 5D and 5E), I showed you some signs about anger management that were used in a classroom for students with significant behavior needs, in an area common to all of the students, set up with a basket of sensory items. In this area was a poster with concrete steps on how to recognize when you are frustrated or angry. This was used to directly teach students to recognize the way their body feels when they are beginning to get frustrated or angry. The next poster (Figure 7.21) gave clear direction on using the sensory items to calm themselves. The entire area was color coded in green. Visual symbols were used with each step. The steps were both simple and easy to understand for students with autism and for students with intellectual disabilities. The key to using sensory items is to teach the student ways of proactively calming themselves.

Schedule of sensory activities

	Choice 1	Choice 2	Choice 3
8:10 – 8:20	Coloring sheets	Bounce on ball	Listen to music
10:00 – 10:15	Run errand	Crunchy snack	Exercise video
12:30 – 12:45	Take walk	Jump on trampoline	Swing
2:00 – 2:10	Wipe off tables	Use lotion on arms	Sand play

Figure 7.21. Sensory diet.

Before they get angry or frustrated and act inappropriately, the student has to recognize the antecedent to the frustration and anger so he or she can intercede before there is an issue. This is a very important life skill that the students can take into adulthood.

Collecting Data

Types of Data Sheets

There are several different types of data collection sheets used to take data on the behavior of a student, regardless of the special need. I am going to provide you with data sheets and tips on how to collect data for

✦ Frequency
✦ Intensity
✦ Duration
✦ Scatter plot

Frequency Data

Frequency data can be defined as *data yielded by counting the number of times a certain behavior occurs within a given period of time.* So when do you use frequency data? Let me give you an example:

CASE IN POINT Amy, a child with autism, has several behaviors that are being addressed by her IEP goals and objectives. One of the most significant behaviors is self-injury. Amy bites her arm when she is upset or frustrated. Mrs. Chalker wants to show the IEP team a baseline for the behavior so the team can better determine the next step.

A frequency data sheet would also be a great one to use if a student with special needs is talking out, biting, fighting, leaving the assigned area, late to class, saying inappropriate things, hitting, or not bringing materials.

Frequency data are typically used to measure specific behaviors that you may want to extinguish and those that can be easily defined. There are several things that you need to remember when you are choosing to use a frequency data chart:

✦ The data are very simple to take as long as the behavior is defined and easily recognizable.

✦ This type of data is also easily analyzed as graphs and trend lines determine whether the frequency increases or decreases without the use of complicated percentages or ratios.

✦ Sometimes frequency data alone may not tell the whole story for several reasons:

  ✪ Several behaviors will come at once and may overlap, making the count of specific behaviors difficult.

  ✪ The behavior may decrease but the frequency may not change and this improvement may not be seen.

  ✪ The intensity may decrease while the frequency remains constant, and even though this is a great improvement you may not know it.

  ✪ A great number of behaviors may occur during one small span of time and no behaviors during other time spans but you may not know this.

Let's look at a frequency data sheet that I have included as Appendix 7J for your use. Look at Figure 7.22.

This type of frequency data sheet is very simple to use. This particular one has room for recording frequency data for three different behaviors. As each of the behaviors occurs, you would put a slash mark through the number, beginning with one. This way cuts out the step of having to count the tick marks that many frequency data sheets require. As you see in the example, data are being kept on only two of the behaviors. It is easy to take the frequency data and summarize weeks of daily recording sheets by creating a simple line graph of the data. This is a great way to present data to parents at IEP meetings.

Duration Data

Let me describe a scenario in which the use of duration data would be very helpful.

CASE IN POINT Billy Bob is a third grader with Asperger syndrome. He is a very bright young man with strong math skills. Mrs. Davis is concerned because Billy Bob has begun exhibiting a few behavioral concerns that seem to be affecting his work in her classroom. When given an assignment that he does not want to do or when denied some type of request, Billy Bob has started pouting. He folds his arms, refuses to do any type of task, and refuses to speak. Mrs. Davis has consulted the special education teacher and has put into place a positive reinforcement system that appears to be making a difference, but she is not sure. She needs some type of data to show improvement. Billy Bob still pouts but he seems to come out of it pretty quickly now. Mrs. Davis has decided that she will begin timing the length of these episodes so she can show they are getting shorter.

Name: Chloe May	School: Smithwood Elementary	Grade: 2nd
Date: March 30, 2010	Teacher: Ms. Winters	Eligibility: Autism

Frequency Data Sheet

Directions: Define behaviors. When behavior occurs put slash through number to indicate number of times the behavior occurs.

Behavior 1

Talking out without raising hand

1	2	3	4	5
6	7	8	9	10
11	12	13	14	15
16	17	18	19	20
21	22	23	24	25
26	27	28	29	30
31	32	33	34	35
36	37	38	39	40

Behavior 2

Making squealing noise

1	2	3	4	5
6	7	8	9	10
11	12	13	14	15
16	17	18	19	20
21	22	23	24	25
26	27	28	29	30
31	32	33	34	35
36	37	38	39	40

Behavior 3

1	2	3	4	5
6	7	8	9	10
11	12	13	14	15
16	17	18	19	20
21	22	23	24	25
26	27	28	29	30
31	32	33	34	35
36	37	38	39	40

Figure 7.22. Frequency data sheet

Duration data sheets (see Figure 7.23; this sheet is available for you as Appendix 7K) are very easy to use, and graphing the data is easy with Microsoft Charts. As stated earlier, progress on some behaviors is best measured by the length of time the student exhibits the behavior. Plopping on the floor and not wanting to get up may be a significant issue for some students. Frequency data may not show progress, but if you record the duration of each, even you may see that the length of time the student is on the floor becomes shorter. This is progress and can only be measured by recording the event's duration.

Intensity Data

Intensity is at what level is the behavior being demonstrated. For example:

CASE IN POINT   John is a child with Down syndrome and he has some pretty explosive behaviors when he is denied certain things. He does not exhibit these behaviors very often, but when he does, they have been quite intense. Mrs. Deale has put into place several interventions that appear to be lessening the behavior. It still occurs but just doesn't seem to be as bad. She wonders how she could show that the interventions appear to be working.

This would be a great situation to begin recording intensity level data.

Intensity is difficult to record. Five people standing in a room watching the same incident may have five different opinions about its intensity level. You have to quantify the data. The Intensity Data Sheet from Figure 7.24 is included for your use as Appendix 7L. This sheet allows for a better defined level of intensity. You can define what the incident would look like at each level so that when the data are recorded they are consistent between raters.

Scatter Plots

Let me give you an example of how to use scatter plots:

CASE IN POINT Don is a child with several learning differences along with medical needs. He has started exhibiting some inappropriate behaviors and has gotten into trouble several times over the past couple of weeks. He has had several altercations with other students. Mr. Lynn has had a difficult time determining what is going on with Don. He wonders what the circumstances are around the altercations and started taking data on a scatter plot data sheet. Through looking at the data taken he determines that Don has about 90% of his behavioral issues between 11:00 and 11:45 before lunch and before his next shot of insulin. Could this be affecting his behavior?

APPENDIX 7K

| Name: | John E | School: | Cooper Middle | Grade: | 6 |
| Date: | May 2010 | Teacher: | Ms. Golden | Eligibility: | Intellectual Disability |

Directions: Define behaviors. Start time using stopwatch immediately upon observing the behavior. Record start time. Circle behavior number. A s soon as the behavior ceases, stop the timer and record the time. Figure the duration length.

#	Behavior definition
1	Noncompliance – plops to floor refusing to get up
2	Tantrum with preferred item is not available
3	

Behavior #	Date	Start time 🕐	End time 🕐	Duration
① 2 3	5 - 1 - 10	8:20	8:25	5 mins
1 ② 3	5 - 1 - 10	9:10	9:26	16 mins
① 2 3	5 - 3 - 10	9:00	9:04	4 min
1 ② 3	5 - 4 - 10	8:30	8:32	2 min
1 ② 3	5 - 4 - 10	1:05	1:12	7 min
① 2 3	5 - 11 - 10	9:30	9:34	4 mins
1 2 3				
1 2 3				
1 2 3				
1 2 3				

Duration Data Sheet

Figure 7.23. Completed duration data sheet.

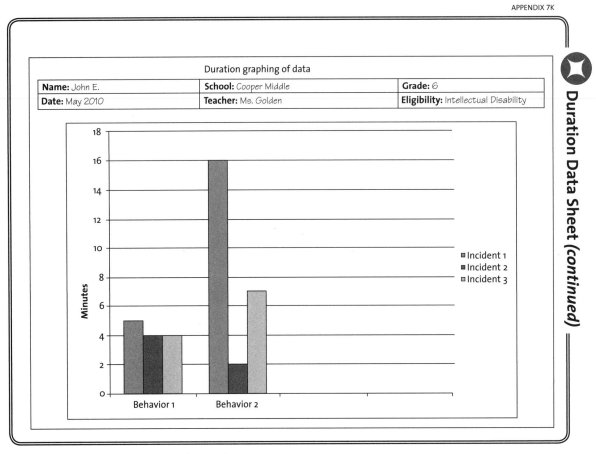

Figure 7.23. Completed duration data sheet *(continued)*.

I feel that a scatter plot is a great place to begin looking at data because it helps begin the analysis process by knowing when behaviors occur (see Figure 7.25; blank data sheet is Appendix 7M). There are several types of information that you can gain from taking scatter plot data about the behavioral issue.

✦ The time of day the behavior occurs

✦ The classroom in which it occurs

✦ The activities the student is involved in when the behavior occurs

✦ The teacher the student has during that time period

After gathering all of these data, you can make better decisions about the function of the behavior so that you can adequately create interventions to use in the classroom.

LEVEL THREE

The information in Level Three will provide you with additional tools to put in your tool belt. These are functional behavior assessments (FBAs) and behavioral intervention plans (BIPs). Not every student in your classroom will require the use of an FBA or will need a BIP written into his or her IEP. So, you are probably asking yourself, *when would I do an FBA or a BIP on one of my students?* The easiest answer is this: If a student exhibits behaviors that are impacting his or her ability to learn and/or progress in the school environment, you may want to investigate the reason for those behaviors and implement appropriate

APPENDIX 7L

Name:	Cindy Low		School:	Grant Middle School		Grade:	7th
Date:	4/15/2010		Teacher:	Ms. Goodman		Eligibility:	EBD

Define Behavior: Refusal to do classwork. This could consist of several different behaviors as seen below.

Directions: Define Behavior. Define Intensity of Behavior. When the behavior occurs, record date and time. Determine at what level of intensity the behavior is being exhibited and mark with an X.

Intensity Data Sheet

		Intensity Level Definitions				
Date	Time	Student sits in desk, maybe w/head down, and may calmly say they are not going to do the work	Sits in desk and verbally refuses or ignores. Doesn't get up from desk.	May raise voice but stays in chair and does not do work. May slam objects on desk.	Pushes objects off of desk, may raise voice, may or may not get up out of desk	Yells, throws objects, get up out of desk, may escape classroom
		1	2	3	4	5
4/15/10	8:30				×	
4/15/10	10:45					×
4/16/10	8:30			×		
4/19/10	9:20	×				
4/22/10	1:00		×			
4/23/10	12:40		×			
4/27/10	10:35	×				

Figure 7.24. Complete intensity data sheet.

interventions. To determine which interventions are appropriate for specific behavioral concerns, you will need to investigate and determine the function or reason the behavior is occurring. This investigative tool is the FBA and the intervention plan is the BIP.

So, you see that all students will not need an FBA or a BIP, but there may be some of your students who could benefit from the use of these tools.

Completing an FBA

What is an FBA?

An FBA can be defined as a process for identifying the function of problem behaviors. Through the use of an FBA, one is able to identify the events that occur in the environment that may be affecting and/or maintaining the behavior (Crone & Horner, 2003). An FBA will provide the user with information that will help him or her determine the context in which a problem behavior is occurring, the antecedent behaviors that occur before the problem behavior and the consequences of the problem behavior event that may be maintaining the behavior. It is a fluid process that provides information so that more appropriate BIPs can be written. An FBA alone is not useful—you have to complete the process by using the information in the development of the BIP.

The completion of FBA and BIP is complex enough to deserve an entire book unto itself, so the following is but a brief overview. I am going to provide you with a simple form

APPENDIX 7M

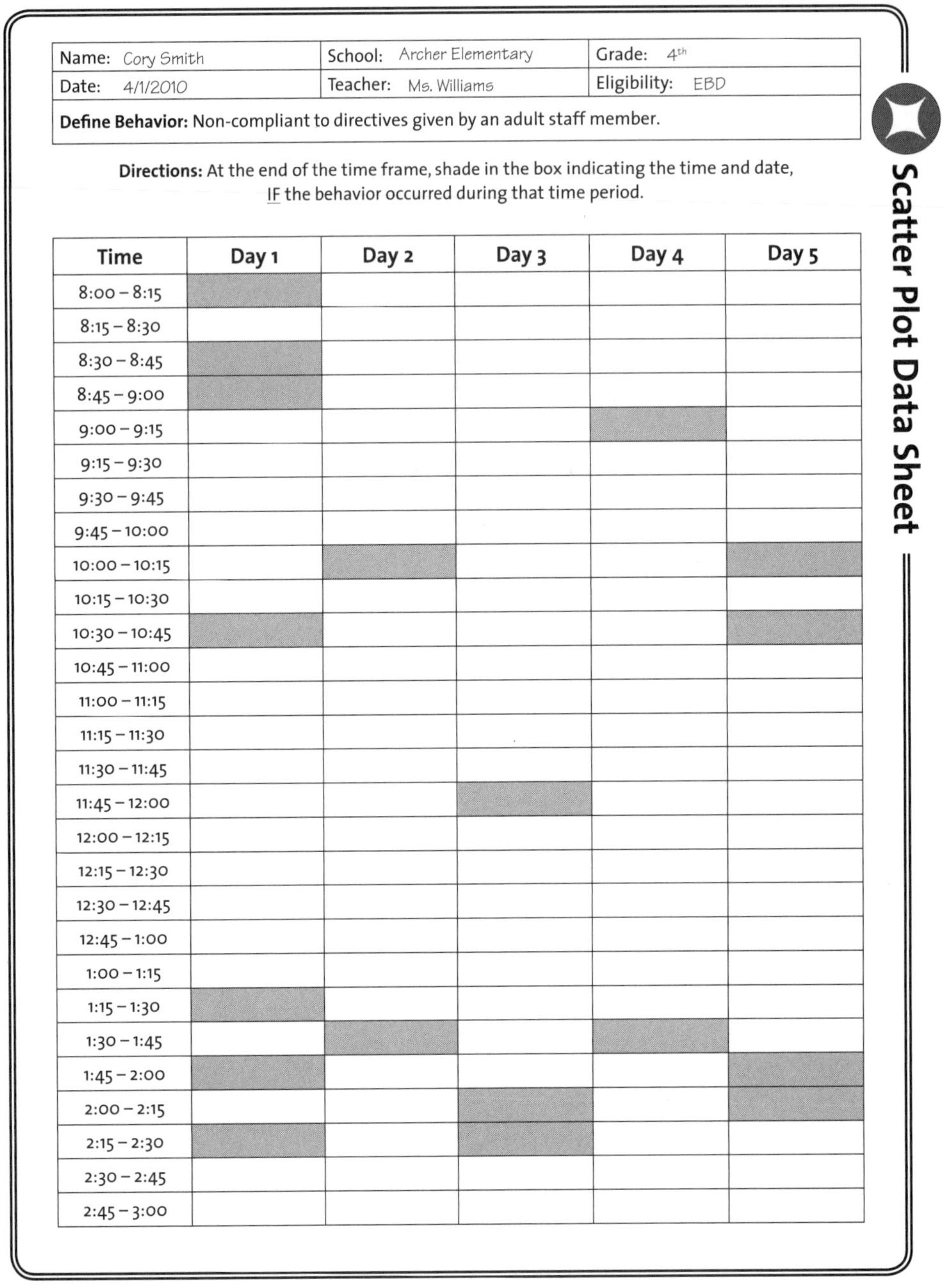

Name: Cory Smith	School: Archer Elementary	Grade: 4th
Date: 4/1/2010	Teacher: Ms. Williams	Eligibility: EBD

Define Behavior: Non-compliant to directives given by an adult staff member.

Directions: At the end of the time frame, shade in the box indicating the time and date, IF the behavior occurred during that time period.

Time	Day 1	Day 2	Day 3	Day 4	Day 5
8:00 – 8:15	▓				
8:15 – 8:30					
8:30 – 8:45	▓				
8:45 – 9:00	▓				
9:00 – 9:15				▓	
9:15 – 9:30					
9:30 – 9:45					
9:45 – 10:00					
10:00 – 10:15		▓			▓
10:15 – 10:30					
10:30 – 10:45	▓				▓
10:45 – 11:00					
11:00 – 11:15					
11:15 – 11:30					
11:30 – 11:45					
11:45 – 12:00			▓		
12:00 – 12:15					
12:15 – 12:30					
12:30 – 12:45					
12:45 – 1:00					
1:00 – 1:15					
1:15 – 1:30	▓				
1:30 – 1:45		▓		▓	▓
1:45 – 2:00	▓				▓
2:00 – 2:15			▓		▓
2:15 – 2:30	▓		▓		
2:30 – 2:45					
2:45 – 3:00					

Scatter Plot Data Sheet

Figure 7.25. Scatter plot data sheet.

that you may want to review when conducting an FBA. There are also many others that I use as resources and that are available on the Internet. Here are just a few.

✦ http://www.usu.edu/teachall/text/behavior/lrbipdfs/lrbiresource_02.pdf
✦ http://www.behaviordoctor.org
✦ http://cecp.air.org/fba/default.asp

✦ http://www.specialconnections.ku.edu/cgibin/cgiwrap/specconn/main.php?cat=
behavior&section=teachertools

✦ http://www.updc.org/fbabip/?searched=fba&advsearch=oneword&highlight=ajax
search_highlight+ajaxsearch_highlight1

There are several key components to an FBA that are consistent with most formats. Figure 7.26 shows one that is shorter and somewhat easier to use. If the student's behaviors are more significant and complicated, you may wish to use a format that allows for entry of additional types of data. Figure 7.26 is a completed example of the FBA template that I have included for your use as Appendix 7N.

Notice that there are several components that are very important to a behavior assessment: background information, psychological assessment data, and previous behavioral data; environmental factors that may affect the student's behavior; and current data of many different types along with recommendations.

There are 10 sections included in this format:

1. Operationally define the behavior: The target behavior has to be defined in such a way that it is clear to everyone what data are measuring.

2. Background information: A child's background information goes a long way in helping put the pieces together. This can be gained through interviewing the student, teacher, and/or parent. This can also been gained through the review of school records.

3. Psychological assessment data: Psychological assessments provide vital information about factors that will impact behavior. Cognitive functioning, academic functioning, and language ability all affect a student's behavior in the school setting.

4. Medical information: Medications, physical disabilities, and medical issues all affect a student's behavior. This information is important when you are completing a behavioral assessment.

5. Summary of previously taken data: Most of the time you will have taken data on the target behavior before the administration of a more formal FBA. It is important to include the data as they help create a more objective approach to research answers to the issue.

6. Current data: This is a summary section for the data that have been collected as part of the FBA. You may also need to attach the data sheets along with the graphed summary of the data.

7. Other factors impacting behavior: This section is where you would include all of the miscellaneous information that is vital to this assessment. This could include the makeup of the class, location of the student's desk, sensory issues, and any other types of environmental information that you feel may help shine light on the behavior in question.

8. Perceived function: Based on the data, why do you think this behavior occurs? Is it to escape or to gain something?

9. Recommendations: These are recommendations based on the assessment and will be used to create the BIP.

10. Plan for continued data collection and monitoring: An FBA is a fluid document because behavior is always changing. Continued monitoring and data collection on the target behavior and any other emerging behaviors will be important as the classroom staff are continually updating the BIP and classroom behavior plan.

Functional Behavior Assessment

Cindy G.	4/18/10	M Ⓕ
Student name	Date	Sex
Anytown elementary	Mr. Smith	
School	Teacher	
Emotional behavior disorder	1-1-2000	4th
Eligibility	Date of birth	Grade

I. Operationally define behavior

Cindy throws her work on the floor, raises her voice, refuses to do some assignments, and will at times cry.

II. Background information

Cindy was in another state before this school year. She has been in special education since the 1st grade. She is currently in a foster care placement and has had a traumatic childhood. She has been under the care of a psychiatrist since coming to this state. She has been separated from her siblings but she doesn't speak of this at all. Family history of domestic violence and addiction. Cindy is quiet and is not able to speak of her frustrations. She cries when frustrated and also does this at home. Foster parents are caring for two other children in their home.

III. Psychological assessment data

Cognitive ability: Full scale 105 SS. Verbal IQ: 85 Nonverbal: 112.

Expressive language: SS-75 Receptive Language: 70

Academic ability: Math SS: 72; Reading Comprehension SS: 74; Spelling SS: 90; Reading Fluency SS: 91

Summary indicated that the student struggles with verbalizing thoughts, understanding reading text, and in math reasoning.

IV. Medical information

Cindy takes Strattera and Tenex. She is diagnosed with ADHD. Also hypoglycemic but it is controlled with diet. Has been diagnosed with an anxiety disorder and is under a psychiatrist's care.

V. Summary of previously taken data relative to behavior

Data taken from 10-09 to 12-09.

Frequency	Average of one episode a day over 2 months	**Latency**	Not applicable
Duration	Average duration of 3.5 mins per episode	**Time sampling**	Shows highest frequency in afternoon during math class
Intensity	(1 to 5 scale: 5 most intense) Average intensity was a 2. Intensity increased later in 2-month period	**Other (ABC)**	Consequence that appeared to continue or escalate behavior was attention being given

VI. Current data relative to the behavior

This report is based on update data from 4-14-10 to 5-1-10. See attached data sheets. This is a summary of the current data.

Target behavior has escalated over the past few months compared with the previous data taken at the beginning of the year.

Frequency	Average of two episodes daily
Duration	5.5 minutes average from initial behavior to return to task.
Intensity	On a 5-level system, student's average intensity is a 3 with 5 being the most intense.
Time sampling	72% of the target behaviors have occurred in math class; 10% in reading; 5% in social studies. Rest were in times of transition.
ABC data	Consequence that appeared to continue the behavior was attention being given to her or drawn to her.

(page 1 of 2)

Figure 7.26. Example completed functional behavior assessment.

Figure 7.26. *(Continued)*

Functional Behavior Assessment *(continued)*

VII. Other factors impacting behavior
For math, Cindy is in a large class of 25 students. It is her first time in an inclusive environment with this many students. She has no friends in this peer group and is very quiet.
Student is new to the school, having just come at the beginning of this year. She is physically smaller than other students.
This is the first year the special education teacher who serves this class has co-taught.
She enjoys one-to-one attention from the regular education teacher. She wants to have a friend but lacks social skills to do this on her own.

VIII. Perceived function
Escape from tasks.

IX. Recommendations
1. Implement a positive reinforcement system that involves attention from the regular ed teacher.
2. Implement a peer-helper system in the classroom.
3. Use a priming method to let student know ahead of time what type of assignments she will be doing. Do this in private. Allow her time to ask questions in private before giving the assignment to the class.
4. Give student a signal to use to let the teacher know that she is frustrated and doesn't understand. This should also be done without the other students knowing. Work up to begin to be able to ask questions in public by raising her hand.
5. Lessen the amount of practice problems she is required to do.
6. In a crisis allow the student to separate herself to a different part of the room away from the other students in order to not bring negative attention upon herself.
7. Teach social skills-friendship making skills to student in a different class. Pair her up with a positive role model and prime this student ahead of time to know how to encourage Cindy.

X. Plan for continued data collection and monitoring
Data collection will continue. Teacher will summarize data and at the end of each week will review it with the classroom staff at a team meeting. Every 2 weeks the frequency, duration, intensity, and time sampling data will be reviewed by the behavior specialist. He will make recommendations as to updates to the behavior plan after reviewing the data every other week. Summary of data and progress will be provided to the parents on a weekly basis.

(page 2 of 2)

Writing BIPs

BIPs are important parts of a student's educational plan. Will every student have a BIP? The answer is no. Students who require BIPs are those whose behaviors are interfering with their ability to learn and their ability to function in a classroom and school environment.

BIPs are written with information and data gained from the FBA. The BIP is not written on assumptions or opinions; it is written based on data. The BIP is also a fluid document and will require the monitoring of the classroom staff as to its effectiveness and the need to update the included interventions.

Writing a BIP

You may have, in the school system in which you work, a specific format for completing BIPs, and, if you do, it is important to use that format. If you do not have access to a preformatted BIP then review the completed BIP template shown in Figure 7.27, which is also included as Appendix 7O to determine if it would work to meet your needs.

As you see this example is formatted to include two separate behaviors. It is important to focus on no more than three different behaviors on your BIP. After reviewing the data from the FBA you may notice that many of the behaviors can be combined and may appear as a cluster of behaviors instead of several different behavior entities. This cluster of behaviors will, most likely, serve the same function and could be intervened with using the same positive behavior plan.

As you can see this is just a detailed plan of how you will intervene with the student to help him or her move toward the goal behavior. Let's briefly look at each part:

✦ Operationally define the behavior: You need a specific definition. "Temper tantrum" is not a behavior that you would include on a BIP. A more appropriate definition may be: "Physical aggression as indicated by hitting, scratching, biting, and/or kicking others, including both peers and adults."

✦ Perceived function based on data from the FBA: Is the behavior occurring or being continued based on trying to escape a task, gain attention, gain an object, escape attention, gain an activity, stimulate sensory system, calm sensory system, and so forth?

✦ Goal behavior: What behavior do you want to see?

✦ Environmental modifications: The manipulation of the antecedents is important. Are there things you could do to the environment around the student to set him or her up for success, such as reducing the amount of work or type of work, increasing attention, changing peer groups, or changing location in the classroom?

✦ Positive reinforcement plan: This is the meat of the plan. This section will include the day-to-day steps involved in intervening with the student. This could be as detailed as you need to ensure that everyone understands the plan.

✦ Data management plan: How are you going to take data on the behavior and what types of data will you need?

✦ Follow up and monitoring procedures: Who will monitor the data and how often? This also takes into account how you will meet as a team to discuss and update the plan, in addition to involving the parents in those updates.

✦ Crisis plan: What if the plan goes awry? You need to have the steps you will follow in the worst-case scenario. Planning ahead for any type of event is important.

If the behavioral needs of the student are not severe, this BIP template may meet your needs. If the behaviors are much more complex and severe, this template may not be detailed enough and may require a much more analyzed plan. Either way, it can serve as a starting point.

Writing a Safety Plan

Students with special needs sometimes have complex behavioral issues and, regardless of the function of their behaviors, their reaction to certain stimuli may create a situation that puts the student in danger. One of the ways to proactively ensure the student is kept safe in the school environment is to write a safety plan. I have provided a safety plan form as Appendix 7P, and an example of a safety plan is shown in Figure 7.28.

This is an example of a simple safety or crisis plan. These types of plans should be developed by a committee after reviewing the student's behavioral data. They may be several pages long, containing specific techniques to use in times of crisis, or they may be as simple as this one. Notice that there are three different behaviors charted on this particular student and for each behavior there is provided a simple progression of steps to implement in the event of a crisis.

Safety plans are very important documents and should be shared with those who have contact with the student for whom it is written. Safety plans should be included in

Behavior intervention plan

Cindy Golden	5-10-10	Anytown Elementary	4th	Mr. Smith
Student Name	Date	School	Grade	Teacher
EBD	1-1-2000	10	1-10-10	12-17-09
Eligibility	Date of Birth	Age	Date of IEP	Date of FBA

Behavior 1	Behavior 2
Operationally define the behavior	*Operationally define the behavior*
Throws her work on the floor, raises her voice and refuses to do the assignment and will begin to cry.	
Perceived function based on data from the FBA	*Perceived function based on data from the FBA*
Escape from task.	
Goal Behavior: What behavior do you want to see?	*Goal behavior: What behavior do you want to see?*
Acceptance of the direction and beginning the task—asking for questions if there is a lack of understanding of the assignment.	
Environment modifications	*Environment modifications*
Place desk close proximity to the teacher and/or a peer helper.	
Classroom work will be examined as to the level and Cindy's ability to complete the task.	
Modification and/or accommodations may be needed depending upon the assignment: do odd/even problems, etc.	

Behavior 1	Behavior 2
Positive reinforcement plan	*Positive reinforcement plan*
Cindy will be "primed" and the instructions given to her individually a few mins before they are given to the class.	
Cindy will have the opportunity to ask teacher questions individually prior to the assignment being given to the group.	
Cindy will be given a signal to use when she is frustrated. At that time the teacher will allow her to get up and go to a different part of the room for a 3 minute break.	
Teacher will then ask Cindy to come to her desk to discuss the assignment.	
Cindy will earn points for completing each assignment. Points to be used as homework passes.	
Data Management Plan	*Data management plan*
Frequency, duration and time sampling data will be taken by classroom staff. Progress monitored weekly.	
ABC data will also be kept to continue gathering information on the types of assignments, subject area, and staff involved.	
Follow up & Monitoring Procedures	*Follow up & monitoring procedures*
Teacher will review the data summary on a weekly basis to determine trends. Weekly progress summary will be sent to parent.	
The team will meet weekly to review the data and determine success of interventions.	
Crisis steps	*Crisis steps*
1. If she disrupts the classroom she will be asked to get up from desk and move to a desk in the back of the room.	
2. If she refuses, administration will be called to the classroom.	
3. If she complies but becomes increasingly disruptive, the administration will be called to the classroom.	

Behavior Intervention Plan

Figure 7.27. Example completed behavior intervention plan.

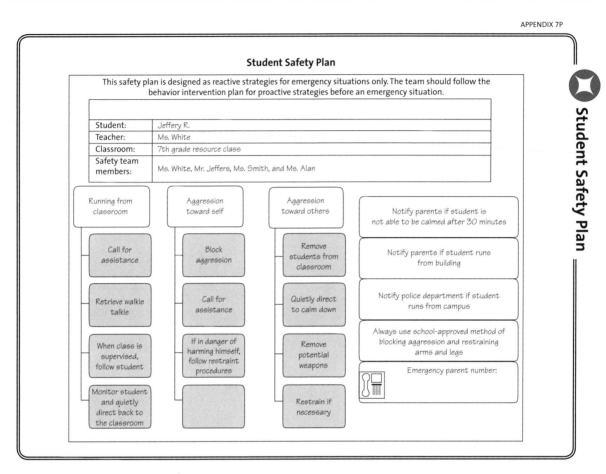

Figure 7.28. Example of a completed safety plan.

Student Safety Plan

the emergency substitute plan book so that they are readily accessible when the teacher is absent. You can post these on a bulletin board in the teacher area; place them on clipboards hung in an area devoted to behavior data; place them inside the lesson plans book located on the teacher's desk; or create a flip chart of laminated sheets and place it on a hook in an area close to the students' work area.

SUMMARY

You are finished with the behavior chapter! But, as a good teacher will do, I plan to review. Let me just hit the high spots:

✦ Remember that behavior is communication. It is important that all students have a way of communicating both needs and desires so they will not have to resort to inappropriate behaviors to communicate to others.

✦ Every student needs to understand what is expected of him or her in the classroom. Remember, if they do not understand what is appropriate and what is expected of them, how can they exhibit the expected behaviors?

✦ Students with autism need direct teaching of social skills. They do not learn as easily from watching others as they do from direct teaching.

✦ Teachers should take a proactive approach to meeting students' sensory needs. Strive to meet sensory needs before inappropriate behaviors occur. This helps set a positive climate in which the students can learn and progress.

✦ Consistency with behavioral expectations is even more important with students who have autism spectrum disorders. Some students have a difficult time with unpredictability and with change.

✦ Watch and intervene when behavioral antecedents occur. These will be more apparent as you go through and analyze each student's behavioral data.

✦ Let the data drive your decisions. Behavior plans are fluid documents, not stagnant annual plans without revisions. The premise of applied behavior analysis is that the decision-making process is built on objective data, not subjective opinion.

You have now addressed the behavior aspect of your classroom. Hopefully, as you continue to work through each of the OMAC layers, you are beginning to feel less stressed and more organized. By creating a system of organization in the area of behavior, you have created a classroom climate that is positive and addresses the unique needs of your students with autism and other learning differences. Now let's move on to organize your paperwork!

Organization of Paperwork

Paperwork—the most dreaded task of a special educator. It will devour the most competent teacher and drown the most organized. However, there is hope. The management of paperwork can be easier than you think.

Let's tackle this problem by using a typical problem-solving technique. We will use a task analysis method of determining the steps needed to deal with this issue. Breaking the problem into small, manageable steps is the only way to tackle an overwhelming issue. After analyzing the tasks you will then tackle one step at a time.

In the area of paperwork management there are three steps:

1. Define the issue: What types of paperwork will I be required to manage?
2. Gather needed materials: What types of materials do I have available to create a system of organization?
3. Determine location for your paperwork system: Where should the paperwork organization system be located within the classroom?

WHAT TYPES OF PAPERWORK WILL I BE REQUIRED TO MANAGE?

Let's begin with determining the types of paperwork that are required for special educators. The area of paperwork can be broken into the following smaller sections:

✦ Lesson plans: Most schools require all teachers to complete plans for academic subjects.

✦ Student information: This includes the management of permission slips, emergency cards, medical information, and so forth.

✦ Data: This includes the organization of all types of individualized education program (IEP) data.

✦ IEPs: This includes the organization of all paperwork involved in writing special education IEPs.

✦ Student work: You will have papers to grade, grade books to keep, and work samples to analyze, so, to keep your head above water, you must have an organized management system.

To organize the massive volume of paperwork that is required of special educators, you need a system. Take a minute to think about the types of paperwork you have to manage, then you can move on to gather the materials needed to develop an organized management system.

WHAT TYPES OF MATERIALS DO I HAVE
AVAILABLE TO CREATE A SYSTEM OF ORGANIZATION?

The suggestions that I am going to make will use materials you have available in your classroom or items that are easily accessible to most teachers. You can probably get your hands on file cabinets, file folders, notebooks, bookshelves, and clipboards. These all work great, but let me narrow the materials down to the ones that will help you create the simplest organizational system. There are several inexpensive generic materials you may want to gather to get started: three-ring binders, plastic document sleeves, colored file folders, plastic file crates, index tabs, clipboards, hanging folders, and construction paper for color coding.

Three-Ring Binders

Three-ring binders are wonderful—especially the larger ones that have the pocket inserts in the front and back covers. They are inexpensive, customizable, and easy to store. They make access to paperwork a snap, can be color coded, and are portable. I recommend the 1-, 2-, or 3-inch three-ring binders with a plastic area for cover customization: These notebooks can be color coded with construction paper, and it is easy to create a customized cover with a digital photo and a word processing program. Use several different sizes of binders depending upon the amount of paperwork you anticipate. Some binders even come in extra-wide widths that allow extra room so the tabbed inserts will not hang over the edge.

Plastic document sleeves that are available at most office supply stores and some larger discount stores are wonderful for protecting pages. Binders can be stored on bookshelves in the teacher area or in file crates or, if they contain confidential information, will even fit in file cabinet drawers.

File Crates

File crates are the best thing since sliced bread. Both open file crates and closed file boxes (see Figure 8.1) are handy tools in the classroom. These can be color coded with construction paper and labeled with the name of the student and the purpose for the materials included in the crate. These crates are for teacher use, but if they are easily coded by color, name, and photo, the student can assume a role in using the organizational management system. The student can independently get his or her own crate and take it to the work area to have the materials ready for the work session.

File crates are inexpensive, readily available in many larger discount stores, portable, and sturdy enough to last years. They can be used with hanging file folders that are also available in many different colors, pocket folders, or simple manila file folders. Another advantage of using crates is that they are large enough to hold three-ring binders and teaching materials.

Figure 8.1. File crates.

| Table 8.1. | Uses of common organizing items |

Three-ring binders with index tabs and plastic document holders	File crates with colored file folders and hanging file folders	Clipboards
Lesson plans	Data	Data
Student information books	IEP materials for specific students	Lesson plans for centers
Data	Lesson plans for centers	Emergency plans
Work samples	Work samples	IEP objectives
Emergency plans		

Key: IEP, individualized education program.

Clipboards

Clipboards are among those items that usually come in the first-year-teacher supply box and are a staple of every classroom. The newest clipboards are even color coded and some have built-in storage boxes with calculators. More typical clipboards are inexpensive, portable, and can be hung on the wall. If you look around you may find colored clipboards, but if not, the wooden ones can easily be painted with a can of spray paint. If you are really feeling creative, try painting the back of the clipboard with chalkboard paint to create a surface for labeling with the student's name or the purpose of the clipboard itself (e.g., IEP data). If you are not feeling so creative you can easily color code the boards by placing laminated construction paper over the board's contents (as was shown in Figure 4.12). This also ensures confidentiality of the material attached. Try looking around for the clipboard storage boxes with calculators. These work great for holding data sheets and the calculator makes it easy to figure percentages of the collected data.

Although you should be creative and determine what works best for you, I've included in Table 8.1 suggested uses for the materials that I have recommended.

Specific information about how to create these will be given later, but for now, just think in general terms about the kinds of things you will need to organize your paperwork.

WHERE SHOULD THE PAPERWORK ORGANIZATION SYSTEM BE LOCATED WITHIN THE CLASSROOM?

Regardless of the type of environment you have, there are several common locations you can use to place your paperwork system within the classroom. This classroom arrangement can be used in a regular education or special education classroom. Figure 8.2 is a sample layout of a classroom setting, and it provides you with ideas of how to integrate a paperwork organizational system into the classroom environment.

As you will notice on the classroom map from Figure 8.2, the same types of paperwork were not scattered around the room but gathered and organized in a central location. All of the student information is held in binders in the teacher area, data collection sheets are placed in a central location, and student work to be graded is all placed in one central location. If materials are organized in this way, the staff, students, and even observing administrators have easy access to all needed materials without asking for your assistance, thus relieving you of a little stress.

Now let's examine each of the five types of paperwork and I will suggest more specific ways to organize each area. Remember that you are to adapt these to fit the specific needs of your classroom and the requirements of your school district.

Lesson Plans

This can be a headache for educators, and for special educators this is especially true. I have heard some special educators comment, "Why should I do lesson plans; isn't the IEP my lesson plan?" Well, the answer to that question is yes and no. An IEP is the overall annual

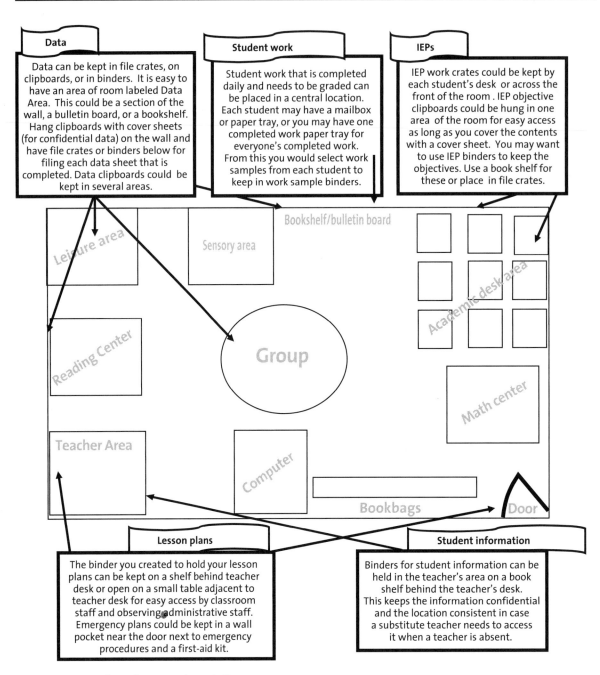

Data

Data can be kept in file crates, on clipboards, or in binders. It is easy to have an area of room labeled Data Area. This could be a section of the wall, a bulletin board, or a bookshelf. Hang clipboards with cover sheets (for confidential data) on the wall and have file crates or binders below for filing each data sheet that is completed. Data clipboards could be kept in several areas.

Student work

Student work that is completed daily and needs to be graded can be placed in a central location. Each student may have a mailbox or paper tray, or you may have one completed work paper tray for everyone's completed work. From this you would select work samples from each student to keep in work sample binders.

IEPs

IEP work crates could be kept by each student's desk or across the front of the room . IEP objective clipboards could be hung in one area of the room for easy access as long as you cover the contents with a cover sheet. You may want to use IEP binders to keep the objectives. Use a book shelf for these or place in file crates.

Leisure area

Sensory area

Bookshelf/bulletin board

Academic desk area

Reading Center

Group

Math center

Teacher Area

Computer

Bookbags

Door

Lesson plans

The binder you created to hold your lesson plans can be kept on a shelf behind teacher desk or open on a small table adjacent to teacher desk for easy access by classroom staff and observing administrative staff. Emergency plans could be kept in a wall pocket near the door next to emergency procedures and a first-aid kit.

Student information

Binders for student information can be held in the teacher's area on a book shelf behind the teacher's desk. This keeps the information confidential and the location consistent in case a substitute teacher needs to access it when a teacher is absent.

Figure 8.2. Location of areas for paperwork organization.

plan that guides educational planning for a particular child. It does not provide specific information on materials you will be using, pages you will complete, when a test on the material is going to be given, and the type of homework that is going to be assigned.

When administrators come into your classroom to observe you teaching a lesson, they will most likely ask to see your lesson plans. But, I have seen a principal or two who do not require lesson plans for self-contained or pull-out resource classrooms that serve only students in special education, as they believe the IEP serves that purpose. Every school and every district is different. Now, let's move forward!

CONTENTS

School-wide activity calendar

Classroom schedule

Weekly group lesson plans

Individual student lesson plans

Support services schedule

Lesson Planning Back Cover

Figure 8.3. Lesson planning back cover.

I think the easiest and most organized way to keep lesson plans is to create a notebook by using a three-ring binder, index dividers for the different sections, and plastic sleeves to hold the permanent documents that you do not have to change. Your school administrator may have you use a certain type of lesson plan book, but you could always consider placing this into a binder so that all of your information resides together. Use a larger size of three-ring binder to create a customized lesson plan book that meets the specific needs of your classroom. Figure 8.3 is an example of a back cover for a lesson plan binder. This example is also included as Appendix 8A for your use.

Notice the back cover. This one book could contain everything related to planning for your academic day. The contents for the book shown in Figure 8.3 will contain:

School-wide Activity Calendar

Why not put a copy of the school calendar in this section? This way you will have a list of dates for school holidays, school-wide testing, report cards, parent conferences, open house, school assemblies, and so forth.

Classroom Schedule

This could hold a classroom schedule that is very general or can be much more detailed if warranted by your particular setting. You may have a self-contained setting where a detailed

APPENDIX 8B

Classroom schedule

Classroom Schedule

Time	Subject	Location	Additional information
8:00–8:30	Reading 6th grade	Room 403	Resource pull out
8:30–9:30	Planning	Room 403 or 6th grade office	Team planning with 6th grade
9:30–10:15	Writing	Computer lab	Will have parapro to assist
10:15–11:00	Math	Room 215 (with Ms. Langley)	Co-teaching 6th grade
11:00–12:00	Reading 7th grade	Room 403	Resource pull out
12:00–12:45	Social studies	Room 215 (with Ms. Langley)	Co-teaching 6th grade
12:45–1:30	Math 7th grade	Room 403	Resource pull out
1:30–2:15	Social studies	Room 320 (with Mr. Johnson)	Co-teaching 7th Grade

Figure 8.4. Completed classroom schedule.

schedule is needed but you may also have a pull-out resource setting that would only need a very general schedule. Figure 8.4 shows an example of a schedule completed for a teacher who teaches several different subjects in several different locations of the school (a blank version of this schedule is included as Appendix 8B). The teacher using this example schedule serves not only as a co-teacher several times a day but also as a resource teacher. This schedule shown in Figure 8.4 serves as the classroom schedule but is specific to the teacher. What a great schedule to enlarge and post on the wall or outside the door so that whenever another staff member or a student needs to know where this teacher is located, they will be able to find him or her. Feel free to modify this schedule to fit the needs of your particular setting.

Weekly Group Lesson Plans

This plan (see Figure 8.5) is one you would use for a large group or an entire classroom. This particular example shows an inclusive classroom with a co-teacher present for three segments a day. The plans indicate the subject areas for which the co-teacher is present and the number of students with disabilities who are present in the classroom during that time (a blank copy of this plan template is available as Appendix 8C).

This type of plan could also be used for the special education resource teacher who may teach three or four different subject areas daily. All of the students in the resource classroom may function at similar levels and may have similar IEP objectives. The lesson plan for those periods may be written as a group plan.

Individual Student Plans

If you need to individualize your plans for individual students, this plan will help you keep organized. This would be especially applicable to a special education setting where several students at different levels are taught. Sometimes in a resource setting the classroom is comprised of more than one grade level or curriculum. Figure 8.6 shows a great way to individualize the lesson plans by the day and is divided into morning and afternoon sections.

Figure 8.6 shows only a Monday morning and afternoon schedule, but a blank lesson plan template you can use for all of the days of the week is included for you as Appendix 8D. You can certainly modify this one by expanding it to show the schedule for several more students.

APPENDIX 8C

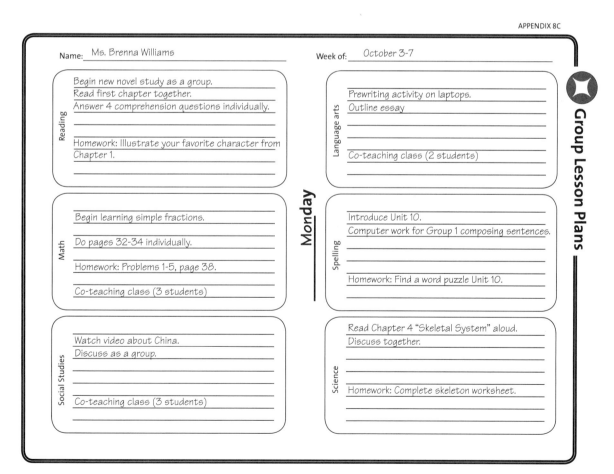

Figure 8.5. Examples of group lesson plan.

Individualized Lesson Plan Template

__Monday__ **Lesson Plans**

(day of week)

Morning/**_Afternoon_**(circle one)

Time	Student names				
	Ann	Bob	Cindy	David	Ernie
8:00 – 8:30	Reading	Speech therapy	Reading	Reading	Reading
8:30 – 9:45	Spelling and writing	Spelling and writing	Spelling and writing	Occupational therapy	Computer
9:45 – 10:00	Recess	Recess	Recess	Recess	Recess
10:00 – 10:30	Math	Math	Computer	Speech therapy	Math
10:30 – 11:00	Speech therapy	Computer	Occupational therapy	Computer	Lunch with Ms. Smith's class
11:00 – 11:45	Lunch	Lunch	Lunch	Lunch	Resource class for math

Daily Lesson Plan Schedule

Figure 8.6. Example completed daily lession plan schedule.

If you need to have a more detailed lesson plan, take a look at Figure 8.7 (a blank version is available as Appendix 8E). It shows another example of a detailed lesson plan that includes not only the IEP objective but also a specific plan for teaching the objective as some students require specific teaching techniques for certain IEP objectives.

Allow me to describe a situation that may warrant the use of this type of lesson plan.

CASE IN POINT Angela is a second-grade student with autism and intellectual disabilities. The teacher has had Angela in her classroom for one and a half years and knows her pretty well. Angela is nonverbal and struggles with basic readiness skills. The teacher also has seven other students in the classroom, with one paraprofessional who supports the classroom. The paraprofessional has no experience with students with autism and the teacher is feeling extremely stressed with trying to do all of the individualized teaching herself. The teacher would like to set up centers and have the paraprofessional work with some of the students individually, but she is unsure about the paraprofessional's ability to use specific teaching techniques. The teacher has to find a way to teach the paraprofessional some of the specific teaching techniques used in the classroom so that she is able to serve the classroom in more areas.

APPENDIX 8E

Individual Student Lesson Plan

Lesson plan

Student name: __Angela Rhodes__   School year: ___2010-2011___

IEP goal/objective

When presented flash cards of eight basic solid colors (black, blue, red, white, yellow, orange, green, purple)

and the name of the color given orally, Angela will choose the correct color from a field of four cards.

Criteria of mastery:
Correctly choose six out of eight colors for eight out of 10 work sessions over a 10 school

day period.

Task instructions

Using three-step prompting technique teach the eight basic colors.

Setup: Arrange the four color flash cards in a line on the table in front of student.

Task instructions:

Tell: "Angela, give me ____ [red]." If she chooses the correct card and hands it to you then present her with four

other flash cards and continue with a different color. If she does not, then go to the next step, which is Show.

Show: "Angela, give me ____ [red]". You should touch the red card to show her to one to choose. If she gives it

to you then go back to Tell and have her do it again. If she does not then move on to Do.

Do: "Angela, give me ____[red]". Take her hand and pick up the red card and give to you. "Great job giving me red,

now your turn." Go back to Show and repeat.

Materials

"Color" flash cards.

Eight basic colors (red, black, blue, yellow, green, purple, orange, white)

Figure 8.7. Example of a completed lesson plan for an individual student.

Look at Figure 8.7. Look at how helpful it would be if the teacher could write up several of these plans that match up with the IEP objectives and place them in the lesson plan book for reference by the paraprofessional. You would only need to do this one time per activity. The materials are listed for each task, along with the setup of the area, the specific instructions for the task, and even the criteria for mastery. What a great way to set up for data collection! This type of plan may be time consuming at the setup, but after a while, when you say to the paraprofessional, "Please use a three-step prompting technique with Angela when you work with her on learning *same* and *different*," he or she will probably understand completely. This way the teaching techniques used in the classroom can be completed with consistency and integrity regardless of who is working with the student.

Support Services Schedule

This is a schedule of services your students receive in the areas of speech and language, occupational therapy, or from other related service providers (see Figure 8.8). It is an organized way to keep up with the individual services for each of your students as it is important to make sure that your students receive all of the services outlined on their IEPs.

Included as Appendix 8F is a blank template for this form. Along with the lesson plan templates, this form can be used as is or modified to create a customized lesson plan notebook. These forms will provide you a creative beginning to the creation of a lesson plan notebook that will help you organize and manage one of the paperwork areas required for your classroom.

APPENDIX 8F

Put date and time that the students receive related services

Student name	Speech-language	Occupational therapy	Physical therapy	Adaptive PE	Other
Cindy G.	Monday and Wednesday 9.00 – 9.30			Friday 9.00 – 10.00	
Ann S.	Tuesday and Thursday 11.00 – 11.30	Wednesday 10.30 – 11.00			
Nate W.	Monday and Thursday 8.45 – 9.15			Friday 9.00 – 10.00	Music therapy Wednesday 2.00 – 2.30

Related Support Schedule

Figure 8.8. Example of a completed related support schedule.

While we are discussing lesson plans, let me suggest one more thing. Imagine this: You are a teacher who has two young boys with autism who are part of your social studies, science, and math classes. It is sometimes difficult to remember what types of accommodations that these young men require to be successful in your setting. The accommodations are written into their IEPs and you are diligent about making sure that you provide what they need. It may be helpful for you to add a column or row at the bottom of your plans to include specific information related to a student's accommodation needs (see Figure 8.9). You do not need to put the names of the students to keep the information confidential, but could use only a first initial.

Substitute and Emergency Plans

Nobody likes being sick—what's worse than being home with the flu? Well, what is worse than that may be what is going on in your classroom! Students with special needs, specifically those with autism spectrum disorders, need consistency, routine, and predictability.

Lesson plans

	Science
Monday	Begin Chapter 3 "Mammals." Read pages 36-40 together and take notes. Homework: Complete questions 1-4 from page 41.
Tuesday	Complete the three worksheets from Chapter 3, video, and discussion.
Wednesday	Complete three worksheets together to serve as a study guide.
Thursday	Lab from page 44, "Eating patterns of selected mammals." Create PowerPoint presentation in pairs of students.
Friday	Quiz on the first part of Chapter 3 and then continue the lab from Thursday.
Special accommodations for students	CG: Provide copy of my notes. Pair up with buddy. Provide 1 extra day to complete the written assignment BW: Provide study guide for tests. NW: Take the test in a small group.

Figure 8.9. Example of completed lesson plans.

When a teacher is sick, most of those three things go out the window, unless you, as the teacher, have worked extra hard to prepare.

When I was teaching in a middle school special education setting, I had a young man, Davie, who had Asperger syndrome. He would tell me on almost a weekly basis, "Please, Mrs. Golden, would you tell us before you are absent, pleeease!" Luckily I was rarely absent, and, of course, when I was I did just that. But one morning I woke up about 5:30 a.m. too sick to lift my head, and one of the first thoughts to cross through my mind was, *Oh, no; Davie is not going to like this.* I had lesson plans and my classroom was organized, but I had no time to *overprepare* for a substitute; therefore, the consistency and routine would most likely go out the window.

So let me give you suggestions of ways that you can over-prepare for an emergency.

To maintain some semblance of order in a time of crisis, I recommend that you have at least 3 days of emergency substitute plans that are kept in a visible place in your classroom. You may be in a school that requires this already, and, if so, be sure to follow your school's procedures. If not, then think about using the tools in the appendixes. Remember, you can always modify these to fit your own environment or allow this idea to get you thinking creatively about ways you could over-prepare for a crisis. Here are a few of my suggestions:

1. Use one of the trusty customizable three-ring binders that you now have. Clearly mark it with a cover as as a *Substitute/Emergency Plan* book. It may also be helpful to color code this binder in red to make it stand out and make it easier to spot. Just slip a piece of red construction paper behind the label in the front pocket, making sure to also label and color code the spine of the notebook.

2. Next, you can use index dividers to section off the *Emergency Plan* binder with different sections. The following are suggestions of items you may want to consider including in your binder:

   ✦ Student roster with photos: This is in case your students are unable to give their names.

   ✦ Emergency contacts for each student: Phone numbers for parents or emergency contacts information.

   ✦ Medical information for each student: This includes information about the medications that are administered at school and other medication information (e.g., does the student have seizures, diabetes, asthma, or allergies?).

   ✦ Staff members who will serve as contacts for needed information: Ms. Smith down the hall may be the special education team leader and may know your students pretty well, so she would be a great staff contact for information.

   ✦ Daily schedule: Just what it says it is! You have this already in your lesson plans notebook, so make a second copy to include here.

   ✦ Location of where materials can be found in the classroom: You may think this is silly but you would be surprised. But hopefully your room is so organized and well labeled that this will not be an issue.

   ✦ Three days' worth of lesson plans: Remember, this is for emergencies only and you should not stress yourself out trying to plan lessons 8 months in advance. How could you plan detailed lesson plans because you are not going to know if the emergency is going to occur when you are teaching multiplication facts, word problems, or fractions? So, the plans should be ones without time limits—maintenance skills to be reviewed just until the emergency situation can be stabilized.

It is helpful to have all of this information in one spot. I know that as you read on, you will find that some of this information may be found in other notebooks, but it would be good if, in the event of an emergency, a substitute did not have to think about looking for information in other places. Remember that this is in the event of an emergency situation, so *make it simple and make it visible*.

Student Information

Imagine taking your students on a field trip. On this trip you have several students with significant needs and a decreased level of communication. Going off campus can be stressful to the adults involved, as safety of the students is the primary focus. Now, suppose there is an emergency and you need to get in touch with a parent, but, in the stress of the moment, you can't find the emergency numbers. You know you have a piece of paper with the information on it in a folder somewhere, but you cannot find it as quickly as you would like. Finally you find it on the bus among student sack lunches, bookbags, and jackets. You come away from this experience feeling a bit stressed and not as organized and prepared as you would have liked to have been.

It is important that information about students be kept

- ✦ Organized
- ✦ Easily visible
- ✦ Easily accessible
- ✦ Portable
- ✦ Confidential

Fortunately, it's easy to create that type of system with a three-ring binder. There are other ways to keep this information organized (e.g., using a crate with hanging file folders or a folder kept in a file cabinet will do the job), but to make it easily portable I feel that a three-ring binder is the best option.

You can do this in two different ways. You can create one *Classroom Information* binder to include all of your students. This is the most user-friendly and most portable, as you can take it on field trips, emergency drills, and so forth. See Figure 8.10 for an example of a table of contents that you could use as a front or back cover to a notebook binder (also included as Appendix 8G). I would make this highly visible by placing a piece of red construction paper behind both covers and the label on the spine of the binder. For most binders there will be an overhang between the cover pocket and the 8.5" by 11" printed binder cover. This is perfect for color coding with a piece of construction paper as the colored paper will be visible. This is easy to do but makes a world of difference in creating a more visible organizational tool.

As you can see, this type of binder will hold

- ✦ School contacts: phone numbers and names of staff members back at the school
- ✦ Roster of students
- ✦ Addresses
- ✦ Phone numbers
- ✦ Photo of each child
- ✦ All types of permission slips
- ✦ Medical information
- ✦ Emergency card information

This is a great binder to just grab and run on fire drills, to take on the playground, and so forth. Let me give you a personal example.

I am happy to say that during all of my years in the public schools, I have only had one incident that involved a fire at school. Part of the building I served filled with smoke

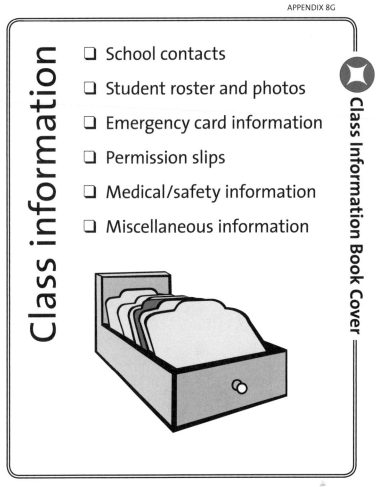

Figure 8.10.   Class information book cover.

from an electrical fire. All of the students in that building were those with significant cognitive and communication needs, and most of the students were diagnosed with autism. All students had significant behavioral challenges and sensory needs and were not functioning independent of intense adult supervision. The smoke was significant and very frightening for the students. It was a true emergency and a test for the staff. The students had to be evacuated and held in a separate location until the fire department could clear the building of smoke. The staff had to scramble to make sure that all students were accounted for, all needs were met, students remained calm and safe, and appropriate interventions were used for the behavioral challenges. It was not easy. But what was easy was to be with those teachers who were prepared ahead of time for emergency situations. These teachers were even able to grab a bag from the back of the door with a student roster, paper activities the students could complete, and special sensory objects that some of the students required to stay calm. This is what I want for you.

If there were to be a fire and you took your classroom out on the school grounds, the administration will probably ask you to bring a class roster and, since some of the students may have significant communication needs, it will be important to include a photo of each child. If you will notice, this is the same type of information that is needed in a substitute emergency notebook, so do not recreate the wheel, just make additional copies.

Now let's think of organizing student information in a different way. You may choose to have a notebook for each student, to hold all information pertinent to that particular student, so I have included as Appendix 8H an example of something you could use as a front or back cover to a binder notebook to house that kind of student information. You may want to use this one or modify it to create your own (see Figure 8.11).

If you choose to use a binder system, then include index tabs for each student, to keep pertinent information related to each student, such as

✦ Student photo
✦ Permission slips
✦ Medical information
✦ Address
✦ Phone numbers
✦ Emergency card information
✦ Bus information

You can even use this more globally to include all information about the student, such as

✦ Copy of the current IEP or summary sheet with goals and objectives
✦ Copy of the current eligibility

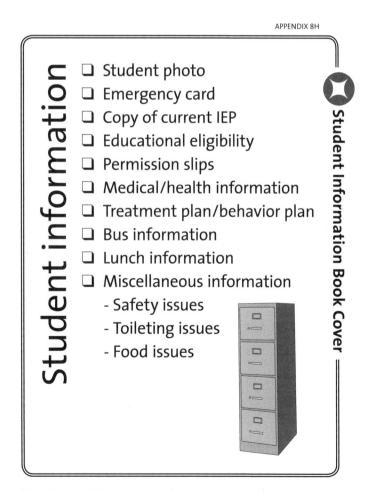

Figure 8.11. Student information book cover.

✦ Copy of the current psychological assessment

✦ Copy of the current behavior intervention plan or treatment plan

Because of the confidential nature of these documents, these binders would need to be kept in a secure location, such as a locked file cabinet.

Having established the need for some type of student information organizational system, now I will provide a couple of examples of different types of forms that you could include within this binder. Make sure to use informational forms that are required by your school system, but if you do not have access to any, then use the ones I have provided in the appendixes. Modify the forms to fit your specific needs. Figure 8.12 is one that may be helpful for organizing basic safety information.

This *Student Safety Information* form (available as Appendix 8I) will be helpful to you if you have students with more significant needs. It allows you to organize and keep all information about the specific safety needs of students in one place. Behind the form you can place detailed information about allergies, medical plans, instruction for the use of a feeding tube, and so forth.

Here is an additional *Emergency Information Form* (see Figure 8.13; Appendix 8J) that may be helpful for you in your organization of student information. You may have one of these from your school, but, if not, this will help you organize all emergency phone numbers and addresses, and even includes a place for a student photo.

Data

As you know by now, special educators' lives revolve around data. We collect data to measure progress on academic goals, data to measure progress on behavioral goals, data to determine why behaviors are occurring, and data to determine what to do when it does. If you do not have a good method for organizing them, you will drown in data.

There are four questions that teachers typically have that lead to the four-part delineation of the data area. These questions are

1. What tools can I use to organize the data collection process?
2. What are some of the ways to easily manage the data collection process?
3. How can I organize the presentation of data at IEP meetings?
4. What are some ways to organize the data paperwork that I collect each week?

I will discuss each of these four questions in detail and provide you with some guidance to overcome concerns you may have in each are

Tools

What tools can I use to organize the data collection process?

I personally love to wander down the aisles of office supply stores. There are so many wonderful organizational tools available. When you think about the tools needed to organize the data collection process, there are a few that stand out as great choices:

✦ Clipboards and clipboard containers with calculators: Clipboards are portable and can be hung on the wall or stationed on a desk. The clipboards with built-in storage are wonderful for data keeping, especially if they have calculators attached, as this makes it easy to figure percentages of weekly data.

✦ Construction paper or spray paint for color coding clipboards: You can easily color code clipboards by spray painting the backs with a different color for each child. Use laminated construction paper to cover the data sheets on each clipboard. This serves

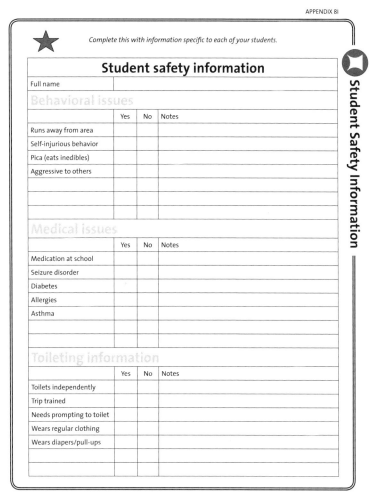

Figure 8.12. Student safety information.

two purposes: It ensures confidentiality of data from prying eyes, and it color codes the clipboard per student.

✦ Colored file folders: Colored file folders are easily accessible at many large discount stores and are an easy way to color code student files for easy organization of data.

✦ Chalkboard paint, magnetic paint, felt sheets, or small plastic pockets:

  ✪ Use chalkboard paint to spray a section of the back of the clipboard so that you can personalize it with the student's name.

  ✪ Paint a layer of magnetic paint on the back of a wood clipboard to create a magnetic surface on which you can use name cards with magnets attached for personalization.

  ✪ Spray glue and felt sheets work great on the back of wooden clipboards because Velcro on the back of a name card will adhere to the felt. This again makes it easy to personalize the clipboard with the student's name.

  ✪ Use duct tape to adhere a small plastic document pocket to the back of a clipboard. This creates a space to slip in a name card for personalization of the clipboard.

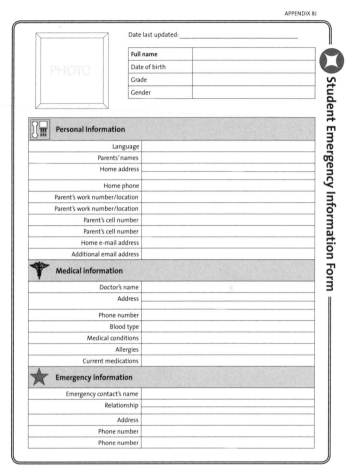

Figure 8.13.   Student emergency information form.

✦   Crates and hanging file folders: You can use crates and hanging files to store data. You can either use one data crate to contain all of the data for your classroom, or use one crate per child with folders for data.

✦   Stopwatch timers and frequency counters: These items come in very handy when you are taking behavioral data. It is very convenient to have a timer and a counter that hangs around your neck if you have students who exhibit behaviors that require you to keep high-frequency or duration data.

✦   Three-ring binders complete with index tabs:

Divide your three-ring binders into different areas. You can have a separate binder for work samples or you can use this same binder for both. On a weekly basis, place the data sheets in the binders from clipboards. Create a cover page and use your own creativity to customize your data binder.

Collection

What are some ways to easily manage the data collection process?

You have gathered tools to use in the data collection process, so now I will focus on the data collection process itself. Let me set the stage to explain further.

 **CASE IN POINT** You are the teacher in an early elementary school class for students with autism. You have eight students. You want to do a top-notch job and are very focused on the data collection part of your day. You have one paraprofessional who assists you in the classroom. She knows very little about collecting data, so it is up to you. You attempt to take data for all eight students, every day, for every subject, and on every IEP goal. You feel like you are always looking for your data sheets and should just keep them hanging around your neck. It is December and you are already exhausted. You feel like you do not have a grasp on the more global aspect of teaching your students and have become hyper focused on the collection of data for the tiny discrete details of every student task. You cannot keep this up but really do not know how to scale back and continue to do a good job.

The process of taking data in a classroom will overpower you if you let it. Allow me to provide you with several suggestions of ways to manage the data collection process:

1. Set the location for your data collection tools for easy access.

   ✦ Try placing your data collection sheets in a binder and house it in a crate with all of the IEP goal information. This way everything is together for when you do the data collection tasks.

   ✦ If you take behavior data on several students, try hanging the clipboards with their data sheets on the wall in a central location of the room. Make sure to place a timer and counter in that same location. This is very helpful if the behaviors have a high frequency or long duration rate.

2. Train the support personnel in your classroom in the basics of data collection. You can expand your options, in terms of ways to collect data, if you have more players with which to work. Use a staff meeting day to examine, train, and practice accepted data collection methods.

3. Schedule times for data collection. Do not attempt to take data on every task you do every day. Look at the way that the academic goals and objectives are written, then divide your week into data collection days and times.

   ✦ For example, try Monday and Wednesday of one week; Tuesday and Thursday of the next, Friday of the next. Remember, this is a snapshot of mastery level. You should probably vary the days and times. Be certain not to take data every Monday morning as that would skew the data of students who perform better midweek.

   ✦ Divide up your day into data collection times. Maybe from 10:00 to 11:00 and from 1:00 to 1:45 are your IEP goal work sessions. This is when you work on the tasks and take data on goals specific to the student's IEP.

4. Try different methods of data collection. If you have additional support personnel in the classroom and you have a classroom of all students with special needs, try round-robin data collection days. To do this, position your staff in centers and locations of the room and have the students move from center to center. When they arrive at certain centers, they complete the tasks for data to be collected at that center before moving on to next.

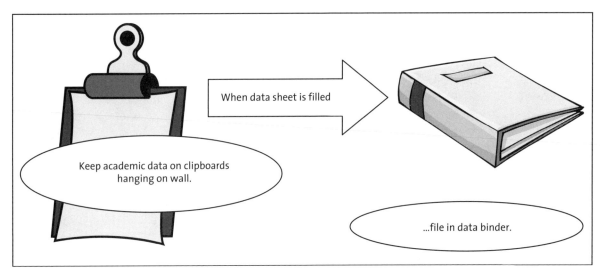

Figure 8.14. Using clipboard and data binder to organize and manage data.

Organization

What are some ways to organize the data paperwork that I collect each week?

I bet that you now have lots of papers clipped to clipboards filled with raw data. Now what? Well, I recommend two ways to organize the data that you collect using the tools that you have already gathered.

Figure 8.14 shows one way, that you just keep the data sheets going on the clipboard until they are filled then you can place them in the data binder. You can also file these on a set schedule such as every Friday plan to file the data sheets and work samples so that you can start with fresh blank data sheets beginning the next Monday.

Another option is shown on Figure 8.15. The single-student crate method is an easy way to manage data. You can pair this with the use of data clipboards to create a system that is quite portable. Each crate can house not only a file for data collection sheets, but also work samples, copies of IEP goals, and the materials you use with the student to collect the

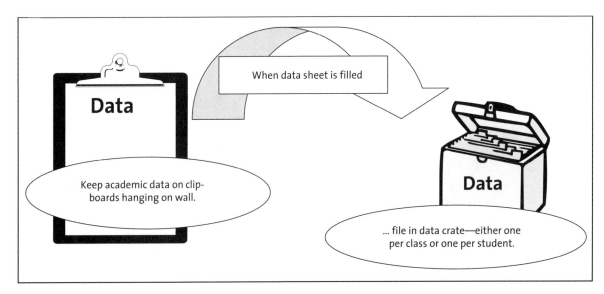

Figure 8.15. Single-student crate method to manage data.

data. This way, each crate contains everything you need. If you would prefer, try combining the two methods and just place the data binder into the data crate. This way the data may be easily taken to an IEP meeting.

Presentation

How can I organize the presentation of data at IEP meetings?

One of the most important steps to the management of your classroom data is turning it into a useable format that will be easily understood by parents and the layperson not familiar with data. Imagine this:

CASE IN POINT You excitedly go into a parent conference with your work sample notebook and data notebook all under your arm. You feel very prepared for this meeting. You are now to the point in the meeting when you get to review the data that you have collected for each goal and objective, so you pull out your data sheets. You have 15 data sheets filled with percentages on every goal: mountains of information. You begin to explain each of the data sheets and you notice heads nodding and eyes glazing over. You have the funny feeling that you have totally lost the group, and you wish you had thought of a better way to show the data you have collected.

The number-one suggestion that I have for a great presentation at an IEP meeting is to graph your data. There are a number of ways to graph data, and the one you choose to use is totally dependent upon your skill level. If you are computer savvy and a whiz with using Microsoft Excel, then you can easily create line graphs that will provide a visual representation of your raw data.

If you are not a whiz in using Excel, as I am not, there are several simple-to-use graphing websites on the Internet that will assist you in the creation of simple graphs. Here are a few:

✦ http://nces.ed.gov/nceskids/createagraph
   This site is called Create-A-Graph. It is a site for students but it is wonderful for those of us who think that simple is best. It produces very professional-looking graphs that are perfect for helping explain student progress data at IEP meetings. Remember that most of the parents are also looking for a simple explanation of the data and not something that looks as if it came from a professional statistician.

✦ http://graphtools.com/line.html
   Graph Tools is another simple way to create simple line and bar graphs.

✦ http://www.onlinecharttool.com/graph.php
   Online Chart Tool is simple to use and like the others will produce simple graphs from the data you enter.

Another suggestion is to use Microsoft Word and insert a quick table. This will take you to an Excel document but will walk you through the insertion of your data in order to create a simple line graph. Remember that line graphs are probably the easiest ones to use to show progress on IEP goals. Look at Figure 8.16.

If you are saying there is no way that you can create a graph by using a computer, then try graphing the data by hand. I created a simple one that I have included as Appendix 8K (see Figure 8.17 for an example). It is a simple graphing plot sheet that may help you to graph simple percentages.

The completed example from Figure 8.17 shows a graph of data over a 4-week period of time. Each of the IEP goals is represented along with the mastery level shown as a dashed

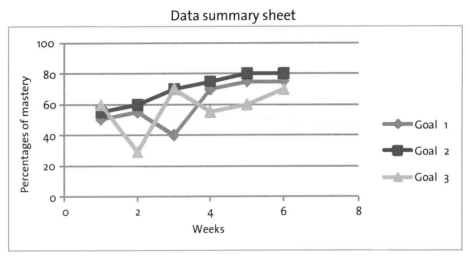

Figure 8.16. Line graph.

line. All information would be color coded as to the goal and corresponding mastery level. No computer skills were necessary but the end result is a pretty impressive visual representation of 1 month of data on four different IEP goals. In analyzing these data for Goals 1 and 2, I would probably say:

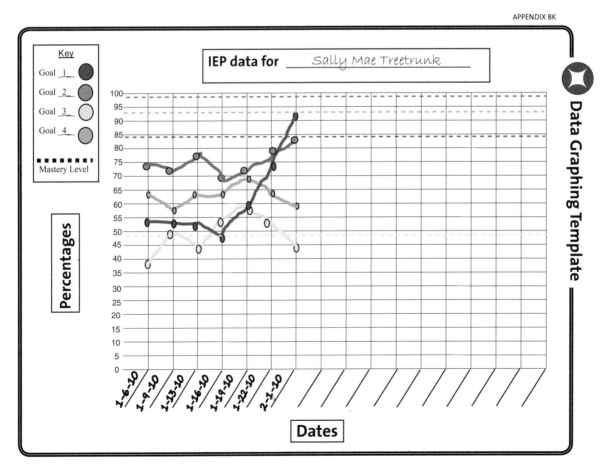

Figure 8.17. Complete data graphing template.

CASE IN POINT "Mr. and Mrs. Smith, I would like to talk about the data that we have been collecting on Sally Mae's four IEP goals. This covers the last 4 weeks of data points. If you will look at goal number 1, shown in red, you see that the mastery level was set at 75% and her baseline showed that she began at about 45% mastery level. During the first 3 weeks she stayed at a pretty consistent level, but you see at about January 19th she began to rapidly make gains. She really began to grasp the tasks and she ended up achieving the mastery level that we set for her by the first week of February! We need to continue to see if she will maintain that level and then generalize that skill to other settings. Let's look at goal number 2 shown in blue. You see that Sally Mae's baseline level was much higher, so, if you remember, the IEP committee set the mastery level at a much higher percentage level. Sally Mae has made slower progress on this goal but if you'll notice, she is very consistent. Do you see the upward trend? If she continues on this upward trend she should reach a mastery level in a couple of weeks, so we'll keep it up."

See how professional you will look and sound? And can you imagine this from the parent's viewpoint? It is easier than you think. You can do this.

INDIVIDUALIZED EDUCATION PROGRAMS

IEP. Those are three dreaded letters. It strikes fear in the heart of every new special education teacher, especially in the springtime when written plans for most IEPs are due. But, take heart. You know by now that the Organization and Management of a Classroom (OMAC) program is grounded in organized simplicity—creating ways of making complicated, overwhelming tasks in the classroom easier to tackle. In this section I am going to provide you with a few tips and tricks to making the management of IEPs simpler. Let's begin with some of the typical teacher questions about the IEP process:

✦ Organization: How can I organize my IEP paperwork?

✦ Timelines: How am I going to keep up with the due dates of all the IEPs?

✦ Paperwork requirements: Is there a way to help me remember everything I have to do to prepare for an IEP meeting?

✦ IEP meeting: Are there ways to organize and manage the IEP meeting in a more professional way?

Having written hundreds of IEPs over the years, I know that each of these questions is a valid concern for teachers, regardless of the type of classroom you teach. So, I am going to discuss each of the four areas and address each question by suggesting organization tips for each area.

Organization

How Can I Organize My IEP Paperwork?

There are a variety of different IEP formats. If you have ever been the recipient of a transfer IEP from another state when a new student moves in, you know that first hand. Even though I have personally read hundreds of IEPs, I still get confused by looking at one from another state. To establish some common ground, let's determine the areas of consistency in the paperwork involved in the creation of an IEP.

The following is a list of some of the items that are typically reviewed when writing an IEP.

- ✦ Academic and behavior data
- ✦ Work samples
- ✦ Psychological assessments
- ✦ Eligibility reports
- ✦ Past IEP documents
- ✦ Current IEP document
- ✦ Behavior intervention plan
- ✦ Other assessment reports (speech-language, functional behavior assessments, etc.)

So, where do you keep these documents? It is wonderful if they can all be kept in a central location, but that may not be possible. Some schools require all psychological assessments to be kept in a central vault. Sometimes they are kept in a central special education office, sometimes in a locked file cabinet within the classroom of the case holder, and sometimes on a networked share drive located within the school system. Find out the requirements of your particular school setting in terms of the location of these files.

Regardless of the location, allow me to make a few suggestions of ways that I have either seen IEP documents organized or have organized them myself:

- ✦ In an earlier section of this chapter, we discussed using a notebook binder to keep student information. Within this binder was included a copy of the student's most current IEP. But what do you do with all of the past IEP documents, work samples, and data? You could certainly have binders for each school year. Within those binders would be held all documents that are included in the student's educational IEP records. These could be kept in a locked file cabinet or even in the vault. Empty copy paper boxes also work well to store these binders and make it easy to access the records. It is much easier to locate an IEP from 5 years ago if it is kept in this type of system than it would be to rifle through mounds of old papers stuffed into file folders.

- ✦ I have recommended that you keep organized binders for different areas of paperwork, so it will be easy to use a plastic crate to house these binders. This one crate could contain your data, work samples, and student information binder. If you do not want to keep the binders, you could certainly use a crate with hanging file folders for each of these areas.

- ✦ There are also several types of cardstock cover folders, complete with section dividers and clips that make wonderful ways of organizing the student's IEPs, special education eligibilities, and psychological assessments. These can be kept in a locked file cabinet to keep the records confidential.

- ✦ Typically I have organized all of my files by using the same format, sometimes flagging (using the sticky-back colored flags available at office supply stores) certain important documents that I knew I would need to access later.

Whatever system you use, it is helpful to keep as many of the documents together as is possible. And, at the end of the IEP, you will need to keep the outdated documents for several years. Keep these organized because you may need to access these in the future.

Timelines

How Am I Going to Keep Up with the Due Dates of the IEPs That I Am Responsible for Writing?

Knowing how to manage timelines in special education is another key to your success! The IEP process is fraught with deadlines. So the use of a calendar is not a suggestion as much as it is a requirement.

There are probably numerous dates that you have to remember as a staff member in your particular school. There are dates for report cards, progress updates, standardized testing, faculty meetings, parent conferences, open house, and so forth. In the world of special education, here are two main dates that you need to remember: the annual IEP review and the eligibility review.

I am going to provide you with a calendar to use specifically for keeping up with these two dates. As a special educator, regardless of the setting in which you teach, you will have a caseload of students for whom you are responsible. I remember my years as a rookie teacher and I remember having a caseload of 24 students. Those are quite a few IEP and eligibility dates with which to keep up. During some of my years spent in the classroom I had a small special education office. I kept a large calendar in that room with blocks for each month indicating when each student's IEP was due. As a psychologist, I did the same. I blocked off an area of my wall for different months and placed in that area the names of the students I was assessing and eligibility dates I needed to remember. Remember, though, these were private spaces away from public viewing as confidentially was important.

The calendar in Appendix 8L and Figure 8.18 may be helpful for organizing your special education caseload.

If you will notice on the *Completed Calendar of IEP Dates* from Figure 8.18, each student has his or her IEP date listed. The eligibility dates are indicated by an "E" but could just be written in a different color ink. This is a great calendar to print onto card stock and place on your bulletin board or place in your lesson plan binder. You can also color code each student for ease of visibility—anything to make it easier for you to stay organized.

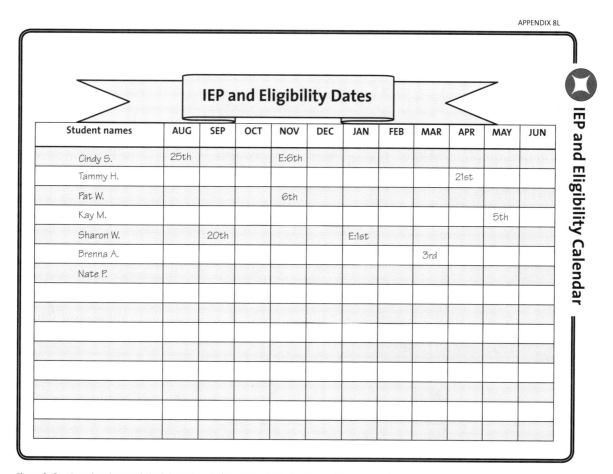

APPENDIX 8L

IEP and Eligibility Dates

Student names	AUG	SEP	OCT	NOV	DEC	JAN	FEB	MAR	APR	MAY	JUN
Cindy S.	25th			E:6th							
Tammy H.									21st		
Pat W.				6th							
Kay M.										5th	
Sharon W.		20th				E:1st					
Brenna A.								3rd			
Nate P.											

IEP and Eligibility Calendar

Figure 8.18. Completed IEP and eligibility calendar. (*Key*: IEP, individualized education program.)

Paperwork Requirements

Is There a Way to Help Me Remember Everything I Have to Do to Prepare for an IEP Meeting?

It is difficult to keep up with all of the requirements of an IEP, in addition to all the steps involved in the preparation. There are committee members to invite, documents to print, signatures to secure, location arrangements to make, and several other things. Because you will probably be juggling several IEP meetings during the same month and all will be at different points of completion, you probably need a checklist of all of the tasks involved in preparing for the IEP. This way you know when things are completed and what you need to do next. It is helpful if you attach that checklist to a pocket folder so that you can keep all of the documents in one place. Here is an example of a checklist that I have provided you as Appendix 8M (see Figure 8.19).

Try affixing this checklist to a folder where you keep the completed items. Keep it in a common location so that the staff members who have tasks to complete can put the items in the folder when they have a chance. Try copying the completed checklist and placing it in the mailboxes of the staff members who have tasks to complete. You may even want to include a coupon (see Figure 8.20) for a mini candy bar or a piece of candy as an incentive to get the tasks completed. If it is completed by the due date, they can turn it in to you for a sweet treat! I have included a coupon template as Appendix 8N that you may want to use.

APPENDIX 8M

IEP Meeting Checklist

Student: Sally Mae

✓	Task	Staff	Date due
	Sign up for conference room	Cindy	2-1-10
	Get date on school calendar	Cindy	2-1-10
	Send invitation and notification to parent	Cindy	2-7-10
	Make copies of current IEP	Ann	2-7-10
	Complete current functioning forms	All teachers	2-7-10
	Invite SLP, OT	Cindy	2-5-10
	Invite all teachers	Ann	2-5-10
	Create agenda	Sally	2-10-10
	Create folders for committee	Sally	2-12-10
	Create PowerPoint of data and work samples	Cindy	2-10-10
	Invite administration	Ann	2-1-10
	Create new IEP draft on computer program	Cindy	2-7-10

IEP Meeting Checklist

Figure 8.19. Example of completed IEP meeting checklist (*Key*: IEP, individualized education program.)

> If you complete the task
> By the date it's due
> A very sweet treat
> Will be coming to you!

Figure 8.20. Incentive coupon.

Just copy, cut apart, and give to the staff members when you ask that they complete one of the IEP meeting preparation tasks.

If you have ever been in an IEP meeting when an important member of the committee failed to show because they forgot, you will understand how important little reminders can be. So, I suggest you pass little reminder notices or e-mails to committee members to remind them of the date, time, and location of the meeting in addition to the tasks they are to prepare before the meeting.

IEP Meeting

There are several professional ways to organize and manage the IEP meeting

One of the best ways to promote a sense of professionalism and respect in parent conferences and IEP meetings is to be prepared. Do not give the impression that you grabbed your materials and rushed into the meeting, out of breath and exhausted. Some days you may have to fake it because you may truly be rushed and exhausted!

Here are a few tips on how not only to *look* prepared and professional but also how to *be* prepared and professional:

✦ Collaborate with parents and all teachers or specialists involved with the student before the IEP meeting. If the student is an older student, it is important to involve him or her in the collaboration process. Teamwork is important in the development of an appropriate IEP.

✦ Create folders for each participant, complete with all copies of all reports, assessments, current IEPs, and material that will be discussed by the committee. Include blank paper and pens to the members of the committee for note taking. This creates confidence in you and shows that you are prepared.

✦ Have a digital tape player ready just in case you need one. Typically if a parent tapes a meeting, you are to tape the meeting as well. Do not bring it to the meeting unless you need it as it will create a climate of defensiveness, but do not let yourself be found scrambling around hunting for a recorder if one is required.

✦ Prepare an agenda for the meeting. Have copies of this agenda for every member of the committee. This will help keep everyone on track and keep the meeting moving. It also provides a place for note taking. Figure 8.21 is a one example of an IEP agenda. A copy of this agenda template is provided for you as Appendix 8O.

I also suggest having a simplified version of the agenda on a large pad of paper or on a whiteboard at the front of the meeting room. This again creates a climate of preparedness and professionalism.

IEP Meeting Agenda

Student name		Contact person	
Sally Mae B.		Cindy Simpson	

Date		Time	Location
2-1-2010		9:00	Conference room

Facilitator	Topic	Notes
Cindy	Introductions	
Cindy	Parent rights	
Ann	Present levels of performance	
Ann	Data from current goals and objectives	
Sarah	Proposal of new goals and objectives	
Sarah	Accommodations/ modifications	
Cindy	Extended school year	
Cindy	Placement options	

IEP Meeting Agenda

Figure 8.21. Completed IEP meeting agenda. (*Key:* IEP, individualized education program.)

✦ If you are using a computer-based IEP program, make sure to set up ahead of time. If at all possible, arrange to be at the meeting or have someone else there about 30 minutes early to set up the computer and organize the room. This is especially important if you are using an Internet-based IEP program and an Internet connection is required to access the program.

✦ Always have a back-up plan. Prepare paper copies of the IEP that you can complete just in case your computerized IEP program is, for some reason, not allowing you to access it.

✦ Have a file folder with several additional forms that may be needed in a pinch; for example,

  ✪ Extra forms for taking minutes, if your district requires a certain form
  ✪ An extra copy of the parental rights form
  ✪ A permission to evaluate form
  ✪ A couple of copies of the permission to release confidential information form

✦ If you have access to an LCD projector and screen, then make use of it in the meeting! It may facilitate communication and participation if the committee members are able to watch as you type in new goals and objectives. Sometimes you may find that it is easier if you can see the changes than if you are just listening to someone talk about the changes that you are making on the IEP document. It will lessen the confusion as everyone is participating on the creation of goals.

✦ Try using Microsoft PowerPoint as a way of presenting the IEP material. I have been to several IEP meetings facilitated by private hospital-type programs specializing in autism. The material for these meetings is typically organized with Microsoft PowerPoint. Slides are created to show data, work samples, graphs, bulleted present levels of performance, speech-language assessment reports, psychological assessments, and so forth. Collaborate with the student and allow him or her to create a presentation that presents his or her strengths, weaknesses, goals, interests, or future plans. Microsoft PowerPoint is typically accessible on school computers and is quite simple to use as it was created for the purpose of giving presentations.

Student Work

There is always so much paperwork involved in grading and keeping up with student work. Because our modern classrooms are much more technologically involved, not as many paper–pencil tasks are used. But even though times have changed, there is something to be said for paper–pencil tasks.

Think about the specific needs of your classroom. All of your students may be students with special needs. You may be the teacher of a self-contained setting and may have students with autism and other types of special needs who are not able to do much in the way of paper–pencil tasks. If that is the case, you may have a great deal of different types of tasks going on at the same time; in other words, *less volume = more variety*.

But you may be in a different type of setting. If you are the teacher in a general education inclusive classroom, you may have a full classroom of students and only a few of those are students with autism or special needs. You may have almost every student doing the same type of written task. In other words, *more volume = less variety*.

Regardless of the type of classroom, teachers have many of the same types of questions and concerns when it comes to managing student work, so let's address each of these.

How Do I Keep Up with Grading All of the Student Work?

Oh, the woes of grading papers. Regardless of the type of classroom, you will almost always have papers to grade. Hopefully, as time progresses and we become more technologically advanced, we may find that this weekend pastime will become a thing of the past. But, for now, we still wrestle with finding time to keep up with grading papers.

As all classrooms are unique, you need to design your own management system. It needs to be one that will allow you time to keep up with the paperwork in your specific setting, but I will provide several suggestions that may get you started. Keep in mind that in certain types of special education classrooms, student work will be limited to work boxes, computer programs, and individual one-to-one work with the teacher using manipulatives. In these cases, the management and "grading" of student work will take on a different slant.

Let me give you several different tips and tricks that may assist you in organizing your system of dealing with student work in the classroom. Modify these to fit your own class-room needs.

✦ Have several plastic dishpans on a bookcase for finished work for each period or subject of the day. Dishpans work well because they easily fit regular-sized pieces of paper without bending them. You can place folders for each student in file boxes on the bookshelf as well, and as the students finish their work they can file their finished work in their own folder. At the end of the day or during planning is when the teacher grades the student's work.

✦ Use plastic pockets hanging on the wall to house completed work. Each pocket could represent a child (if you have a smaller class size). As each child finishes written work, they place the work in the pockets.

✦ Hanging nylon file pocket holders are available in school supply catalogs. These work well in housing folders that will provide a place for students' finished work.

✦ Use a large crate that includes hanging folders for the different periods, segments, or subject areas of the day. As each child completes his or her assignment, he or she is in charge of filing the folder. This way the system is portable for the teacher.

✦ Have one file folder per child with a *To Do* side and a *Finished* side. As the student completes the tasks in the *To Do* side they place it in the *Finished* side. The student then places the file folder in a predetermined location for the teacher to grade at a later time. Make sure to color code these folders for easy student access.

Here is a little trick that I do with the mail from my mailbox. It is easy if you create a system where you do not have to touch the mail but once or twice. My habit is to check my mail when I am coming home from work. While I am sitting at the mailbox, I go through the mail and place all parts of the junk mail that are recyclable into a bag. I also place other types of mail that need to be shredded into a bag to be shredded later. Items that can be thrown away are placed in a trash bag. I then throw the trash bag in the outside trash can. I only carry into the house the mail that I need. Upon entering the house I place all catalogs in a basket to read when I am bored and all bills go in a plastic pocket of my bill binder. That about does it for the mail and it never piles up unopened. Do the same for the paperwork in your classroom. Create a system where you only touch the papers once or twice and are not constantly shifting the piles and finally putting them in your *To Do* box that never gets seems to get done.

How Do I Manage the Collection of Student Work Samples?

To keep good data of the student's ability to complete tasks, teachers typically gather written work samples from the students in their classroom. This does not mean save all of the student's best written work and it does not mean save all of the student's worst work; it means save a sample of both.

As a psychologist I have asked teachers for an opportunity to view a student's work samples in a particular area such as math. I have had the pleasure of perusing through a wonderful collection of analyzed samples of a student's work and this gave me a great overview of the types of things the student was able to do in that area. I have also had the

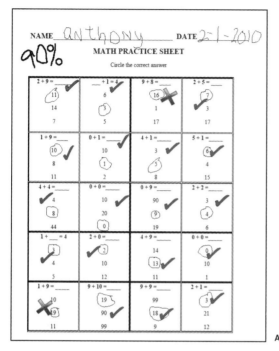

Figure 8.22. Student work samples.

distinct pleasure of wading through mounds of written math worksheets and tests completed by a student, some graded and some not. However, even the papers that were graded were not analyzed, so it wasn't clear how the student had carried out the task. This created a stressful, time-consuming task for me and one that did not give a great impression of the particular teacher's ability to manage this area of his or her classroom.

So, what do I mean by analyzing work samples? Let me give you an example. Look at Figures 8.22A and B.

At first glance, which of these appears to be more helpful in determining exactly what the student is capable of? I will give you a hint: it is not Figure 8.22A. The grade on this paper is deceiving as it would indicate that the student was able to independently complete 90% of the math problems with accuracy. Was he? No, he was not, but this is not indicated on the page. In looking at Figure 8.22B you will see a small sticker that is placed at the bottom of the page. This is one way to easily analyze work samples. Let me discuss that small sticker (see Figure 8.23) in a little more detail.

Student work samples are typically analyzed in two ways: level of accuracy and the accommodations that were needed to complete the task. Figure 8.23 shows a close-up view of the work sample analysis sticker that is affixed to the math work sample shown in Figure 8.22B.

A teacher could have written notes on this work sample indicating exactly what was required for the student to complete the task, but that is very time consuming. This sticker creates an easy way to do that same task. The analysis sticker shows that even though the student was able to complete the task with 90% accuracy, it required

✦ Adult support
✦ Multiple attempts at the task
✦ Extended time to complete the task
✦ Use of manipulatives
✦ Problems read aloud to the student

Independent		Analysis	
Hand over hand		Multiple attempts	x
With gestures		Extended time	x
Visuals		Adult support	x
Manipulatives	x	Peer support	
With model		As a group	
Read aloud to	x	As homework	
Percentage correct		90%	

Figure 8.23. Work analysis sticker.

This gives a much better picture of the student's ability to do the task than Figure 8.22A. To keep the work sample without proper analysis would be somewhat deceiving. I have provided you with a copy of these work sample analysis stickers. They are great way of easily analyzing work samples. These labels (Appendix 8P) are formatted to be printed on whole-sheet adhesive labels and then cut apart into 2" X 4" labels. You can also print on plain paper and tape onto work samples. When you choose to keep certain samples, they will already be analyzed. You can also just use these stickers as an example for creating your own labels to fit the specific needs of your classroom.

Be sure to remember that as you choose the samples to save, you will need samples of all levels of the student's work because you want a global picture of the student's ability to complete the work tasks. These analyzed work samples are now filed with the student's IEP as documentation of functioning on certain goals.

So, hopefully you now have a good grasp on how to analyze work samples once they are collected, but what about the overall management system for collecting them? If you were to keep every paper of every child, you would never get them organized.

The following list will give you one idea of how to manage the entire process:

1. Student completes paper–pencil task. Staff members place sticker on work to indicate level of accommodations used.
2. Student places work in *Finished* tray.
3. At end of day, staff member scores work for accuracy and puts percentage on sticker.
4. Staff member then places analyzed work sample in child's folder in teacher work area.
5. At end of week, teacher chooses work samples to keep and file in work sample notebook and sends rest home to parents.

You will notice that the teacher chooses the work samples from the already analyzed group. After choosing several samples the teacher then sends the others home to the parents. This will keep parents informed as to the accommodations needed to complete tasks. Because the samples are also labeled as to which ones were homework assignments, it will also show the difference in the student's ability to complete the work at home versus completing the work at school.

What Do I Do with All of the Work Samples?

I recommend two ways of keeping up with analyzed work samples and I bet you know what those are: binders or file crates.

There are advantages to both methods of keeping up with work samples, depending upon your specific needs. After determining which of the work samples you want to save, it is fast and easy to place the samples in file crates if you have crates positioned close by. You can have one crate with individual student folders to hold all work samples for your entire class, or, if you have a smaller class, you may want to have one crate per student and divide the work samples into folders for each subject or IEP objective.

Three-ring binders are of course very easy and portable but are limited in the amount of work samples they will hold. I discussed including work samples in the data binders, but you may want a separate notebook for work samples only. If you want separate binders for each student then clearly label each binder and use index tabs to separate them into different subject areas or IEP objectives. Store a three-hole punch close to your work area to make it easy to place the work samples in the notebooks. You can also place plastic sleeves in the binder to store the work samples. These are easy to take to IEP meetings.

Are There Other Ways I Could Keep up with Student Work without All of This Paper?

One of the newest ways to keep up with student work is to scan it for storage in a digital format. This follows in the footsteps of the online portfolios used in the world of academia, in addition to the digital management of paperwork used in the financial and business worlds. Although this method may not be for you at the present, it is a foreshadowing of things to come.

If you are brave enough to try this method you may find that it is very simple. There are some plain paper copiers used in schools today that will turn your paper copy into a PDF format and will send it to your school e-mail account. You can also scan work samples onto a small computer thumb drive or USB drive and use this to load the files onto your computer. Having these work samples as digital files opens up innovative ways of presenting data and information at parent conferences.

SUMMARY

The management of data and paperwork in the field of education, particularly special education, is cumbersome. It is a significant challenge that is easier to manage if you have a system. Sometimes the technique that will make the most profound difference in your ability to manage this paperwork challenge can be as simple as a sticker.

You have only one more chapter to go before your completion of the entire OMAC system. So, hang onto your hats; you are almost finished!

Organization of Classroom Staff and Home Supports

Are you beginning to see a difference? You should be. Your classroom has been slowly transformed into a model classroom. You should be feeling more organized and less stressed. You should also be seeing your students exhibit more independence, fewer inappropriate behaviors, more appropriate social skills, improved academic achievement, and better communicative skills in the classroom.

So, let's address the final issue. First let me ask you a couple of questions. Do you feel that you are able to adequately support the needs of the staff who work with you in the classroom? Are they knowledgeable and informed in a way that is helpful to you in working with the students? What about the parents of your students—is there a reciprocal trusting rapport between you? Are you all on the same team, so to speak?

Providing support to the staff who support your students and to the parents of your students can be a challenge. Few things are more stressful for teachers than a strained relationship with the paraprofessional, teacher's aide, or the support personnel who serve the students in your classroom. If there is dissension among the ranks, how can you move forward? You all need to be on the same team—teacher, parents, and support personnel working together—supporting each other with one goal in mind: the advancement and progress of the student.

Remember, you are the teacher in the classroom. You are the one who is charged with overseeing the management of the environment. But it is not always easy to establish yourself as the one in charge. It can be difficult for those of you who are young, new to teaching, and have a classroom staff who have served in that position for a number of years before you. You veteran teachers are not off the hook, either. You also interact with several school staff members who may require a great deal of support to both attain and maintain a close working relationship. It will make your life much easier if you encourage a positive relationship and support those who support your students.

The management of a classroom involves not only knowledge of best practice as it pertains to teaching students with special needs; it also involves a certain level of people skills. These people skills are used to establish a trusting, respectful environment where all of the adults work as a team and fully support the common goal of the classroom. Also remember that to gain respect from other adults—both parents and support personnel— a teacher needs to be confident, organized, and supportive to those with whom he or she works.

This chapter is one of those with no rubric of supports. However, you do not get away that easy; there is a *Home and Staff Supports Checklist* (see Figure 9.1) included as Appendix 9A that may be helpful in guiding you to the areas where you need to focus.

Place a check mark in the appropriate box. Use this to help yourself
determine the needs of your classroom

	Yes	No	Sometimes/maybe
Staff supports			
I have several staff members who work in my classroom.			
Staff are trained in autism and in other specific special needs areas.			
Staff are trained in data collection and in the specific teaching methods used in my classroom.			
Staff meet together to discuss classroom issues.			
Staff work together as a cohesive unit.			
All classroom staff members are independent in using their time appropriately in the classroom.			
The school administration allows me to do training with my classroom staff.			
The classroom staff members have a common time that we meet for training and to discuss the needs of the classroom.			
I feel that I have the respect of all the members of my classroom staff.			

	Yes	No	Sometimes/maybe
Home supports			
We have a communication system between home and school.			
Parents are aware of the events of the classroom.			
I would like to have more parent involvement.			
We have a classroom newsletter that goes home to parents.			
I have a supportive relationship with all the parents of students in my classroom.			
There are ways that I could improve the relationship I have with parents.			

Home and Staff Supports Checklist

Figure 9.1. Home and staff supports checklist.

The *Home and Staff Supports Checklist* will assist you in determining your present level of performance, so to speak. It will also direct you to the areas on which you should focus. But, keep in mind, every classroom is different and some of the items on the checklist may not be applicable to your particular setting. In other words, you may not have a use for the first part of the checklist and, if you don't, then skip it! But before you do, let's think outside the box.

You may not have paraprofessionals who serve in your classroom, but you may be a special educator working with a regular education teacher and feel that a common time of planning, training, and discussion about issues that pertain to the student you serve would be important. In that instance you can certainly use some of the information, as doing this will not only make your job much easier but will also indirectly support the students. As with all of information in the Organization and Management of a Classroom (OMAC) system, you glean from this chapter the ideas that you can and that are applicable to your setting and let it be a way to get your creative juices flowing.

So go on and complete the *Home and Parent Support Checklist* and then let's get started talking about this final chapter. Are there areas where you could focus? Use your responses not as a test but reflect on them to determine if there are areas that you would like to make changes to add, update, or just beef up a little. This will help prepare you to put the final touches on your model classroom.

THE CLASSROOM AS AN ORCHESTRA

You, as the teacher, are the conductor of the *classroom orchestra*. Every section has its purpose. The education of your students is your sole purpose; therefore, it should always be directly in front of you. It should be your constant focus. However, there are three other competing entities that will vie for not only your focus and attention but also your time.

First, you have the parents of your students. The parents of your students can provide a great deal of support for you as the classroom teacher. A reciprocal relationship that is positive is very important to cultivate.

Next, you have the additional classroom staff members that support your students. Remember, for special educators this applies to a variety of different disciplines. These staff members may include

+ Your co-teacher (general or special educator)
+ A paraprofessional coming into your classroom to support a particular student
+ Support therapists such as speech-language pathologists or occupational therapists
+ Paraprofessionals who work with you in your self-contained classroom

Last but not least is the group watching from the side—the school administration. School administrators will be a support for you in the classroom, but they will also ask for your time and attention. It is important that the special educator seeks opportunities to involve the administrative staff so they will be aware of the issues you face in the classroom. You can see that if you have these sections organized and a plan of management in place, then the classroom orchestra members can work as a team with one clear purpose.

Classroom Staff Support and Management

A conductor has many responsibilities. He or she has to set the focus for the performance, make the selection of music, make sure that all of the performers have the skills they need to perform as a group, and direct everyone in the group as they perform as a unified body with one focus. Think about how the performance would sound if a trombone took the lead, if everyone played a solo in a different key, if no one was in tune with each other, and if no one respected the conductor enough to follow his or her lead. It would be a pretty poor performance and you would probably walk out early.

As the conductor of the classroom orchestra, you have the same responsibilities. One of the first and most important things to do is to know you are in charge. You are responsible and you are the one who determines what needs to be accomplished for your students during the school year. As you have worked through the OMAC system, you have probably formed a pretty good idea of the way you want your classroom to run. You want it greased up and moving forward with as little stops, starts, and stutters as you can get. Your focus is to create an environment that promotes student success. Now you need to find ways of getting everyone who is involved in the education of your students focused on the same game plan. And with a student with special needs, that game plan is the individualized education program (IEP).

If we are honest with ourselves, we know that the management and support of other adults working in the classroom is sometimes more challenging than the management of students. If you think about it, you probably spend more waking hours in close contact with the adults at school than you do with your own family. You are bound together with one purpose: to educate your students. To create a model learning environment, you need skills not normally taught in graduate school. Let me tell you a little story to set the stage.

CASE IN POINT   A young woman named Allison went to college to be a special education

teacher. She loves kids and is so excited to begin her career. She took classes in autism, teaching methods, data collection, and special education law. Allison graduated at the top of her class and has now been hired as a first-year teacher. She begins pre-planning with so many ideas for her classroom. Allison will have eight students with special needs in her self-contained classroom. She has 2 days to work before the paraprofessional who will be assisting her will return. The returning paraprofessional, Phyllis, has been at the school for the past 20 years. Phyllis not only knows the other teachers and the administration but also knows the students and their parents. Allison is nervous about arranging the classroom and creating a schedule of responsibilities, and is afraid her management style will be much different than what Phyllis is used to. She is beginning to lose the confidence she needs to get started. She is more afraid of Phyllis than she is of the students.

I wish I could say that this story was a fairy tale, but it is not. Depending upon the personalities of those working in the classroom, the young teacher may have a difficult time attaining proper control of the room and may not feel the freedom to do what she knows she needs to do. This has the potential for causing dissension in the staff ranks and creating quick burnout for the young teacher. It is especially difficult if a new teacher, fresh out of college with a degree in education and no experience, enters a situation with students who have been in the same classroom for 4 or 5 years and the supporting classroom staff (i.e., teacher's aides or paraprofessionals) have been with the students the entire time. Few things are more difficult. Young teachers may have had numerous college courses in educational theory, teaching methods, and educational law, but very few, if any, have had courses on how to build positive staff relations.

This scenario does not just happen to the rookie teacher. It could happen to veterans who are coming into a new setting, a teacher starting a new co-teaching arrangement, or a veteran teacher who has a new staff member working in his or her classroom where there seems to be a personality conflict. This can happen to anyone. But take heart—I have included strategies in this chapter that you can use to give this story a happy ending.

One of the easiest ways to get started is to spend time in your classroom alone. As I said at the beginning of this book, it is ideal if you are able to get into your classroom alone before the beginning of the year. Summertime is the best time to begin setting the stage. Taking control of the classroom environment early will boost your confidence. As the conductor does, you should spend time away from other staff members planning your focus, setting a goal, and putting into place the strategies you need to reach your goal. It will be difficult if you begin the year with all members of the classroom staff making suggestions on how to manage your classroom, especially if you are going to make changes from the way it was organized and managed in the past. Change is difficult. So, get by yourself and plan before others drop by to "help" you out.

Administration

Off in the wings is the administration. You know they are always there, but they may not be aware of the day-to-day struggles you face in your classroom. It may help to sit down with your principal or other administrator to get his or her expectations of the classroom and the classroom staff. What is the supervision hierarchy in your school? Does the teacher's assistant directly report to you, or is there an administrator or supervisor with this responsibility? If things don't go as planned in your classroom, to whom do you report the issue? Can you schedule a time in your classroom to meet with the classroom staff? You need guidelines before you begin.

Support Staff

Next are the staff members who support your students. This staff may come in the form of teacher's aides or paraprofessionals. They may also come as therapists who come into your classroom and give support to your students in the room. Some students with special needs may only receive consultation services from a therapist, so he or she may be working with you to indirectly provide support to the students in specific areas.

You will want to define your own set of expectations for your classroom. Again, most assistants are not educators; they learn through experience. *You* are the one who spent years in college studying the art and science of education. *You* are the one with knowledge of the theoretical basis of education and knowledge of evidence-based best practice in the field. *You* are the one who has a big picture of what needs to happen in your classroom during the school year to promote student achievement. And *you* are the one solely responsible for what happens to each and every student in your classroom. Later in this chapter, I will suggest several ways that you can help support those who serve your classroom. These tips and tricks can also be used to assist and support those in co-teaching or inclusive environments.

Parents

Parents of children with special needs may have particular concerns that have to be addressed by the school. Parents need to be able to relax, knowing that their child is a safe environment, one that is designed to enhance the child's ability to progress and become the best he or she can be. Parents need to be able to relax, knowing that if the child is unable to care for himself or herself there will be reliable and competent assistance from the adults in the school setting. Parents need to be able to relax, knowing that if the child is unable to communicate adequately, they will receive consistent communication from the school. The home can become an extension of the classroom, one that supports the educational plan by creating an environment conducive to the generalization of skills the student learns at school.

ENHANCING THE MANAGEMENT OF CLASSROOM STAFF RELATIONSHIPS

Let me preface this by reminding you that you will have to pick and choose the items that fit the needs of your particular setting. Some may be applicable and some may not. This will serve as a way to get your creative juices flowing in the right direction.

1. Begin having classroom staff team meetings.

   I have facilitated classroom meetings with several different groupings of classroom personnel, such as:

   ✦ Special education teacher and the two paraprofessionals who serve the classroom

   ✦ Special education teacher, speech-language pathologist, occupational therapist

   ✦ Special education resource teacher and the regular education teacher who serve a particular group of students

   ✦ Special education teacher, paraprofessionals, psychologist who serves the students

   These meetings are not IEP meetings—they are team meetings with the focus being to build the rapport and skills of the classroom staff. Isn't it easier to tell something to a group than to have to keep repeating yourself to individuals? Wouldn't it be easier to train a couple of people in how to use a specific teaching method than to have to constantly correct as they used it incorrectly? This will help create a well-run classroom environment, where everyone is knowledgeable, informed, and can be much more independent.

   You will need to be creative in determining a time to hold these meetings. These meetings can be held during a planning period, before school, after school, or during the students' physical education or lunch period. They do not have to be formal, but the meetings do need to be consistent, be organized, and serve a purpose, as you do not want the meetings to just be a gripe session. There is nothing better at bursting the confidence bubble of a teacher than that.

   During the meetings, you can discuss several different topics.

   ✦ How things are going in the classroom

   ✦ Specific student issues, teaching interventions, or behavior interventions

   ✦ Communication issues between staff

   ✦ Issues around the organization and management of the classroom

   ✦ Training in data collection, autism, specific area needs

   ✦ Celebrating progress and building camaraderie

2. Create a schedule of daily duties for each member of your staff.

   This alone may solve numerous issues, especially if you have numerous staff serving one classroom. It takes the personal aspect out of managing the classroom staff. Here is an example of how this could solve potential problems.

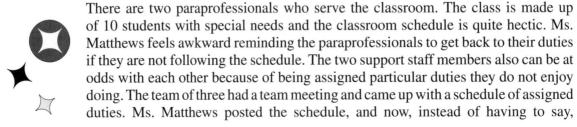

CASE IN POINT   The teacher of a classroom, Ms. Matthews, is new and fresh out of college. There are two paraprofessionals who serve the classroom. The class is made up of 10 students with special needs and the classroom schedule is quite hectic. Ms. Matthews feels awkward reminding the paraprofessionals to get back to their duties if they are not following the schedule. The two support staff members also can be at odds with each other because of being assigned particular duties they do not enjoy doing. The team of three had a team meeting and came up with a schedule of assigned duties. Ms. Matthews posted the schedule, and now, instead of having to say,

"Ms. Jones, could you please begin working with Michael," she can just remind the class as a whole, "Everyone check the schedule." This takes the aspect of criticism out of the interaction and creates a more respectful rapport among the staff members and a more self-sustaining classroom environment.

Included in this chapter is a template for a *Staff Duty Schedule* (Appendix 9B, see example in Figure 9.2).

This schedule can be blown up to poster size, laminated, and posted on the wall to be easily viewed by all. You can also use electrical tape to section off an area on a white board to use for your schedule or just post it on the bulletin board you use for communication items (e.g., lunch menu, school calendar). It does not matter where you post your schedule; however, the fact that you post it does matter.

APPENDIX 9B

Time/activity	Ann	Julie	Ben
7:30 – 8:00	Bus	Organize materials for 1st activity	Room to greet students
8:00 – 8:30	Check home folders	Bathroom duty	Monitor morning activity
8:30 – 9:15	Lead calendar group time	Calender group time	Organize materials for centers
9:15 – 9:45	Reorganize calendar	Gather items for snack	Facilitate centers

Staff Duty Schedule

Example

Figure 9.2. Example of a completed staff duty schedule.

Using a *Staff Daily Duty Schedule* will make the distribution of tasks less personal and will certainly free up time for the teacher. Be creative in using this schedule as it could also pertain to the schedule of services that your students get during the day (e.g., speech, occupational therapy, physical therapy) or in a co-teaching situation. I served as a co-teacher in a middle school science and social studies classroom, and it was difficult to remember some of the things I needed to do as I went into several different teachers' classrooms. See Figure 9.3 for an example of one that can be used in a co-teaching environment.

3. Create a classroom expectations booklet. You can use three-ring binders to create a booklet for each staff member, or just create one to be used as a reference guide for the classroom. Add your own touches to the book and use your team meetings to put it together as the team goes over each section. You can even put the minutes from team meetings as one section of the book.

    One of the model classrooms I worked with used this idea, and the staff coming into the classroom were always well informed, knowledgeable about the activities

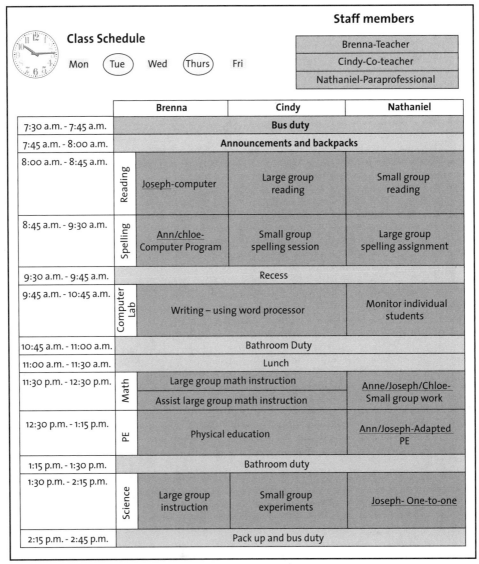

Figure 9.3. Staff daily duty schedule used in a co-teaching environment.

they were involved with in the room (i.e., teaching methods), and also educated about autism and how it affects learning. I was quite impressed at the confidence level of the staff. It was like working with a classroom of teachers instead of one teacher and two paraprofessionals.

The following are suggestions of things to include in the book.

+ Information about autism spectrum disorders and other types of disabilities

+ Classroom staff expectations or job descriptions

+ Information about specific teaching methods such as three-step prompting, discrete trial training, or the Picture Exchange Communication System. Staff members may refer back to these if they need to use a different teaching method. Support personnel may want to include specific information about the areas of speech-language or occupational therapy.

+ Resources about data collection, best practices, and websites that would be helpful

4. Do special things for the staff. Time and money may be in short supply, but small things you do will go far in helping build camaraderie and rapport. Remember that this also works for speech-language staff, regular education teachers who serve your students, and, guess what—it also works on the custodian, secretary, and principal.

Here are ideas of ways to treat the staff you work with to build relationships and confidence:

+ Bring donuts or goodies in for breakfast.

+ Give a drink and snack on a break.

+ Cover a duty for them (e.g., lunch duty, bus duty, hall duty).

+ Put goodies in their boxes (so many cute ideas for this online).

+ Celebrate birthdays—the students aren't the only ones who have birthdays.

+ Use a little note to say something positive about the work they do and just to say *I appreciate you!*

+ Praise them in front of the administration—this goes miles in helping build confidence in their work.

Included as Appendix 9C is a template (see Figure 9.4) that you can use to praise your staff. Staff members will be fighting each other to get to work in your classroom.

In thinking about the management of support staff, OMAC refers to the items in Figure 9.5 as "Note-Ables". They are important tidbits of information you should file in the back of your mind. They will help guide the decisions you make in your classroom.

ENHANCING THE MANAGEMENT OF PARENT COMMUNICATION AND RELATIONSHIPS

Home communication and support is another vital area in the creation of a model classroom. You will soon learn that communication is essential to establishing a good rapport and maintaining a good relationship with the parents of your students.

Put yourself in the shoes of a parent for a moment. You have a child with special needs. Your child is functioning at a low developmental and cognitive level. Your child communicates using picture cards and has difficulties with spoken instructions. Your child also has some significant behavioral issues. Knowing that this particular student is virtually dependent upon adults in his or her environment for his or her very survival at school, you, as the parent, will try to protect the child from as much harm as possible. You bring the child to school and leave him or her in the care of a stranger for 7 hours a day. Wouldn't you be defensive, suspicious, and distrusting at first? What if days went by during that first week

Figure 9.4. Staff member award template.

without ever hearing a word from the teacher? Worse than that, what if you *had* heard things but those things went something like this:

✦ Monday: "Mrs. Martin—Johnny didn't have a good morning."

✦ Tuesday: "Mrs. Martin—Johnny had a rough afternoon."

✦ Wednesday: "Mrs. Martin—Johnny must not have had his meds today."

✦ Thursday: "Mrs. Martin—You must talk to Johnny's doctor about his tantrums."

✦ Friday: "Mrs. Martin—You must come in for a conference immediately on Monday— we need to speak to you in person regarding Johnny's behavior. Have a good weekend."

Negative, negative, negative. Be honest with yourself: Do you do this in your classroom? Go back and take a second look at the home communication log you use. What was the ratio of positive to negative comments? Put your own child's name or imagine your own name in the comments and read it again. Feel different about what was said?

Although it certainly may be an accurate account of what is going on in the classroom, this is probably not the best way to communicate with parents. You need to inform while building relationships and enlisting support. By Friday afternoon, poor Mrs. Martin is probably getting angrier by the minute, and by the time the weekend is over she is ready to rumble. What a way to start a conference!

Let's rewind. Every day, the student, regardless of what happens in the classroom, has done something you can brag about—*so brag*. While being honest about the issues in the classroom, you should remember that how you frame your communication is of utmost

Communication to the parents should always come from the teacher.

The teacher should be the one in control of the situations that occur in the classroom.

Open communication is key. If something should be done in a different way, you should discuss it at a classroom staff team meeting.

Classroom staff will need duty-free breaks away from the responsibility of monitoring students.

Use your staff's talents. Is there an artist in the bunch? Use those talents.

Figure 9.5. Things to remember about building staff rapport.

importance. Always try to sandwich a negative between two positives. Do this in a face-to-face parent conference also. Do not begin the meeting with negative issues.

If parents feel that you care about their child, they will more readily listen to the less-than-positive information about their child. For example, consider the following note sent home:

CASE IN POINT   Mrs. Martin,

Johnny had a better day today! He was really focused in science and completed his worksheet independently. We still have work to do, but he only had three episodes of inappropriate behaviors. Let me know how he is doing at home so we can work together to come up with a reinforcement system that will work. Thanks for all of your support!

Mrs. Smith

So, what do you think? Mrs. Smith was still able to tell the parents that Johnny had inappropriate behaviors or tantrums, but it is framed in a positive, hopeful way. It is not the end of the world. This is the job of special educators, after all. Yes, Johnny still has a ways to go, but together they can work on a reinforcement system that has the potential for meeting his needs and helping him make behavioral progress. And, remember, this also applies to academic issues.

Here and in the appendixes for this chapter, I present three items that may assist you in supporting the parents of your students with autism spectrum disorders and other types of special needs. These can be used in any type of classroom and will also help prime you to come up with even more ways of supporting the parents of your students.

1.   Home communication book
2.   Classroom newsletter
3.   Letters

Home Communication Books

Home communication with parents of students with disabilities is really not an option—it is a necessity. Special education teachers are in environments that require a constant flow of information to and from the home setting. Teachers typically take student progress data that parents need to know about. Parents typically have information about the student functioning in the home setting that is vital to the day-to-day progress in the classroom. For example:

✦ Johnny only slept 3 hours last night.

✦ Marylyn did not eat all of her breakfast this morning.

✦ Sally spontaneously played with a friend yesterday after school.

✦ Joe's sick grandma moved in with us over the weekend.

Isn't this useful information? Regular communication with a student's parents is the best way to avert communication lapses or miscommunication that can, in turn, generate a great deal of grief for everyone involved. Whether this is on a daily basis for those younger students or on a weekly basis for higher-functioning, more independent high school students, communication is important.

Home communication books can be as simple as a spiral notebook, a teacher-made homework agenda, or one that is purchased from the school store. This type would be applicable for the older student or a student who is functioning with more independence. This type of communication book may contain homework assignments with a short daily note from the teacher and a signature from the parent. If the students are seeing several different teachers, the book might be coordinated by the special educator who serves as the student's case manager. This way there is constant communication among teachers, as each one can be informed as to how the student is doing in other classrooms.

Younger students or students with more significant communication needs and less ability to function at an independent level may require more intensive communication between school and home. Let me explain the steps involved in creating a more intensive communication book. Figure 9.6 is an example of the cover of this home communication book. Copies of these covers, in addition to the social story, are included as Appendix 9D.

Step 1

This book can be placed in a three-ring binder that has pockets on the front and back cover. It can be personalized with a copy of the school's photo on the front instead of the one shown. Laminate the social story, punch holes, and place it as the first page. This social story helps the students understand and become a part of the use of the book. This social story also helps bring meaning to the task of taking the book back and forth between home and school.

Step 2

The meat of the book should include two separate sections. One section includes paper copies of a form you create to communicate back and forth with parents. Be creative about the type of form you use and make it simple for both you and the parents. For an example of a form, see Figure 9.7. This form is also included as Appendix 9E if you choose to use this one. This section could also just include blank paper on which you write short narrative notes.

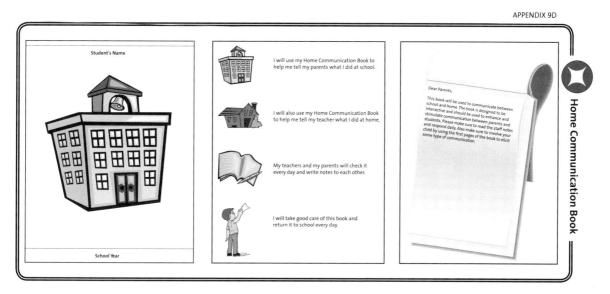

I will use my Home Communication Book to help me tell my parents what I did at school.

I will also use my Home Communication Book to help me tell my teacher what I did at home.

My teachers and my parents will check it every day and write notes to each other.

I will take good care of this book and return it to school every day.

Student's Name

School Year

Dear Parents,

This book will be used to communicate between school and home. The book is designed to be interactive and should be used to enhance and stimulate communication between parents and students. Please make sure to read the staff notes and respond daily. Also make sure to involve your child by using the first pages of the book to elicit some type of communication.

Home Communication Book

Figure 9.6.   Home communication book.

Step 3

The front section is different as it is interactive for both students and parents. It is a great teaching tool for teaching functional skills. This section could include the following types of pages (see one example in Figure 9.8):

✦ *All About Home:* This gives students a way of communicating activities they did at home the night before. It becomes a wonderful communication prompt during a morning group time.

✦ *All About School:* This is a way of enhancing the students' communication to parents at home. This will serve as communication prompts for describing the activities of the school day. This is a great end-of-the-day activity that teachers can use to summarize the school day.

✦ *All About Me:* This can be used in the morning group session or at the beginning of the day to help the students generalize and practice basic functional skills.

As you see in the example, sample photos were used to show how the page could look when personalized for the student. Blank copies of these pages are included as Appendix 9F if you choose to recreate the book. Make sure to create your own pages, specific to the needs of your students. The pages can be copied onto card stock and laminated. Hook and loop tape is then placed on the page so that picture symbols or photos can be used. A choice of several pictures can be placed below each sentence, and the one that is appropriate for the child's activity is chosen and can be placed in the box to complete the sentence.

Look at the multiple purposes the use of this type of home communication book serves.

✦ As communication to the parent from the teacher

✦ As communication back to the teacher from the parent

✦ As an enhancement of basic functional skills (recognition of people, recognition of home photo, recognition of name, etc.)

✦ As a communication prompt that is used to elicit communication to parents about school activities

Date: _____

From the teacher:

_____

_____

_____

_____

_____

_____

From the parent:

_____

_____

_____

_____

_____

_____

_____

_____

_____

Home–School notes

Figure 9.7. Home-school notes.

✦ As a communication prompt that is used to elicit communication to teachers about activities the students did at home the night before

Newsletters

What better way to keep communication going between school and home than with a simple class newsletter? You'll find a sample newsletter in Figure 9.9. After formatting your newsletter, you can easily change it from month to month or season to season. You may want to use Microsoft Publisher or a simple Microsoft Word newsletter template that can be downloaded for free. If you have older students or students who function at a

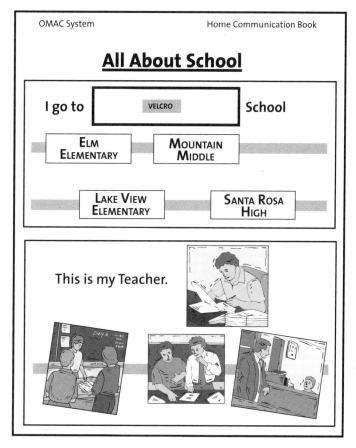

Figure 9.8. Example of a school page.

higher level, you can add the creation of this newsletter to the weekly classroom writing activities.

Your newsletter will be a wonderful way of eliciting support from parents for both special activities and everyday events. You can also add a section to the newsletter to teach about a certain subject, such as sign language, using visual supports, or specific teaching methods. You could also enlist the help of the therapists involved with your student. The speech-language therapist could have a small column on enhancing communication skills with everyday activities in the home and community settings. If you have older students or classroom peer mentors for your students, this may be a great way of having them support your classroom while enhancing their own writing abilities.

Letters

If you do not have enough time to prepare a newsletter each month, then how about a letter to the parents? Many people write "holiday letters" to slip inside Christmas cards to keep family and friends abreast of what is going on in their lives. The same can also be accomplished with a class letter. It could be produced once a month or once a semester. A sample letter can be found in Figure 9.10.

If you have older, more capable students, then get them involved in the writing process. Add pictures of the class activities. However, at the beginning of the year, always get a permission form signed for each of the students to have their photos in class publications.

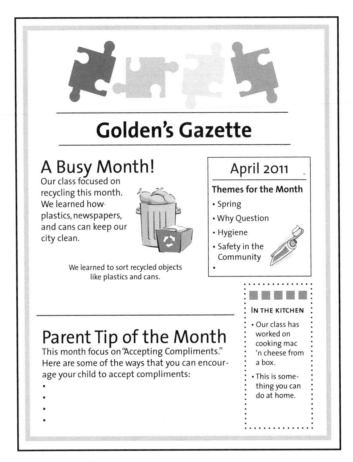

Figure 9.9. Sample newsletter.

Are you at the higher end of the technology spectrum? Many schools and classrooms have web pages or blogs. A newsletter or letter is something that can be easily uploaded to those types of sites and can be downloaded and printed by the parents at home.

Other Ways to Support Parents

There are so many ways that you can foster a positive relationship with the parents of your students. I am sure that the teachers within your special education department could come up with quite a list of things they are currently using. Here are a few other ideas.

Helping Parents Set Up a Home Environment

You are the expert on the students' ability to function cognitively, socially, and academically in the school setting. You, as the teacher, are also the expert in child development. Teachers have so much knowledge and expertise that they rarely get to share with parents. Here are ways you can support the parents of your students by using your academic and communication expertise:

✦ As you print picture symbols for each student, make an extra set for the parents to use at home.

✦ Advise the parents on how to set up a communication area on the refrigerator at home. This is a common location and will be easily accessible during the day.

What's going on in our classroom this month?

Dear Parents,

OMAC System

Figure 9.10   Sample letter.

✦ Help parents set a morning and nighttime routine and provide visuals to use. For consistency, use the same format you are using in the classroom.

✦ The student may have a difficult time going to the dentist, the doctor, a church, a shop, or a restaurant. You may use some of the same interventions you use in the classroom to advise the parents in ways of helping the student become more efficient in these types of activities.

✦ Assist parents by providing them with tips or information on organizing the student's bedroom. Color coding and visual supports not only help the student's classroom environment but can also assist the student to function more independently at home.

✦ Sign language will only become an effective means of communication if it is used consistently in all settings. Hold a training session in basic sign language for the parent. Provide a weekly instruction sheet on using sign language at home, adding one sign a week.

✦ If the student is having a difficult time in knowing how to use unstructured time or leisure time, provide guidance to the parents on activities you use in the classroom. Teaching students to use leisure time is a great skill to learn and one that will carry into adulthood.

Providing a Recipe Book

Extra supports go a long way to helping the parents of your students in the home environment, and if they are supported, then you will probably reap the benefit of that support in the way of enhanced trust, respect, and a positive relationship. You do so many activities in the classroom that will help parents in the home. In turn, this will help enhance the student's ability to generalize learned skills to other environments.

Now, I know that not all classrooms have cooking at school, but you may have a classroom that does. You may have students you support who are in a home economics course, or students who require a more functional curriculum for which cooking may be part of the week's lesson plan. Let's expand the reach of that activity and help the students generalize those skills to another environment—the home. There are a couple of different ways you could do this:

✦ At the beginning of the year, send home an empty, blank three-ring binder. Each time you cook in the classroom, send home a copy of the recipe you used with the students to be included in the book. This will create a classroom recipe book that can be used at home.

✦ Each time you cook in the classroom, run extra copies of the recipe. Create a recipe book using a three-ring binder. At the end of the year, present this book to the parents as a parting gift. The cookbooks also make wonderful gifts for the students to give their parents for a holiday or special occasion.

Either way you do this, it will promote generalization of learned skills by allowing the students an opportunity to practice, at home, the recipe they made at school.

Be creative in how you use this idea. You may not cook, but you may do other types of functional activities such as vocational tasks (e.g., software use or landscaping), functional tasks (e.g., cleaning house, choosing clothing, or taking care of personal hygiene/grooming tasks), or even leisure tasks (e.g., crafts, music, or simple games). Try creating a book for the parents to use at home that includes these types of tasks. If you have visuals associated with those tasks, parents can use these to promote generalization of these same skills in the home setting.

Holding a Make and Take

"Make and takes" provide parents an opportunity to get their own copies of tools used in the classroom such as visual schedules. It can be a very fun activity. Parents normally do not have access to visual symbol computer software; some parents may not even have access to a computer, a color printer, or a digital camera; and most will not have access to a laminator. So why not have a make-and-take session one afternoon or on a Saturday morning? Get some of the special education classes together and spread the preparation jobs around to several staff members. You may even get your parent–teacher association involved.

1. Gather materials: card stock, laminator, paper cutter, Velcro, computers, color printers, and copy machines.
2. Determine your goal. Is it to create picture symbols, a picture activity schedule, or something else? Before the event, send a survey to the parents to determine their needs. Set up stations or classrooms for different types of visuals. Teach the parents how to use what they create at home. This is a good way to generalize the skills the students are learning at school. Offer stations for make-and-take activities such as these.

    ✦ Visuals for organizing the home environment
    ✦ Visual supports for behavior reinforcement systems for the home setting
    ✦ Visual schedules for home routines

Consistency across settings is key to mastery and generalization, and this will have a great impact!

Providing Trainings

The same idea used in the make-and-take sessions is true for training sessions. However, neither do you have to hold the sessions nor do you have to do the teaching yourself. For example, you may want to have an annual "Autism Boot Camp for Parents." Keep it simple. Maybe have a workshop with one speaker or a small conference with several rotating sessions. This is a great function for April, which is Autism Awareness Month. Some suggested trainings include

✦ Helping your child with academics at home

✦ Sign language and communication interventions

✦ Encouraging independence at home

✦ Organizing your home environment

✦ Creative ideas for the summer

✦ Dealing with unstructured time at home

✦ Dentists, doctors, and haircuts, oh my! How to get students through these three activities

SUMMARY

Can you believe you made it through? If you stayed to the end and implemented some of the ideas, you now have some wonderful things in place to help you support not only the classroom staff but also the parents of your students. And, in supporting them, you have supported yourself and made your life much easier to manage and much more organized.

Conclusion

Congratulations. You have completed the entire Organization and Management of a Classroom (OMAC) system.

Take a look around your classroom. Do you notice a difference? I bet the environment is not only organized but also clutter-free and color-coded. I bet you and the students are able to find the materials you need without wasting time. I also bet that the students are much more independent in the classroom.

Remember back to Chapter 1?

This is a diagram of the three-fold objective outcomes for the OMAC system. My goal was to help you create an environment that would be manageable and organized. This organization and management system would enhance the student's ability to be independent, help decrease inappropriate student behavior and decrease the stress level of the classroom staff. With each of the OMAC layers now in place, let's do a final checklist to show you some of the things you have put into place that have helped you progress toward meeting these objectives.

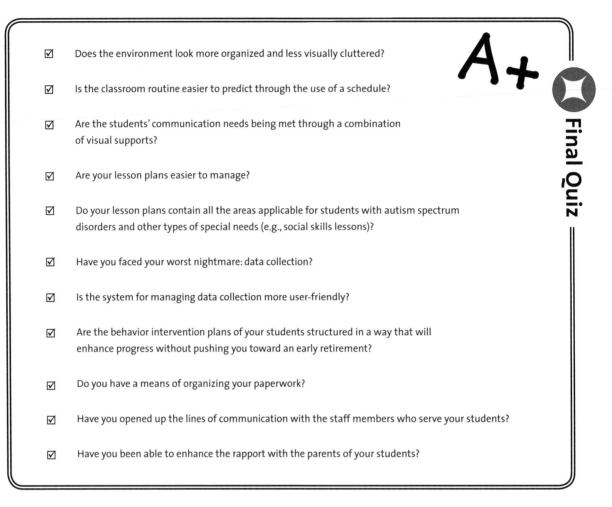

☑ Does the environment look more organized and less visually cluttered?

☑ Is the classroom routine easier to predict through the use of a schedule?

☑ Are the students' communication needs being met through a combination of visual supports?

☑ Are your lesson plans easier to manage?

☑ Do your lesson plans contain all the areas applicable for students with autism spectrum disorders and other types of special needs (e.g., social skills lessons)?

☑ Have you faced your worst nightmare: data collection?

☑ Is the system for managing data collection more user-friendly?

☑ Are the behavior intervention plans of your students structured in a way that will enhance progress without pushing you toward an early retirement?

☑ Do you have a means of organizing your paperwork?

☑ Have you opened up the lines of communication with the staff members who serve your students?

☑ Have you been able to enhance the rapport with the parents of your students?

A+

Final Quiz

If you have at least completed a few of the items, you are well on your way to creating a model environment! One layer at a time will get you where you want to be, if you don't give up. *Remember that Rome was not built in a day,* and neither is a model classroom, but if you hang with it, both you and your students will reap the benefits and become a tremendous success!

References

American Speech-Language-Hearing Association.(2006). Roles and responsibilities of speech-language pathologists in diagnosis, assessment, and treatment of autism spectrum disorders across the life span (ASHA position statement). Retrieved from http://www.medicalhomeportal.org/link/3445

Aspen, A., & Austin, M. (Fall 2003). How to visualize success in the treatment of autism. *CSHA Magazine*, 33(2), 10–12.

Autism guidebook for Washington State. (July 2009). Olympia, WA: Washington State Department of Education. Retrieved from http://www.doh.wa.gov/cfh/autism/guidebook/default.htm

Autism Society of America. About autism. Retrieved from http://www.autism-society.org

Blacher, J. (2007). Unlocking the mystery of social deficits in autism: Theory of mind as key. *The Exceptional Parent, 37*(8), 96–97.

Bondy, A., & Frost, L. (2001). The picture exchange communication system. *Behavior Modification, 25*(5), 725–744.

Boswell, L., & Nugent, P. (2002). *Freeing the child: Using action research on visual learning strategies to develop children with autism.* Paper presented at the Annual Meeting of the American Educational Research Association in New Orleans, April 1–5.

Browers, A., & Tomic, W. (2000). A longitudinal study of teacher burnout and perceived self-efficacy in classroom management. *Teaching and Teacher Education, 16*, 239–253.

Bruner, D.L., & Seung, H. (2009). Evaluation of the efficacy of communication-based treatments for autism spectrum disorders: A literature review. *Communication Disorders Quarterly, 31*(1), 15–41.

Bryan, L., & Gast, D. (2000). Teaching on-task and on-schedule behaviors to high-functioning children with autism via picture-activity schedules. *Journal of Autism and Developmental Disorders, 30*(6), 553–567.

Chiang, H.-M., & Carter, M. (2008). Spontaneity of communication in individuals with autism. *Journal of Autism and Developmental Disorders, 38*, 693–705.

Cooper, J., Heron, T., & Heward, W. (2007). *Applied behavior analysis.* 2nd ed. Upper Saddle River, NJ: Prentice Hall.

Crone, D.A., & Horner, R.H. (2003). *Building positive behavior support systems in schools: Functional behavioral assessment.* New York: Guilford Press.

Dalrymple, N.J. (1995). Environmental supports to develop flexibility and independence. In K.A. Quill (Ed.), *Teaching children with autism: Strategies to enhance communication and socialization.* New York: Delmar Publishers Inc.

Dawson, G., & Osterling, J. (1997). Early intervention in autism: Effectiveness and common elements of current approaches. In: M.J. Guralnick (Ed.), *The effectiveness of early intervention.* Baltimore: Paul H. Brookes Publishing Co., 307–326.

Dawson, G., Toth, K., Abbott, R., Osterling, J., Munson, J., Estes, A., & Liaw, J. (2004). Early social attention impairments in autism: social orienting, joint attention, and attention to distress. *Developmental Psychology, 40*, 271–283.

Dettmer, S., Simpson, R., Myles, B.S., & Ganz, J.B. (2000). The use of visual supports to facilitate transitions of students with autism. *Focus on Autism and Other Developmental Disabilities, 15*(3), 163–169.

Dewey, J. (1944). *Democracy and education* (pp. 18–19). New York: The Free Press.

Diagnostic and statistical manual of mental disorders, fourth edition, text revision.(2000). Washington, DC: American Psychiatric Association.

Fortunato, J. A., Sigafoos, J., & Morsillo-Searls, L.M. (2007). A communication plan for autism and its applied behavior analysis treatment: A framing strategy. *Child Youth Care Forum, 36*, 87–97.

Frith, U. (1989). *Autism: explaining the enigma.* Oxford, England: Basil Blackwell.

Ganz, J.B., Kaylor, M., Bourgeois, B., & Hadden, K. (June 2008). The impact of social scripts and visual cues on verbal communication in three children with autism spectrum disorders. *Focus on Autism and Other Developmental Disabilities, 23*(2).

Gray, C.A. (1995). Teaching children with autism to read social situations. In K.A. Quill (Ed.), *Teaching children with autism* (pp. 219–241). New York: Delmar.

Gray, C., & Garand, J. (1993). Social stories: Improving responses of students with autism with inaccurate social information. *Focus on Autism and Other Developmental Disabilities, 8*(1), 1–10.

Halle, J. (1982). Teaching functional language to the handicapped: An integrative model of natural environment teaching techniques. *Journal of the Association for the Severely Handicapped, 7*(4), 29–37.

Heflin, L.J., & Hess, K.L. (2011). *Enhancing instructional contexts for students with autism spectrum disorders (EIC-ASD).* Retrieved from http://education. gsu/autism/

Heflin, L.J., & Simpson, R.L. (1998). Interventions for children and youth with autism: Prudent choices in a world of exaggerated claims and empty promises. Part 1: Intervention and treatment options review. *Focus on Autism and other Developmental Disabilities, 13,* 195–211.

Hill, E., & Frith, U. (2003). Understanding autism: Insights from mind and brain. *Philosophical Transactions of the Royal Society of London, 358,* 281–289.

Holdheide, L., & Reschly, D. (2008). *Teacher preparation to deliver inclusive services to students with disabilities.* Washington, DC: National Comprehensive Center for Teacher Quality.1–25.

Horner, R.H. (1994). Functional assessment: Contributions and future directions. *Journal of Applied Behavior Analysis, 27,* 401–404.

Horner, R., Carr, E., Halle, J., McGee, G., Odom, S., & Wolery, M. (2005). The use of single subject research to identify evidence-based practice in special education. *Exceptional Children, 71*(2), 165–179.

Hume, K., Loftin, R., & Lantz, J. (2009). Increasing independence in autism spectrum disorders: A review of three focused interventions. *Journal of Autism and Developmental Disorders, 39,* 1329–1338.

Hume, K., & Odom, S. (2007). Effects of an individual work system on the independent functioning of students with autism. *Journal of Autism and Developmental Disorders, 37,* 1166–1180.

Kasari, C. (2004). Teaching joint attention and play skills to students with autism. *Autism News, 1*(3), 4–7.

Kayikci, K. (2009). The effect of classroom management skills of elementary school teachers on undesirable discipline behavior of students. *Procedia Social and Behavioral Sciences, 1,* 1215–1225.

Kim, Y.S., Leventhal, B.L., Koh, Y.J., Fombonne, E., Laska, E., Lim, E.C., et al. (May 9, 2011). Prevalence of autism spectrum disorders in a total population sample. *American Journal of Psychiatry in Advance.*

Koegel, L.K. (2000). Interventions to facilitate communication in autism. *Journal of Autism and Developmental Disorders, 30*(5), 383–391.

Lovaas, O.I. (1977). *The autistic child: language training through behavior modification.* New York: Irvington.

Marckel, J., Neef, N., & Ferreri, S. (2006). A preliminary analysis of teaching improvisation with the Picture Exchange Communication System to children with autism. *Journal of Applied Behavioral Analysis, 39,* 109–115.

Marzano, R.J. (2003). *Classroom management that works: research-based strategies for every teacher.* Alexandria, VA: Association for Supervision and Curriculum Development.

McClannahan, L., & Krantz, P. (1999). *Activity schedules for children with autism.* Bethesda, MD: Woodbine House.

McCloskey-Dale, S. (2000). *Environmental communication teaching.* Paper presented at the 20th Annual Southeast Augmentative Communication Conference; Birmingham, AL; October 1–2, 1999.

McGee, G., Morrier, M.J., & Daly, T. (1999). An incidental teaching approach to early intervention for toddlers with autism. *The Journal of the Association for Persons with Severe Handicaps, 24*(3), 133–146.

Mesibov, G.B., Shea, V., & Schopler, E. (2005). "The Culture of Autism" from The TEACCH Approach to Autism Spectrum Disorders (pp. 19–32). New York: Kluwer Academic/Plenum Publishers.

Mitchell, D. (2008). *What really works in special and inclusive education: Using evidence-based teaching strategies.* New York: Routledge.

National Autism Center. (2009). National Standards Report. Retrieved from http://www.nationalautism center.org

National Institute of Child Health and Human Development. (2011). Autism spectrum disorders. Retrieved from http://www.nichd.nih.gov/health/topics/asd. cfm

National Research Council. (2001). *Educating children with autism.* Washington, DC: National Academies Press.

No Child Left Behind (NCLB) Act of 2001, Pub. L. No. 107-110, § 115, Stat. 1425 (2002).

Ogletree, B.T., Oren, T., & Fischer, M.A. (2007). Examining effective intervention practices for communication impairment in autism spectrum disorder. *Exceptionality, 15*(4), 233–247.

Ohio Developmental Disabilities Council. (2007). *Ohio parent's guide to autism.* Retrieved from http://www. ocali.org/_archive/pdf_family/Parent_Guide.pdf

Ohio State Department. (2004). *Service guidelines for individuals with autism spectrum disorder/pervasive developmental disorder.* Retrieved from http://www. ocali.org/up_doc/Autism_Service_Guidelines.pdf

Ozonoff, S., & Miller, J.N. (1995). Teaching theory of mind: a new approach to social skills training for individuals with autism. *Journal of Autism and Developmental Disorders, 25,* 415–433.

Ozonoff, S., Pennington, B., & Rogers, S. (1991). Executive functioning deficits in high-functioning autistic individuals: Relationship to theory of mind. *Journal of Child Psychology and Psychiatry, 32*(7), 1081–1105.

Pries, J. (2006). The effect of picture communication symbols on the verbal comprehension of commands by young children with autism. *Focus on Autism and Other Developmental Disabilities, 21*(4), 194–210.

Probst, P., & Leppert, T. (2008). Brief report: Outcomes of a teacher training program for autism spectrum disorders. *Journal of Autism and Developmental Disorders. 38,* 1791–1796.

Quill, K.A. (1995). Visually cued instruction for children with autism and pervasive developmental disorders. *Focus on Autistic Behavior, 10*(3), 10–20.

Quill, K.A. (1997). Instructional considerations for young children with autism: The rationale for visually cued instruction. *Journal of Autism and Developmental Disorders, 27*, 697–714.

Savage, T.V. (1999). *Teaching self-control through management and discipline.* Boston: Allyn and Bacon.

Schopler, E., Mesibov, G.B., & Baker, A. (1982). Evaluation of treatment for autistic children and their parents. *Journal of the American Academy of Child Psychiatry, 21*, 262–267.

Seida, J.K., Ospina, M.B., Karkhaneh, M., Hartling, L., Smith, V., & Clark, B. (2009). Systematic reviews of psychosocial interventions for autism: An umbrella review. *Developmental Medicine and Child Neurology, 51*, 95–104.

Siegel, B. (2003). *Helping children with autism learn: Treatment approaches for parents and professionals.* New York: Oxford University Press.

Skinner, B.F. (1953). *Science and human behavior.* New York: Macmillan.

Smith, T., & Ingersoll, R. (2004). What are the effects of induction and mentoring on beginning teacher turnover? *American Educational Research Journal, 41*, 681–684.

Smith-Myles, B., Trautman, M., & Schelvan, R. (2004). *The hidden curriculum: Practical solutions for understanding unstated rules in social situations.* Shawnee Mission, KS: Autism Asperger Publishing Company.

Wang, M., Haertel, G., & Walberg, H. (1994). What helps students learn? *Educational Leadership, 51*(4), 74–79.

Watson, J.B. (1913). Psychology as the behaviorist views it. *Psychological Review, 20*, 158–177.

Weyandt, L.L., & Willis, W.G. (1994). Executive functions in school-aged children: Potential efficacy of tasks in discriminating clinical groups. *Developmental Neuropsychology, 10*, 27–38.

Yang, X., Ge, C., Hu, B., Chi, T., & Wang, L. (2009). Relationship between quality of life and occupational stress among teachers. *Public Health, 123*, 750–755.

Yoder, P., & Stone, W. (2006). Randomized comparison of two communication interventions for preschoolers with autism spectrum disorders. *Journal of Counseling and Clinical Psychology, 74*(3), 426–435.

Index

Tables and figures are indicated by *t* and *f*, respectively.